A GATHERING OF EXTRAORDINARY INDIVIDUALS

Thomas Mack Wilhoite / Kenitra American High School, Morocco, 1956-1976

Edited by Douglas E. Campbell

A GATHERING OF EXTRAORDINARY INDIVIDUALS

Thomas Mack Wilhoite / Kenitra American High School, Morocco, 1956-1976

Edited by Douglas E. Campbell

SYNECA RESEARCH GROUP, INC.

A Gathering of Extraordinary Individuals: Thomas Mack Wilhoite/Kenitra American High School, Morocco, 1956-1976

ISBN 978-1-387-98464-0

Direct all inquiries to Douglas Campbell at dcamp@aol.com.

Cover design by Michelle Rekstad at Rekstad Graphics, rekstad@aol.com.

Acknowledgments

First and foremost, this book would not have been possible without the Thomas Mack Wilhoite/Kenitra American High School alumni wanting this to actually be possible. Your heartfelt memories from decades ago and your willingness to share them only prove the heightened experiences we all shared from that day and age. More so, many of these experiences would have never occurred without the support, implied or otherwise, from our parents, who gave most of us teenagers enough leeway to experience Morocco as only teenagers could have. And even more importantly to many of us, a thank you to our TMW/KAHS faculty and staff who molded our young minds, using Morocco as their backdrop, to ensure our success in the future. Whether we joined the military, went off to college or simply entered the workplace after graduation, the experiences of high school life in a foreign country (well, foreign to those who weren't Moroccan students!) was enhanced by their guidance and direction. We can't thank any of you enough.

Foreword

We are a gathering of extraordinary individuals who met under extraordinary circumstances. Coming of age in a small high school in Morocco decades ago, we have something unique in each of us yet in common with each other, and decades later that feeling has somehow never left us. We are the *Sultans* of Thomas Mack Wilhoite/Kenitra American High School. Be it the first graduating class of three Seniors in 1956 to the last Class of 1976, our experiences as students were sharply tuned to our environment. We were not strangers in a strange land; we were welcomed by the Moroccan people as if we were visiting relatives. The sights, sounds, tastes and smells of Morocco were absorbed by hundreds of students and no matter what span of years we were there, the similar experiences of living in Morocco can be shared by all. Proof of that is reflected in our high school reunions in which alumni 10 or 15 years apart in their graduation years can relate, and laugh at, similar experiences of their teenage years growing up in and around Kenitra/Port Lyautey, Mehdia and Bouknadel beaches, Rabat, and nearby military bases. Within this book are the memories of those days as told by the former students and teachers of our school.

The basis of this book began to form after the Facebook site "TMW-KAHS Sultans in Exile" echoed a lot of entries by alumni who started with "I remember...". Many of those stories are reflected in this book. Subsequently, a request was made for other former students and teachers to sit down and write more about their experiences. As the editor, and a KAHS Class of 1972 graduate, it is my pleasure to present to you this book, capturing our collection of memories of those days past.

Douglas Campbell

Table of Contents

Introduction

Morocco was the first country to officially recognize the newly independent United States of America in the year 1777. They formally recognized the United States by signing a treaty of peace and friendship in 1786. Full diplomatic relations began in 1905. Morocco entered into the status of a French protectorate from 1912 to 1956, and normal diplomatic relations were resumed after U.S. recognition of Moroccan independence in 1956. Also, in 1956 was the naming of a military dependents' school on the Port Lyautey base to Thomas Mack Wilhoite.

Who Was Thomas Mack Wilhoite? Thomas Mack Wilhoite was born on February 12, 1921, in Guthrie, KY. He enlisted in the Naval Reserve on June 16, 1941, in Atlanta, GA, and received his aviation indoctrination training at the Naval Reserve Air Base in Atlanta. On August 7, 1941, he reported for flight instruction at the Naval Air Station (NAS) in Pensacola, FL, and was appointed an aviation cadet the following day. Transferred to NAS in Miami, FL, on January 15, 1942, for further training, he became a Naval aviator on February 6, 1942. Three days later he was commissioned an Ensign and at the end of February had reported to the Advanced Carrier Training Group, Atlantic Fleet, NAS in Norfolk, VA. There he joined Fighting Squadron (VF) 9, then preparing to go to war. He became the Assistant Navigation Officer for that squadron. Operation Torch--the World War II invasion of French North Africa--saw VF-9 assigned to the aircraft carrier USS RANGER (CV-4). It was that aircraft carrier that provided air superiority during the amphibious invasion of German-dominated French Morocco (commencing early November 8, 1942). It was still dark at 6:15 a.m. that day when RANGER, stationed 30 miles northwest of Casablanca, began launching her aircraft to support the landings made at three points on the Atlantic coast of North Africa. Each section of the squadron had drawn assigned tasks on that morning, the first day of the amphibious landings. Wilhoite flew one of five Grumman F4F-4 Wildcats which attacked the French airdrome at Rabat-Sale, the headquarters of the French air forces in Morocco. Despite heavy anti-aircraft fire, Wilhoite pressed home a determined attack and set three French bombers afire with his guns. In a second strike directed at the Port Lyautey (now Kenitra) airdrome later that day, Wilhoite flew his Wildcat, Bureau Number (BuNo) 02023, as part of the RANGER's third flight. He destroyed one fighter--a Dewoitine 520--by strafing. However, the Vichy ground gunners served their weapons well; and Wilhoite's Wildcat took hits from the intense flak and crashed about one mile from Port Lyautey. After all was said and done, the RANGER's aircraft destroyed more than 70 enemy planes on the ground and shot down 15 in aerial combat, immobilized 21 light enemy tanks and destroyed 86 military vehicles. Casablanca surrendered to the Americans on November 11, 1942. Thomas Mack Wilhoite received a Silver Star posthumously, for displaying "conspicuous gallantry and intrepidity" during the strikes at Rabat-Sale and Port Lyautey. The citation also cited Wilhoite's "superb airmanship and tenacious devotion to duty" in pressing home his strafing attacks.

Before the school was named Thomas Mack Wilhoite it was simply known as "Navy 214." Bobbie Nagle attended Navy 214 from 1954 to 1956 and relays these memories: "I can only speak as the child I was back then, but the time in Morocco was the happiest time for my brother and me in our childhood. My dad, LT M. H. Nagle, Jr., was stationed at the Naval Air Station there from '54-56. I spent my first 6 months in Morocco living in Rabat, in the oldest French-built house there: 6 Rue de Poitou—right off the Avenue Victoire! (My brother and I would climb up into the trees lining the Avenue Victoire that were cut like hedges and shoot the green berries from the trees through pea-shooters on very stuffy French people. How they would howl and carry on! It was a kids' paradise.) My brother and I spoke no French, yet we had a lot of French children in our neighborhood with whom we played. Our front yard was full of wisteria vines, wrought-iron balconies, and tangerines. We took trips with our French landlord and his family to Meknes (the "Happy Valley"), Ifrane in the Atlas, and had such a wonderful time, and drank their champagne and ate French bread with butter and sugar piled on! Later we moved to Port Lyautey on the outskirts of town: 95 Rue de Cathedral de Reims. I had quite a few American dependent children to play with. We used to run wild, unhobbling horses and donkeys, screaming what we thought were horrible things to the poor Arabs who lived over the hill. One of Ben Yousef's sons, I believed lived nearby. Six months before we had to go back to the States, we moved onto the base into a Quonset hut, right behind the Marines gym on the Band Field. And for a kid, that was the BEST! We had the Oasis Snack bar, roller-skating, movies, the pool, Media Beach. Also, the French had a bunch of Lancasters as you were going into the NAS, which were of endless fascination to us. I remember my dad had always been a flyer, but somehow, an LST appeared on the Oued Sebou, and my dad was given command of it! We all thought it was very funny, since I don't think he knew anything about ships."

"We got to take trips on the R5D to London and Naples—I always threw up on them, which made me very popular. I was fine on the bucket seats, but when we children had to sit on the floor...oh, the poor Sailors that were sitting next to us! I remember the Connies and the Super Connies making trips back and forth between Port Lyautey and the States. I remember that many of them went down, too."

"Morocco got its independence from France while we lived there. For a month we couldn't go down to the Medina—people said the Arabs were bouncing French babies on their bayonets (I don't think so—but it was a colorful saying). So many things happened there. Daddy had to sit on courts-martial sometimes when some of the men got drunk in front of the main hotel (I have forgotten its name—was it the Mamora?—and were diving into the fountain pool trying to wring the necks of the swans—it happened more than once! He laughed so hard telling us about it! He thought it was great."

"I ran into one of my little boyfriends who lived there when I was there—John Bunce. He is now an oceanographer living in New Orleans, and his brother was a SEAL. They were sent off to school in England after I left. Our school was named "Navy 214" -- later Wilhoite. It is sad, because we can never go back. But it was great while it lasted!"

Bobbie Nagle

History Lesson: The first Fleet Intelligence Center (FIC) was established in May 1953 by Commander in Chief, U.S. Naval Forces, Eastern Atlantic and Mediterranean (CINCNELM) and was activated at Port Lyautey, Morocco, in March 1954. Look closely now - does the FIC building look familiar?

It is the high school, of course!

Cece Canton

Sans the front porch & a few palms...

Suzanne McQuagge Nagy

Yeah, they dressed it up for us kids. It does look naked!

Cece Canton

I would have known... no matter how many years ago!

Brenda Cozad Nutt

I loved sitting around out there in the morning

Gloria Outland Kemery

Hey, where's the Roach Coach??? It was always at the curb in the forefront.

Pamela Jean Myers Richert

Someone's sick joke to put a school in an Intel building!

Doug Campbell

I seem to remember a big vault door in my Algebra class on the lower floor, so I could believe it was an Intel site at one time. May have been a good place to stay during a storm. I remember standing over a steam grate to keep warm.

David Neumann

We had study hall periods underneath those trees that were numerous in back of the school with a cool breeze coming off the river that flowed behind the school. No A/C in the classrooms and we endured triple digit heat when the winds came off the Sahara Desert in August. Our year started 3rd week in August.

Robert Oberkehr

Pam, here's the original Roach Coach from the 1960's!

Here's a text from Donna Sadler who attended Thomas Mack Wilhoite School before it was named TMW...

"My father, Homer C. Lucas, was a Warrant Office with a FasRon unit based at Port Lyautey in the early 1950's. I am his oldest daughter, Donna, who travelled with her mother and four siblings from Norfolk, VA, to Patuxent Naval Air Station, MD, where we flew on a "cargo plane" to Port Lyautey. At the time I was eleven years old, and our ages went down to nine months. We departed Pax River NAS three days before Christmas and flew from there to Newfoundland where we ran into a horrible blowing snowstorm and two of our motors on the plane froze up. The passengers onboard were a Captain, two enlisted personnel, two naval stewards, six of us, the pilot and co-pilot, not to mention one side of the plane was filled with cargo. There was a row of "bucket seats" on one side of the plane and four "regular" seats in the back of the plane. No heat on the plane and we were bundled up in blankets and huddled together to keep warm. Coffee was frozen in the coffee pot and could not be offered to the adults. We landed safely in Newfoundland where the enlisted men on the plane and enlisted personnel from the "terminal" came to our rescue in helping with the younger children so they wouldn't be blown away. We were in this one-room terminal for about four to six hours where we were kept warm and given hot coffee and chocolate.

Once the storm had died down a little and all four motors were running properly we were helped back to the plane where we continued on to the Azores for our last stop before landing in Port Lyautey. We spent about three or four hours in the Azores where we were taken to the enlisted cafeteria for breakfast. We finally landed on the air strip in Port Lyautey about 10 hours late with a much-worried father watching us taxi into the terminal. It was now a little less than two days before Christmas. After many hugs and kisses and tears my father put us in a very small car, for the size of our family, and the funny thing was a "wooden block" under the back of the seat is what held the seat up.... yes, my father had the experience of having the block move from under the seat but he was alone in the car at the time and no injury occurred."

"One of the wives of one of the enlisted men had a Christmas dinner waiting for us (God Bless her - she tried her best to keep the food as warm as she could). Mom and all of us kids were tired, hungry and sleepy and couldn't wait to get to our new home in a foreign land. I must admit it was nice to get off the airplane in such a warm climate with the sweet smell of flowers as we travelled down the road into the city. Once having left the city we headed to Mehdia Beach where my dad had rented a one-bedroom bungalow on the third level. The road to the beach passed a 'whaling station' where the blubber was boiled down and what a horrible smell. This was the first home we lived in with no hot water, no electricity and no drinking water!! We moved several months later to the first level and into a two-story building. Again, no electricity, no hot water, no drinking water, and only a galvanized tub for bathing, unless you wanted to take a cold shower in a room off from the garage. A year later we moved into the city where we had a bath tub, no hot water but we had electricity so we had lights in the house."

"After about two years we left Port Lyautey and dad was stationed in Quonset Point, Rhode Island. I have often wanted to go back to Port Lyautey and see what changes had been made. As a young person, I thoroughly enjoyed living and meeting new friends in a strange place and will always remember the sweet smell of flowers in the area of the Officer's Club. My father's commander had housing in a Quonset hut across the street from the club and when I would babysit for them and the windows and doors were open the sweet smell would blow through the house. I might also add that I was in the 8th grade now and we "moved" into the "new" school down on the water. I experienced things that none of my friends had ever or would ever experience. My mother and father are dead now but I know it was one of my mother's favorite places to live as a military wife, inconveniences and all. Memories, thank God we have them."

Donna Sadler

CLASS OF 1956

1956 witnessed an increase in living standards and a focus on education which helped to fuel the increase in college education - one in every three high school graduates were now going off to college. Television shows included the premier of "As the World Turns" and "The Price is Right". Mothers could now buy disposable diapers and tefal non-stick frying pans. Elvis Presley appeared on the Ed Sullivan show and entered the music charts for the first time with "Heartbreak Hotel". IBM released the first computer with a hard drive, the IBM 305 RAMAC. The machine weighed about one ton, measured about 16 square feet and stored about 5 megabytes. "My Fair Lady" opened on Broadway starring Julie Andrews as Eliza Doolittle and Rex Harrison as Professor Higgins. The movie star Grace Kelly married Prince Rainier of Monaco and became Princess Grace of Monaco. In late 1955, in the middle of what came to be known as the Revolution of the King and the People, Sultan Mohammed V successfully negotiated the gradual restoration of Moroccan independence within a framework of French-Moroccan interdependence. The sultan agreed to institute reforms that would transform Morocco into a constitutional monarchy with a democratic form of government. In February 1956, Morocco acquired limited home rule. Further negotiations for full independence culminated in the French-Moroccan Agreement signed in Paris on March 2, 1956, and the following day Morocco gained independence from France (the Anniversary of the throne). On April 7, 1956, France officially relinquished its protectorate in Morocco. The internationalized city of Tangier was reintegrated with the signing of the Tangier Protocol on October 29, 1956. The abolition of the Spanish protectorate and the recognition of Moroccan independence by Spain were negotiated separately and made final in the Joint Declaration of April

1956. In the months that followed independence, Mohammed V proceeded to build a modern governmental structure under a constitutional monarchy in which the sultan would exercise an active political role. He acted cautiously, intent on preventing the establishment of a one-party state. He assumed the monarchy in 1957.

I Remember:

I am Becky Hornsby (now Snow), Class of 1956, first graduating class of Thomas Mack Wilhoite High School in Port Lyautey, Morocco. Our military school was located on the base. It was the first year of the school and there were 3 seniors: Larry Miller, Pat Le Fleur and me. The other grades had a few more students.

After all these years, the three of us had settled in California, within about 70 to 80 miles of each other. We had a 50th (I think it was the 50th!) reunion in a restaurant in Thousand Oaks and had a great time reliving our senior year. We never all got together again at the same time.

Last week I was reading the local paper and saw where Larry had died in his sleep. It was a sad déjà-vu. He had done well, being an official in a local college and I had seen him in his robe at my daughter's graduation but didn't talk to him on that occasion. Pat and I were planning another reunion with Larry, as before, but just didn't get around to it. I called her today and told her, then decided I'd let any classmates who remembered him know.

Becky Hornsby Snow, September 15, 2014

I'm the third graduating senior,1956, from TMW High School. Larry, Pat and I got together for a senior reunion several years ago for dinner at the Hungry Hunter in Thousand Oaks. We are all three living in Southern California. Pat and I went to a TMW/Kenitra reunion a couple of years ago in San Diego. It was fun seeing those who came after us. The times in Morocco were enjoyable and basically carefree. I stayed a few months after graduation until my Dad was transferred. I worked in the office at the Navy Exchange and my hobbies were riding the Arabian Stallions at the stables, going to different functions on the base, and trying to stay out of trouble! I gained a hearty respect for dueling animals, and still have a hard time relating to docile horses after the experiences of the spirited horses in Port Lyautey. My career was real estate and I still maintain my licenses.

The entire Graduation Class of 1956! From left to right, Becky (Hornsby) Snow, Pat Le Fleur Jones and Larry Miller.

This picture brings back memories and I'm still into the 50's music. My dress was pink and I ordered it out of a catalog. Don't wear glasses much anymore since contacts came in. I was in Port Lyautey from August 1954 to August 1956. We got to Morocco in 1954 just as I was going into the 11th grade. At that time there was one senior and several juniors. We had correspondence courses from the University of Nebraska and all sat in one big room. Our teacher or "monitor" was Mrs. Duborg, the base Captain's wife. In my senior year we had another school with real live teachers. Our English teacher, Mrs. Ryan was a Shakespeare lover and she celebrated his birthday. In those days we diagrammed sentences. Sure was a good way to learn sentences. By that time there were about 7 juniors. Chemistry class was read and memorize. No lab. Our principal was Mr. Humperdinck. These were civil service teachers. Both Becky and Larry lived in outlying areas so only saw them at school. In 1954 we lived in town and then moved on the base - in back of the Marine Corps barracks - in a Quonset hut. Very convenient because I dated

Marines. Spent many evenings watching my date spit shine his shoes. Who can forget the outdoor movie theater??? The base movie was about all there was to do on the base but spent a lot of time at the Red Cross Center in town. I was allowed to drive our car so had transportation for the "gang." The first year we were there, I was chosen Navy Relief Queen. Every time someone bought a ticket for a new car, they got to vote for a Queen. The winner of the car didn't even give me a ride.... My Dad was LCDR Ernest J. La Fleur, VR-24 Terminal Officer, so I also spent time at the terminal and "Greasy Spoon" as they called the snack bar. On Saturday, some of the girls took turns putting on a radio show called "Teen Timers," which was on Armed Forces Radio. We had scripts and selected our own songs to be played. Our graduation was at the Seabee auditorium. All three of us sat on the stage while the glee club sang. Graduation was June 5, 1956. We left Morocco in August 1956 and I went to Florida State University. My Dad was stationed in Pensacola at the time. To this day, I keep in contact with Becky (Hornsby) Snow, Leila (Griffin) Applewhite, Sue (Greksouk) Kerry, Larry Miller and some of the wonderful people I met at the reunion last year in Imperial Beach, CA. Let's have another reunion before we all get too old to travel. Enjoyed remembering the "good old days."

Pat Le Fleur Jones

My Dad, CAPT Bill Kopfler, CEC, USNR RET was in Port Lyautey from 1954-1955 as Assistant Public Works Officer, under then CDR Sam Gill. I believe my Dad was either a LT or LCDR at the time. In reading the Kenitra High School memories of the first class I got a laugh when they mentioned Mrs. Duborg, the base CO's wife as their teacher - she was my fifth-grade teacher! My Dad is in the early stages of Alzheimer's but is really enjoying the pictures on your site. He does remember Port Lyautey fondly, as does the whole family. Thank you for your wonderful efforts,

Dixie Kopfler Susalla

The Class of 1956 did not have a Yearbook.

Who Remembers the Stables?

I rode almost every weekend!

Chloe Camry

We were civilians and my dad was actually working on the northern and eastern areas of the Mediterranean. Mom loved Morocco and we had good friends there in the community so we lived in town for a while then moved to the beach. As an American I could go to the school and we could use the base. It was nice and we utilized all the facilities there. I started with my riding instructor, Mr. Hoyer, in 1954 at La Chenaie and then he moved to the stables there on base. I rode every day with him there until October '58. He had been on the Dutch Olympic Equestrian team at the '36 games in Berlin but didn't medal. I leased 3 horses ("Babbul", "Sharron" & "Bushadea") so I could ride with him every day. I used to ride out the back gate and to the beach, over the hills or to the old Moorish fort. No fences and in those days but cork forests and tall grasses. I almost got killed in '58 though when he asked me to take a steeplechaser that had had bowed tendons and been pin-fired. They wanted to see if we could make him a jumper. I think he was in such pain he was nuts. He threw me into 2 jumps then the final was he started for the arena fence and threw me into a post and then attacked me. I was blind, deaf, no memory and a damaged inner ear from that one. I didn't fully recover for a full year. I've spent my life with horses though and still ride. I know Mr. Hoyer had no family and had fled Europe because he had been in the resistance. I hope he found the horses a home after we gave up the base. We lived out at the beach and had 2 burros. Unfortunately, one of them disappeared. I still own a burro today. I have a long story about a ride Mr. Hoyer took me on with his friends that they did several times a year called "La Chase". It almost killed me. It was basically follow the leader and jump what the leader jumped. Crazy, crazy memories.

Sharon Grandy Vinson

From '59 to '61...I was riding almost every day...that was such a luxury. Mr. Hoyer was trying to teach me to jump and the house kept refusing. I continued over the jump without the horse several times. I insisted it was the horse's fault and of course Mr. Hoyer jumped with no problem. I spent a lot of time at the stables and Mr. Hoyer was so patient.

Susan Bernet

We were there from 1969 to 1972 and the riding stables were still there and in use. Besides getting to ride horses, the stable had a mascot burro named Taco which was a real trip to ride. His little legs would about rattle your teeth out, but he was good sport about it and never tried to throw us. We never did get anyone to show us how to jump, but we did like barrel racing. I had a few tumbles myself, so hearing you guy's stories tells me it's just part of the deal.

David Neumann

Mr. Hoyer was my coach in 1957.

Sylvia Torrey

I also had some lessons at the stables there. Mr. Hoyer was a nice man, very patient as I remember.

Melinda McLaughlin

I liked to rent the burros and take them up the narrow paths on the cliffs. Glad that they were sure-footed. I weighed 118 back then and didn't feel like I was breaking the backs of the burros after seeing bigger and older men in town riding them using a stick on their neck and cursing them in Arabic, LOL.

Mike Crumpton

Rode a couple of times. Then one stumbled and threw me. Didn't ride them after that.

Tony Collins

My first summer we rode a lot. Jody Ballard had a horse, and I remember riding behind Bill Bradley a couple of times. We'd take the horses to Mehdia Beach. We would take them into the water. We'd have bread and gouda cheese sandwiches for lunch and then ride them back to base. Fun times!

Nancy Lukas-Slaoui

We went riding horses from the stables to Mehdia Beach. We would ride the horses in the water. I wasn't much of a rider, but that was fun. I remember the donut man at the beach.

Bill Bradley

Jody's horse was named Tougy. Rode Tougy quite a bit after Jody's family left Morocco. I loved that horse.

Kathleen Therese Campbell-Marble

I have a photo of Rudy, next to a corral with horses. I never rode. My mother forbade it. She was afraid I would be seriously injured. My loss.

Viki Lasher

We had a horse that looked pathetic when we bought him. We named him Brochette. He filled out. All he could do was trot. We think he was a cart horse. He eventually learned to run and I'd take him to the beach with Jody Ballard and Cheryl Bradley. I was not a good rider but Cheryl Woodward and Jody were. It was fun but scary.

Marguerite Golden Bright

Riding got me thru a lot. We sure had some good times. Some Jody and I have will still just keep between us!

Cheryl Woodward

I was always told Brochette was Charlene's horse. He was a small, short thing with stiff bristles in his hair. I rode him a few times. He was not terribly responsive to signals. I do remember thinking the "stable" crowd was multigenerational and busy and tight. I remember going to picnics and dances at the stable, and they all seemed to know one another. I was not a good rider either, only did the trails with a Moroccan guide, I think.

Carla Golden Callaghan

Yes, my horse was Brochette, the best horse there. He sure made one little girl very happy. My Dad bought him off base at a livestock sale, or their equivalent of one. When we brought him on base he had to be quarantined for a month from the other horses.

Douglas E. Campbell

Dad paid 75 bucks for him. Some of the other horses were named Satan, and Sultan.

Charlene Golden Coke

    I use to ride with Tami Desrocher and Kelly Bates. I think both of them had horses. I was terrified of the steep trails!!

Michele Fetterly

    My sons, John and Mike [ages 13 14], would ride ['58 -'61], here's one of John's stories: "There was the manager named Gallagher at the stables... for 50 cents he would saddle up the meanest Arabian Stallions for my brother Mike and I, and wish us good luck... we rarely made it out of the stable yard... as my horse would either jump on Mike's horse or throw us though/over the inner ring fence... I think Gallagher had a sense of humor... he always offered us the brown horses but Mike and I would not have any part of it. Would often try to be there to watch Grace Clark ride an Arabian Stallion... she was poetry in motion"

Joan Ellen Bernard

    I had a horse - his name was Destiny. Katherine "Natalie" Gibbs Metzger was my riding buddy. Loved it!

Karen Ruth Butler

OK, not quite the Stables, but this is me riding a camel on base at Bouknadel. Another happy memory with my Daddy. He loved those camels! LOL YES, I am shooting the peace sign!

Beverly Beardsley

CLASS OF 1957

1957 saw the continued growth of bigger taller tail fins on new cars and more lights, bigger with more powerful engines and an average car sold for $2,749. The Soviet Union launched the first space satellite Sputnik 1. Movies included "Twelve Angry Men" and "The Bridge Over the River Kwai", and TV showed "Perry Mason" and "Maverick" for the first time. The music continued to be Rock and Roll with artists like "Little Richard". The popular toys were Slinkys and Hula Hoops. The continued growth of the use of credit was shown by the fact that 2/3rds of all new cars were bought on credit. Some of the areas that would cause problems later were starting to show: South Vietnam was attacked by Viet Cong Guerrillas and National Guard troops were sent to Arkansas to enforce anti-segregation laws.

I Remember:

My father, Thomas Tennent Garland, was a 1st Class Storekeeper in charge of the warehouse for the base Navy Exchange from 1954 through 1956 or early 1957. We lived in the town on a street I think was called Rue de la Mamora. I went to school on the base during the week and at a local Catholic school in town on Saturdays. My brother, Bruce Garland, was born in the base hospital on 2 April 1956. I have fond memories of my childhood there (I was 5 when we arrived, and 8 when we left). Thank you and blessings to all!

Linda L. Garland Oestreich

This is just unbelievable, just reading the wonderful letters from you all has cleared up many things I had forgotten. I too lived at the American hotel, the first one was small but later we moved in a much larger one and we could go up on the roof and sun tan. My Mother was a great cook and she would make big pizzas for everyone that lived on that floor. Does anyone remember that? My Dad was Air Force (I got a lot of teasing from that) and stationed in Rabat.

Back in '57 there was no high school there and I was the oldest civilian female there all of 17. I was jeeped to school every day back and forth (sometimes in a six-by) for a while. I was the only high school student stationed in Rabat. We also lived in Port Lyautey, still took the bus to school but don't seem to remember much of that. I remember the McBride twins I was real close to one of them.

I remember the awful bus accident, I cried a lot. I have been looking for them for years but can't find them. Years ago, I found out that when they came back to the States, the girls went and lived with their grandmother and for the life of me I can't remember where. That was back in 1964. After my life got busy and time just got away, but now as I get older and things are more or less at a standstill I have time to reflect.

Paulette Kaczmarski

I was at the NAS during the period 1956-1957 as a high school student while visiting my father who was a civilian employee. We lived on the circle and I enjoyed my stay in Morocco very much.

Glenn Snider

The 1957 Yearbook

Administration: CAPT C. H. Duborg, USN (CO) ; LT F. B. Morse, USN (Information and Education Officer); Mart A. Murphy (Superintendent of Schools); and Mauro F. Caputo (Principal).

Faculty and Staff: Nancy Armstrong; Janine Courson; Miriam H. George; Natalie Haglund; Frank A. Hedrick; Marjorie R. Poe; Mona Riggs; Bernard L. Quinlan; and Rosina L. White. **Staff:** Mrs. Thomas (Secretary).

The 16 graduating Seniors of 1957: Lynn Alles (President); Glenda Mathis (Vice-President); Donna Hamilton (Secretary); Glenn Snider (Treasurer); Joe Basha; Joanna Coleman; Diana

Dice; Sherrie Greenwood; Irene Hannum; Jan Kassell; Sylvia Lasell; Robert Plank; Ruby Lee Shuping; Linda Snider; Carol Thayer; and Anita Vermillion.

CLASS OF 1958

1958 found Americans in a recession and with a large increase in unemployment - over 7.0% (5.2 million people) - inflation dipped below 2% in 1958 so those working were earning the average of $3,851 per year and were considered quite well off. Cars continued to get bigger and heavier with larger engines, but imports continued to grow now with Datsuns and Toyotas entering the marketplace. America's first satellite was launched from Cape Canaveral. This is also the year that the microchip was first developed - which is the very early stages of Personal Computers that now make up our daily lives. This was also the year of the Munich air disaster on February 6 in which seven Manchester United soccer players died. In Morocco, the northern strip of Spanish Sahara was ceded to Morocco on April 10. Ten days later Morocco demands the departure of Spanish troops and on December 23 Abdallah Ibrahim forms the government of Morocco.

I Remember:

I lived off base in Kenitra across from the MIMOSA French cafe/dance hall for one year only. I am sort of a member of the 1958 and 1959 class though I graduated in Kingsville, TX. Class members were John Schlict (deceased), Sandy Walsh, Rhona Toonk, Vicki Wakeman, Alta Smith, Lee Barnette, Gigi Keene, Gary Kirkindall, Margi Kemp, Kathi McMichael, Sandy Spies Fredric (seen her a few times), Karen Crane, Sherry DeHart, Judy Hill, Shirlee Egan, Tom Silvey, Deanna Greenwood (saw her at New Orleans reunion), & Mike Corder. I have been in contact with others, but I lost my yearbook! I distinctly remember Aicha Lahgzouai and Faiza Sbihi. Any word of them?

Patricia Mattingly Wallace

My father (Grant Lawrence) was stationed at Sidi Yahia from 1956-58. We lived on the base and I graduated from the dependents High School in June 1958. Would love to hear from anyone who remembers my dad (who unfortunately passed away in 1995) or me. My brother Glenn and I were at Sidi Yahia in 1958. After we went back to the States, I married a guy I met there and my brother joined the Navy and got sent to Port Lyautey. He said it sure was different being a sailor or an officer's son. A few years later, my cousin who was making a career of the Navy was sent to Sidi Yahia! But wait there's more! My brother later was driving a semi-truck and trailer and got snowed in somewhere in the Midwest at a truck stop. He spent some time talking to everyone, especially this sailor. The guy said he was being shipped to a new duty station. My brother asked him where he was coming from and he told him: "Probably somewhere you never heard of, Sidi Yahia, Morocco", and, as it turned out, he shared a room with my cousin while he was there!! Top that one!

Sue (Lawrence) York

The Class of 1958 did not have a Yearbook but here's a photo of the Cheerleaders!

My Dad, Lt. Comdr. Jack James, USN-SC, was stationed at Port Lyautey from 1956-58 when I was age 10 - 12. We lived in the town of Port Lyautey. Earlier this year my sister and I decided to revisit Morocco. However, we were unable to gain access to the base which is now part of the Royal Moroccan Air Force. Before we went, we tried every angle we could to get on the base....contacted the Moroccan Embassy (courteous but non-responsive), contacted an acquaintance who is teaching at the American School in Rabat (his Moroccan contacts were not able to help). I got the feeling that if we greased the palm of someone we might have gotten somewhere. Anyway, we did go through Port Lyautey and had it grown! We were unable to find where we used to live in the town but drove around the town which was very congested. We did learn that the base was used for some flight line scenes in the movie "Black Hawk Down." Sale near Rabat was used for other scenes in that movie and the Green Zone. Morocco has really changed. Well-built four-lane toll roads stretching from Marrakech to Fez to Tangier. Large farms and modern farm equipment. The young women wear blue jeans, sunglasses and wear makeup. About 25% of the older women wore the traditional djellabas and women drive cars. In the arid eastern part of Morocco, the government is putting in water lines. Everyone loves the King and will tell you so to the point that I became uncomfortable. Police and Army are present most everywhere. Roadblocks are a common experience. We were there in March 2011 after the conflict with Libya had begun and security was tight even at the airport in Casablanca (formerly Nouasseur AFB). The people were very friendly and always extended an outstretched palm looking for a tip (that aspect of daily life has not changed). It was fun but I do not think we will ever go back (too old).

Elizabeth James

Sherrie Greenwood was Deanna Greenwood's younger sister. Although not a Class of 1958, her comments are most appropriate here:

The only time I ever ran into anyone I knew in Morocco was in Honolulu in 1971, thirteen years after leaving Morocco. We lived in Waipahu for 18 months while my husband was on one of the old Apollo tracking ships that docked at Pearl Harbor. My mother was visiting us and while eating at a restaurant, we both thought that a gentleman eating with his family at another table looked familiar. Curiosity got the best of me and I went over to ask if we might know each other. I'm sure no one's surprised that we knew each other from Morocco. He was an airman, stationed at Sidi Slimane in 1957 and we sang in the same choir on base. Until being reunited with my best bud, Glenda Mathis through Classmates.com, that was my only shocking Morocco-related experience. I also vividly remember the Sidi Slimane evacuation incident. I had graduated and was working at the PX (AFEX) in Slimane. Sister DeAnn was at school in Kenitra, but parents picked up younger sibs and I, and we drove a distance from the base where many cars lined up alongside the road, where we waited and waited and waited. Seemed like forever before we were allowed to go back. I recall some pretty scary times during the revolution while living at Mehdia. We'd get a knock on the door, ordering us to close shutters on windows, keep doors locked and not venture out. At the time I recall feeling apprehensive, yet excited.

Sherrie (Greenwood) Hendrix

Student entertainment, from left to right: Sandy Spies, Cheryl Boudrou, Colene Piercy and DeAnn Greenwood.

Oh my goodness, I remember this night so well. TMW had an International party and we were lip synching to Youngblood. I do believe this was in 1958 which was my last year in Morocco. What a fun time we had!

DeAnn Greenwood

Who Remembers the Mamora Hotel?

My folks and I stayed at the Mamora during summer of 1962 before getting a villa in Kenitra and my starting my sophomore year at Thomas Mack Wilhoite. I really liked the hotel, the pool, and the little coffee shop. The market outside was fun and a great way to start a two-year tour in a cool city.

Barry Click

3rd floor right in the curve we had a two-room suite, stayed there for 3+ weeks.

Terri Spring

Our family was there almost 100 days waiting on housing. We arrived in summer 1970 left after graduation summer 1974. Pool was green and mossy the whole time.

Mark Roberts

Our family stayed there when we first got there. I remember loving to watch the swans.

Kathleen Therese Campbell-Marble

My fondest memory in Morocco besides all the cool friends I made was the swimming pool at the Mamora Hotel in Kenitra. I stayed there in summer of 1971! I finally got Charlie Beggs to jump off the high diving board at the hotel's pool!! He wimped out several times but finally took the plunge when Harry LaDue kept busting his chops about not jumping!! Harry LaDue's daughter was Sheri LaDue who was in the 7th grade in the 1971 - 72 school year. FUN TIMES IN MOROCCO!!

Robert Oberkehr

We did!!! Loved it. Met a dressmaker named Vincent Mari who specialized in wedding dresses and dated his brother Tony Mari who worked at a pharmacy across from the clock in the center of town. Also became friends with the French hairdresser and his partner who was American. They had their shop just around the corner of the building. Vincent's shop was the third shop down to the left in this picture. I dated Tony and brought him to the prom in '66. Everyone called him my Latin Lover!!!

Bonnie Arey Fowler

We stayed at the Mamora 30 days in '68 and 30 days in '70 on the 2nd floor. Maxine Fetterly had tea there in 2000, while at the reunion.

Juanita Cornette

We stayed in the Mamora from September - December 1970 and it was really quite a classy place especially with the white swans in the pond across the street. Unfortunately, they had just drained the pool for the winter months so didn't get to try it out. The Navy bus picked us up and dropped us off right in front. We moved out in town for several months, and then we were assigned some base housing. In the hotel we felt relatively safe, but out in town was a little rough so we were thankful to get on the base plus everything was convenient. I really enjoyed the 5 course meals at the Mamora, but you had to hold back on the hors d'oeuvre tray or you would fill up before the main course or worse, the desert. I still remember the flambé style desserts with the flaming brandy. While we were there at the Mamora, Kenitra hosted a grand prix car race with them passing right in front of the hotel so it was an exciting weekend. It's nice to see some of the old buildings even though Kenitra is modernizing around them. My mom used to try her French out at the Marché, while my brother, John Eric Neumann, and I would love to check out the fish and the meat market.

David Neumann

We were there until Jun 5, '67 when the Six Day War started. We were evacuated from the hotel to Bouk, moving in without our household goods. Daddy came to check on us only to find the Jarheads had dug a foxhole in the back yard overlooking the Bouk gate. Daddy believed they were guarding the new teenage girls who had moved in. Neighbors fed us because we did not have access to the commissary or kitchen stuff.

Deborah Robin Kafir

The Mamora was the last place we stayed before leaving Morocco. We lived not far from it, for 4 years. We left when I was 12 in May 1970.

Carmen Byrd Bohn

We stayed there coming and going!

Bill Bradley

That's where I met George and Renate Phillips. The Fleming's lived just around the corner (I Think).

Lee Sichter

Great mint tea. Thursday was best day to swim in the pool (after it was drained and cleaned!). Stayed there Summer 1972.

Patrick Senf

Was there in '66 for about a month. I remember the Mercedes bus that took us to school.

David Aiken

This was my first home in Morocco for 4 months until our base housing opened up. My sister and I shared a room that overlooked the pool and into Faraj's backyard. We used to shout to each other from the window. Good news. I was visiting with Chakib Loudiyi, Class of 1973, last week and he said that the Mamora Hotel is still there. They didn't tear it down like the guide told us at the 2012 Rabat reunion. Hurray!

Nancy Lukas-Slaoui

Lived there for about 5 or 6 weeks while waiting for base housing, Dec. 65-Feb. 66!

Brenda Cozad Nutt

I don't remember how long we stayed but do remember me and my brother being picked up there for school on base which we ended up living right next to. I was 10.

Tannis Wa

Ours was a two month stay at the Mamora hotel!

Jerold Jenkins, Jr.

Loved the Mamora! I remember croissants and real, unsalted butter...too good!

Barbara Ford

Some fantastic salads at dinner, so tasty and fresh!

Mary L. Zamora Thompson

We stayed in officer's barracks at the bottom of the hill from the Oasis and a few blocks up from the bakery the French sailors had then....1960.

Cece Canton

Yes, we all stayed there until we were moved into a Quonset hut...and then to a big house where we spent most of our three years '58 -'61.

Joan Ellen Bernard

I spent a month there upon arriving!

Katherine Gibbs Metzger

We spent a month there before leaving. We stayed at Hotel Rotunde when we arrived. Both hotels are still there and operating. Last year I went for a swim in the Mamora pool while there...Still a well-kept-up swimming pool.

Kathy Sacra-Anderson

We stayed there a couple months in 1966 when we arrived. My friend and I got caught throwing water balloons from the roof at people across the street watching the swans. Boy did we get in trouble. LOL They dried the motels sheets on the roof too. I was in 7th grade.

Robert Goodreau

Stayed there briefly in 1960...then down the street to the Regina. I was in the 8th grade. We did the water balloon thing also but didn't get caught. Used to put firecrackers in the donkey poop...did wonders to the white-washed walls. Ahhh, to be young again!

Patrick Foley

John Fleming became (according to legend) a "Free-throw Guru" from his experience of throwing eggs off the roof....and made it into professional basketball.

Charlene Bratton

When I first arrived in Kenitra, we stayed at the Mamora Hotel. In the evenings, I would chat and play cards with a retired somewhat famous soccer player (or so he claimed) named Eduardo who seemed so worldly and spoke more languages than I could imagine. Sitting in the draped nooks seemed like a romantic spy novel. And, of course, he wanted to know who everyone was that came and went and also told me who everyone was that he knew! In the plaza out front it seemed so Parisian. I browsed the bakery where they made the pastries and the baker told me they painted them with apricot jelly to keep them fresh and sooooo good! When the car races came to Kenitra, the family hung out the window to see them speeding through. We had croissants with shell-shaped butter and apricot jam and of course chocolat chaud! Poured from two pitchers into one cup from at least a foot above! I did feel so special!

Jessie Smith Allen

HOTEL MAMORA

BAR
RESTAURANT
SALON DE THE
JARDINS
PISCINE

LE SALON

LE BAR

CONSTRUIT en 1952, selon la dernière technique hôtelière, l'hôtel Mamora est un des grands établissements touristiques des plus perfectionnés de l'Afrique du Nord.

L'hôtel Mamora allie le privilège de son heureuse situation en plein centre de la ville, aux avantages d'une tranquillité particulière aux abords des jardins des Services Municipaux.

L'hôtel dispose d'appartements privés et de 72 chambres, avec téléphone, salle de bain ou douche, et radio pour la plupart.

Le restaurant, où l'on se réclame des grandes traditions de la cuisine française, forme, avec le bar et les salons, un ensemble fort coquet qui complète merveilleusement cet hôtel de tout premier ordre.

PLACE DE L'HOTEL - DE - VILLE
TELÉPH. 30-06, 30-07
TÉLÉGR. MAMOTEL

PORT - LYAUTEY

BUILT in 1952, according to the latest data of modern hotel technique.

The hotel Mamora represents one of the largest and most perfect touring establishments of North Africa.

The hotel Mamora combines a privileged position in the very heart of the city, with the advantages of a quiet peaceful site by the town gardens.

The 72 rooms are all equipped with telephone, bath, shower and some with radio.

The restaurant wich is famous for maintaining the great tradition of french cooking makes a fine expanse with the lounges and the american bar.

The 14 graduating Seniors of 1958 (Incomplete – based on Junior Class of 1957): Bob Averitt, Eddie Diamond; Eli Hendrix; Sue Lawrence; Beth MacNeill; Pat McCool; Donna Melcher; Nancy Naureckas; Judy Odbert; Darrla Paddock; Colene Piercy; Jeanne Pitcher; Sharon Williams; and Joni Wirz.

CLASS OF 1959

1959 saw the U.S. unemployment problems ease to 5.5%. Television programs included "Rawhide", "Bonanza" and "The Twilight Zone." Movies included "Some Like It Hot", "Ben Hur" and "North by Northwest". Alaska was admitted to the Union and became the 49th state; the Territory of Hawaii then became our 50th State. The Boeing 707 Jet Airliner comes into service and little girls fell in love with the Barbie Dolls created by Ruth Handler and made by Mattel. Fidel Castro came to power in Cuba.

I Remember:

I was in Morocco in 1957, '58, '59. I attended school at Brown HS in Casa in '57 and '58 and stayed in the boarding house during the week, returning to Ben Guerir AFB on the weekends. In the spring of '58 we moved to Sidi Slimane and I traveled daily to Port Lyautey with others on the bus. Now that was quite a ride!!! I remember passing Sidi Yahia on the way to school in our packed bus. At times there were mobs carrying red flags, and it was fairly scary. Can't imagine living there. Remember the Arab that always rode in the back of the bus? What I remember most about being in school at Wilhoite HS was the daily killing of a hog next door and the horrible sounds coming from it. I actually had the bus driver drop me off at the base library on the way to school one day so I could study for an exam. That was my one and only time to skip school and some way my folks found out and I got in trouble. Seems like I was with another girl ... maybe Lynn (can't remember her last name). I started working that summer at the base exchange on Sidi and ended up running the gift shop for the next year. Didn't go back to school but took correspondence classes.

Would have graduated in 1959 if I had used the good sense I was born with, but I opted to go to work at the BX. Thought the long ride every day to Wilhoite was a waste of time, I guess. I spent a lot of time at the swimming pool and theater...also remember trips to Mehdia Beach. All in all, I loved Morocco. I remember Sandy Spies, DeAnn and Colene very well.

Linda DeLashaw Gilliam

October 6, 1959

GRIDIRON GIRLS

The Cheerleaders pictured above from left to right are: Back row: Dee Dee Hale, Roxie Hughes, Grace Clark, and Beverly Johnson. Front row: Judy Perry, Jean Kosin, Susan Kelly, and Sandy Boudrou.

Cheerleaders
For '59 Season

The try-outs for the six positions as Cheerleaders were held on September 23. The judges, Mrs. Spears, Miss Walston, Mr. Price, Mr. Mercer, Mr. Stebbins and three Seniors, Barbara Wilson, Karl Mohns and Wayne Smith had a very difficult task of choosing the girls from a group of twenty eight. They gave each girl a number and used a point system.

Two freshmen, Grace Clark and Susan Kelly; one Sophomore, Beverly Johnson; two Juniors, Roxie Hughs and Judy Perry; one Senior who is Sandy Boudrou; and two substitutes, Jean Kosin, and Dee Dee Hale were the lucky girls choosen as the ones responsible for the enthusiasm and spirit for Wilhoite's football games.

We know these girls will do a very capable job.

In 1959, Miss Margaret Walston taught 8th Grade English and History to her students. She found the whole experience fascinating. "You had a very interesting situation in that school," she said. "As part of President Eisenhower's People to People program, some children from the local communities attend, and I had three French children in my classes and also two little Moroccan boys who only spoke Arabic at the beginning of the year. And do you know, those boys picked up English grammar faster than our American children did! And the American children had lived all over the world, almost. You start to teach a unit on Japan, for instance, and you find you have a student who lived in Japan for three years." The school, Thomas Mack Wilhoite, was housed in a former military barracks, she said. "It was adequate, not plush, certainly." But she said the local schools were pathetic. "Our Red Cross project last year was to get pencils and paper for a Moroccan school near us that had none." The thing that impressed Miss Walston the most was the extremes in Morocco – between wealth and poverty, and between the new and the old. "There are the few who are extremely rich and the many who are desperately poor. I got so tired of seeing filth and poverty. Morocco has some of the most modern buildings in the world and it has people who live exactly as their ancestors did a thousand years ago. You see people in ancient costumes coming out of modern apartment buildings. You see herds of camels being driven down the main streets." With other teachers at the base, Miss Walston did a lot of traveling. "On weekends we'd take bus trips or tours, and we saw most of Morocco that way. We went to Fez, Marrakech and Meknes, for instance. We were near enough to Gibraltar that we went there a few times. I did not get to Agadir before the earthquake, though some of the other teachers did. They said it was a lovely modern resort area. It was, of course, completely flattened and we weren't allowed to go there after the quake. In January and February we went skiing in the [Atlas] mountains. Before I went to Africa I wouldn't have believed it if you'd told me they had snow enough for skiing there – but they do, in the mountains. Along the coast where we were it doesn't ever get cold, of course. The climate is perfect – warm and dry and always a pleasant breeze from the ocean." At Christmas time Miss Walston and her roommate spent their two weeks' vacation traveling in Europe. Easter vacation they spent driving through Spain and Portugal. By then she had a little MG, which she ordered through London through Tangiers. She said she found living costs very low in Morocco. "Maid service was $1.15 a week and we ate most of our meals in clubs or restaurants. You could get a complete steak dinner for $2 and in my book, you can't cook for that." Shopping, she said, was most interesting. "Moroccan handiwork is most interesting – leather goods, brass trays, hand-woven blankets. I had all my Christmas presents for this year bought before I left Africa. There were French shops where you could get the latest things from Paris and there were open-air markets where you bought fruits and vegetables and haggled over prices. At first I used to pay anything they asked until I found out that bargaining is expected and sort of a sport with Arab merchants." Were the fruits and vegetables safe? "We washed everything in chlorine solution before we ate it." Miss Walston said that the experience or teaching and traveling in Morocco was wonderful because theirs was such a different culture. "In Europe, too, you can find different cultures. But in Morocco it's all around you – you can't miss it."

Miss Margaret Walston

Attended TMW from February 1958 through February 1959. Lived off base at Rue de Oranges.... outside of Kenitra. Rode a bus to school, and often rode local busses, etc., to get to the base. We rented a villa from a French farmer who grew oranges as well as other crops. Hung out at the Teen Club, Oasis, etc. Left after only one year due to sickness in the family.

Gary Skiff

I was there '54 to '59 so it was the longest station with my dad. Lived in Kenitra, then a Quonset hut, then moved into like a townhouse on base.

Barbara Benson Rogers

My father, Vincent "Roy" Willever, was stationed in Port Lyautey from 1955 through 1959. He was a Dental Technician at the base Dental Clinic. I was only 5 when we were transferred to Morocco, but it was an adventure I will never forget. We lived in town when we first arrived; there were other military families in the apartment complex. Our time in this country covered many varied things, from the bombing of the French homes across the street when we lived in town, the Arab doorman who stood outside with his large knife, the visiting Women's Fast-pitch Softball team; living in the Quonset hut on base and going to the base school. I have many pictures and film of our stay there and have shown it to my children and grandchildren. My youngest sister was born on the base there. It was a troubled time and our return stateside was not an easy one. We had to fly to Cadiz, Spain and stay there until a steam liner could transport us back to the States.

Peggy Willever Johnson

My father, Leonard Culjat, was stationed in Port Lyautey from 1957 to 1959; he served as comptroller and as industrial relations officer (most likely human resources today). [NOTE: He was also President of the TMW Board of Education]. He made many friends with French and Arab employees of the base, some of these friendships spanned over 40 years until his death in 2000. Our family enjoyed Morocco immensely and it set the foundation for my own interest in exploring different cultures particularly through the Peace Corps and through teaching ESL to refugees. My parents always let me take the "French bus" from the base into Kenitra by myself and I would explore the market, the "tout a 100 francs" store and return to the Mamora Hotel where we lived for 5 months until a Quonset hut opened up on the base. When we returned to the States, my mother would make cous cous at least once a year and they had packets of it (the traditional cous cous, not the instant) shipped to the States and they would freeze it. For years, we were in touch in Jeanne Fuentes, Jeanne Mortier and Jeanine Cacace as well as Maurice Cohen who moved to Rota, Spain. I went to Jr. High at Thomas Mack Wilhoite and was in touch with Anita Counihan, Anita Pitcher, and Kathy North for a few years in the 1970s. I recall fond days of horseback riding with Mr. Halter and other students, a day trip along the beach and through to a park. I was fortunate to have the chance to revisit Morocco in 1992 and Jeanne Mortier arranged a quick visit to the base where I saw the theater, the chapel, the PX and the pool--our house had been torn down but it didn't affect me as the memories are the ones I keep with me wherever I go. Whenever I swim at an outdoor pool, I think of Morocco and the pool and warm sun. I revisited the Mamora Hotel and the market where I savored the preserved lemons that we can now buy in the US. If anyone one knew me or my parents, Leonard and Marget Culjat, please feel free to contact me at cscdlc@nwfirst.com. My sister Terry also made many friends. I also baby sat for many young officers and their families including the Portos and the Prathers.

Dorothy Culjat

Having read a number of remembrances of those who were in Morocco, I would like to add a few notes of my own. I first arrived in Casablanca aboard the USNS (MSTS) General Geiger in September 1953. We went directly to Port Lyautey where my dad was living even though he was working as a base engineer at Sidi Slimane since 1952. We stayed at several hotels including the Mamora and then into a series of private homes on Rue de Lyon, Avenue de la Gare, Avenue de Lorraine and the Route de Rabat.

In 1953, I was in 7th grade and always remembered waiting for the Navy school bus and watching the French kids approximately my age then walking to school carrying a baguette and a bottle of red wine. Things were certainly different then. The only persons I can remember from the school bus days are Chris Navarro, Bill Griffin, Leila Griffin and Lapred Brady. I had many good times there. I graduated 8th grade in 1955 and came back to the US and did my freshman year here and then went back to Morocco via MATS to Nouasseur for my sophomore year 1956-57. I would have been a 1959 graduate of TMW.

I can remember Brian Burke, Pat Perkett and Mrs. Riggs but few others. I lost my copy of the "Sultan" many years ago, so I go by memory only.

Most people seem to have been in Morocco in the years following my stint. I do remember the French Navy cooks slaughtering the pigs or hogs in the open on the street directly below the school. Sanitation was not a requirement. I have many other remembrances of Morocco.

Vince Bailey

You may remember me as the daughter of an Air Force Chaplain. I was Class of '59 and married in '59 and have one daughter and one son, two grandsons and one granddaughter. After 15 years, I divorced. Eight years later, I remarried and we have been together 22 years. Currently we are living in the mountains of North Carolina and enjoying our retirement riding these roads on our motorcycle.

Linda Delashaw

From the Chillicothe Constitution-Tribune (Chillicothe, Missouri), 11 May 1959:

> ## HELPS TEENAGERS WITH OVERSEAS GOOD WILL
>
> A school dance had an international atmosphere recently at the chief petty officer's club at Port Lyautey, Morocco. The student council of the Thomas Mack Wilhoite High School welcomed guests from the College du Kenitra and the colorful background included American, French and Moroccan flags.
>
> The sponsors were Russell E. Dayton, son of Charles Dayton of Chillicothe, and Mrs. Virginia Reed, members of the school faculty.
>
> There was a program as well as dancing.
>
> The khalifa of the Pasha of Kenitra, H. E. Thami Serouillou, told the students he was highly impressed with the feeling of friendship shown by all students.

The 1959 Yearbook

Administration: CAPT Verne A. Jennings (NAS Base Commander) ; CAPT John L. Counihan, Jr. (COMNAVACTS Commander); LCDR James E. Waldron (School Officer) ; Mr. Mart A. Murphy (School Superintendent) ; CDR Leonard M. Culjat (President of the Board of Education) ; Mr. Robert I. Tharp (High School Principal) ; and Mr. Elwin B. Dell (Elementary School Principal) .

Faculty & Staff: High School Faculty: Mrs. Alice F. Affolter; Mr. John C. Aliano; Mr. Robert J. Boula; Mr. Steven Bogden; Miss Gail Buttler; Mr. Russell E. Dayton; Mr. Guy T. Hagan; Mrs. Lois I. Harris; Madame Anne Moussu; Mrs. Carol Parrent; Mrs. Mary Perez; Mr. Eugene Quinn; Mrs. Janine Quinn; Miss Caroline Smith; Mrs. Lois F. Smith; and Miss Marie Vines. **Staff:** Mrs. Trudy K. Kane (Secretary to Superintendent) ; Mrs. Violet Diamond

(Secretary to High School Principal) ; Mrs. Dorothy Sutton (Secretary to Elementary Principal); Mrs. Elizabeth A. Smith (Elementary School Librarian) ; and Hohmane Ben Jilali.

The 13 graduating Seniors of 1959: Shirlee Egan (President) ; Sandy Walsh (Vice-President) ; Sandy Spies (Secretary) ; (no Treasurer); Elaine Ball; Mike Corder; Gigi Keene; Margaret Kemp; Pat Mattingly; Sue Mitchell; Donald Shockley; Alta Smith; Rhona Toonk; and Jerry Weeks.

CLASS OF 1960

1960 saw the Cold War become colder as the distrust between the two superpowers increased, culminating in the shootdown of Francis Gary Powers' U-2 spy plane near Moscow on May 1. John Fitzgerald Kennedy and his vice president Lyndon Johnson won the election with one of the smallest margins in history – by 113,000 votes out of 68.3 million cast. The sexual revolution of the 1960's had begun with the use of birth control pills and Hugh Hefner opening the first of his Playboy clubs in Chicago. The "Flintstones" is shown on television for the first time and movies this year included "The Magnificent Seven" and "Psycho." Notable technical achievements include the invention of the Laser and a Heart Pacemaker. France tests its first atomic bomb and joins those countries with nuclear bomb technology. Notable names that appear in the limelight that year include "Cassius Clay" (the boxer Muhammad Ali) and "Sir Francis Chichester" (winner of the world's first solo transatlantic sailing race in *Gipsy Moth III)*. The US sends its first troops to Vietnam following the French withdrawal in 1954 in the fight against communist North Vietnam. In Morocco, the Agadir earthquake in Morocco kills a third of that town's population (12,000-15,000) on February 29. Born in 1960 was the Moroccan singer Samira Said on January 10, and Saïd Aquita, the Moroccan 5K runner (Olympic gold 1984), who was born in Kenitra on November 2.

I Remember:

I have many fond memories of our 2 years there - we had a ball! The base swimming pool, where most of us spent all our daylight hours during summer vacation, the "Boy Scout Camp" they had on base at Sidi Slimane, shopping in Port Lyautey, my Mom bargaining with the vendors, etc. And that NASTY mint tea! My gosh, we drank a lot of that stuff, as part of the bargaining process. Yellow headlights. NSU Mopeds. Gross French cigarettes. Our maid, "Heymore" (I never knew her real name). Sand and ice plants for a 'yard'. Pet chameleons. My dad and I liked to build box kites and fly them using an old salt-water rod & reel with 50-pound test string. Once, we built one that was 7 feet tall and 2.5 feet wide - and got it up almost 200 yards. Then the AP's came to the house and asked us to bring it down, because they were picking it up on radar!

Tom Krueger

I remember Mademoiselle Couson marrying Mr. Quinn–not really surprised. This is so neat–I thought a chapter of my life that was long forgotten would never be prodded into my conscious mind again. I remember having to dissect–first a worm, then a frog-in Mr. Quinn's class. I also remember the Gutenbergs. Twenty-five Gutenbergs was his standard punishment - "When and by whom was the first printing press discovered as far as is generally known? Gutenberg, about 1450." For as long as I live I will always be able to answer that question. Mrs. Riggs was our PE teacher, and Mr. Boula the music one. I'll have to look in my yearbook for the typing teacher, a woman, but that class was invaluable throughout the rest of my school years and my career as a special-ed teacher.

I remember having to give a 5-minute speech in English class, and I was shaking so hard when I turned over my written speech it rattled loud enough for the next classroom to hear, I swear. I recall a girl in my class, who I always sat behind because we were seated in alphabetical order, telling me how good my speech was. Yeah, right. Her name was Sandy Gill. Also, my best friends were Karen Crane and Kathy Williams.

The Teen Clubs on Port Lyautey and Sidi Slimane held formal dances – exchanging – first on Port, then Sidi Slimane. We were doing the bunny hop and in the middle of it my ugly half-slip, not the pretty crinolines, fell down around my ankles. I had to stop hopping, step out of it, and grab it and run to the girl's room. I was mortified. In my '57 yearbook, someone drew a sketch of me with my slip hanging down to the floor and asked if I remembered. As if

I could forget! Do you remember those slips under the full skirts? They were so full, we had to tuck them between our knees when sitting so we could see over our skirts!

Then there were penny loafers or saddle shoes, and sweater sets. The beehive hairdos weren't in yet–the page boy was popular then, or a good old-fashioned pony tail. Then the shift dressed came in–made us look shapeless–straight up and down. Ah, for the good old days.

Back in '57 or '58, our bus ride was made even more dangerous. Our driver was a small man who spoke only Spanish, and there were no adults on the bus other than him. One day when the base was surrounded by rebels, when we got to the gate to board the bus, the Marine on guard duty slung his gun over his shoulder and walked us out. Once on, again no adult, and off we went towards Port. Soon there were fighters shooting at each other across the road, and our driver drove us around via a detour over the open terrain. I don't recall being frightened but was fascinated by the adventure. Too young and stupid, I guess. We all had to keep a bag packed at Sidi in case we needed to evacuate immediately.

Then there was the incident from Sidi Slimane where one of the SAC bomber planes crashed on take-off and the base was evacuated into tiny Sidi Yahia. Us high schoolers were in school in Port Lyautey, but my younger siblings went to school in Sidi Slimane and were part of the ensuing mess–just before lunch, wouldn't you know. It was all kept pretty hush hush for a long time. I have been able, finally, to find the incident on line, but it is quite incomplete and speculative. The nuclear bomb on the plane was aboard, but not armed, but in the fire there was a possibility it could have gone off.

I have a story about the day we arrived in Morocco. My dad had already been there for a few months, when my mom, siblings, and I (I was the oldest at 15) took a slew of buses to Norfolk and flew out from there. The whole trip was quite, uh, interesting. Our first stop was in Bermuda. We took off, wearing our Mae Wests, (October, 1957, but hot), and after we started to level off, one of the plane engines caught fire. Of course, on military transport, there were no stewards to tell us what was going on. Finally, the engine stopped and the fire went out. Then the navigator came back to talk to us. We had a row of seats facing backward, with our luggage on the other side of the same level–real "seat-of-the-pants" flying. He said we could make it to the Azores with the 3 remaining engines, but if we lost another, we would have to jettison our luggage. After they circled, dumping all the fuel they had just loaded, we landed back in Bermuda. Then we could finally get out of those hot Mae Wests. After four hours of waiting in the terminal, the plane was repaired and off we went.

We landed in the Azores for breakfast. Then as we neared Morocco, someone announced we couldn't land in Port Lyautey as the Sultan was supposed to land there and the base was opened up to the Moroccan people. So, we headed for Casablanca. Then another passenger spoke up, announced he was an Admiral, and we would land where he damn well pleased. We turned back to Port Lyautey.

We landed and the Moroccans all pressed forward–seemed like a million of them they were so crowded, thinking it was the Sultan's plane. We couldn't disembark.

Finally, a laundry truck pulled up and we were hustled into the back of it to be taken to the terminal. It took many days to find all the natives and get them back off the base. About the same time, a shipment of furniture arrived, wrapped in orange plastic. Some enterprising native collected the plastic and cut slits in them and made raingear and sold them off base. I remember natives riding their bikes or walking around in those flowing orange outfits.

Then we got the classes about what was safe to eat and learning how to soak the local vegetables in Clorox (yuck) to make them safe to eat and all. Quite an introduction to Morocco. But I really loved it there and would love to go back to visit someday.

Also, don't know who "blew" it, but… does anyone remember when us kids from Sidi Yahia hid behind the guard shack instead of getting on the bus? Then we caught the liberty bus into Kenitra but got off in town instead of going on to school. We wandered around one of the local schools, talked to those kids when they were on a break outside, until their principal came out. He asked us our names and of course we gave him phony ones. He said he would arrange for us to visit his school with our principal if that was what we wanted. Then we caught the next liberty bus to get on base, went to the Oasis for lunch, as it was "almost" lunchtime anyway, then went to school. We were standing in the principal's office explaining how we missed the bus and had to wait for the (later) liberty bus, when the phone rang. It was the principal of the French school. The principal repeated the names we had given the other guy, looking pointedly at us. He gave us a break, though, but warned us not to be late again. He knew what we were up to, but couldn't prove it, exactly, so we had gotten away with our Half-Day Hooky. We met some of the kids from the French school later at the International Dance. Looking back, high school was more fun than I thought at the time.

Judy (Hill) Swanson

My father, Frank Boudrou was stationed with his family at Sidi Yahia from March 1957 to June of 1960 when I graduated from high school at Thomas Mack Wilhoite High School on base at Port Lyautey NAS. Anyone remember working with him? He was a court reporter and worked in administration. We loved living there and enjoyed the pool and outdoor movies between the buildings in the summer. I think it cost us a dime to see them. Spent many days at the beach in Kenitra. Have my yearbooks and many pictures.

I have my 1959 yearbook out now and so I started hunting the others down this afternoon.... without any luck. It helps to look up everyone and see pictures! Has anyone kept in touch with Aicha Laghzaoui? She was a junior in 1959 with my class and was one of the Moroccan diplomatic students. We were good friends and her family lived in Rabat. Her father was chief of police and a bodyguard to the king. A big limousine would pick us up at school and take us to her home for the weekend. Wonderful house, servants, etc. I remember being surprised and a bit embarrassed when her maid came to wash my feet! The other Moroccan girl gave a big slumber party at her house and we watched movies and ate my first croissant! Anyone remember that party? We stayed up all night.

Enjoying the memories of time spent in Sidi Yahia and I just have to add some more! We came to Morocco in March 1957 when I was a Freshman and lived at the hotel until we found an apartment in downtown Kenitra. We were on the top floor (108 steps I remember!) and looked at the Mamora Hotel. We were there until we got housing at Sidi Yahia. Lived on base until June of 1960 after graduating from Thomas Mack Wilhoite....my sister was a junior (Cheryl Boudrou) . I have my yearbooks with pictures of us getting on that bus. We were pretty rowdy! We used to bring a loaf of Wonder Bread, share it and have spit ball fights! We would sing sometimes for the entire hour and hassle the Marines who got on to check all of our ID's at the gate in Port Lyautey-singing the Marine anthem, etc...

Others on base were Kitty Favor, Gayle and Mike Corder. We were all best friends. Swam at the pool, took lifeguarding lessons there and went to the movies between the buildings. My mom, Cheryl and I (and Gayle) were all on the Women's Sidi Yahia baseball team! Ha ha I still have a pic of us.

Remember riding the big truck back and forth on the weekends? We would go to Kenitra and the base to play-horseback ride, bowling (where we setup our own pins) and, of course, the Navy Exchange and lived on French fries and cokes. We had lots of slumber parties and would sneak out the window and roam the streets of Kenitra meeting our friends. Got caught by shore patrol one night and never did it again! I believe Anita Jones was with us that night! No fears in those days.

Sandra "Sandy" Boudrou

Do You Remember the Agadir Earthquake?

The 1960 Agadir earthquake occurred on February 29. Between 12,000 and 15,000 people (about a third of the city's population of the time) were killed and another 12,000 injured with at least 35,000 people left homeless, making it the most destructive and deadliest earthquake in Moroccan history. The main shock took place on the third day of the Muslim observance of Ramadan, immediately collapsing many hotels, apartments, markets, and office buildings. Underground water mains broke and sewer systems crumbled. The Kasbah, a dilapidated fortress which had stood for centuries, crumbled on the side of a hill. With no water pressure and most fire stations having collapsed (killing their occupants) many fires were left burning in this resort city with few firefighters and resources to fight them. With nearly seventy percent of the city in ruins, no rescue operations were able to be initiated or arranged from within Agadir. By morning the French army and sailors from the United States Sixth Fleet approached the coast, anchored, and prepared for the rescue process.

"Sponsored by Captain John L. Counihan, Jr., Commander Naval Activities, Port Lyautey, Kenitra, Morocco, was a festive 'Friendship Day' on May 5, 1960, as part of the "People to People Program." This successful event drew over 5,000 visitors from the local community to witness a demonstration of a helicopter rescue, Navy firefighting, a huge picture display depicting Navy friendship in action during the Rharb Valley floods and the Agadir earthquake, and the fly-over by the USAFE Skyblazer jet team. Pictured above are people from the local community walking through an R5D "Skymaster" of Fleet Tactical Support Squadron TWENTY-FOUR based here at Kenitra. Included in the throng who visited this day were approximately 1,500 school children who took time off from their school studies to visit this magnificent display." Official U.S. Navy photograph.

"Pictured above is a Quonset hut, a gift of the Naval Base at Port Lyautey, Kenitra, Morocco, to the city of Kenitra for an international library, being lowered into place on its foundation. Because of an ever-increasing need for library facilities due to the English language teaching program by the Navy Wives in the Takadoun School, this community project was undertaken. Stocked initially with approximately a thousand books, divided among Arab, French and English titles, this international library was dedicated in the presence of high state and governmental officials on the 4th of July, 1960, as the highlight of the gala 4th of July celebrations hosted by Commander Naval Activities, Captain John L. Counihan, Jr., U.S. Navy." Official U.S. Navy photograph.

"Pictured above is part of the thousand books initially stocked in the new "International Library," presented by the Naval Base, Port Lyautey to the city of Kenitra, as part of the continuing program of "People to People" and "Community Projects." In response to an increasing need for library facilities because of the popularity of the Navy Wives English language teaching program in the Takadoun School in Kenitra, this library was built and dedicated with formal ceremonies in the presence of high state and Moroccan governmental officials on the 4th of July 1960, as the highlight of the Navy Base 4th of July celebrations hosted by Captain John L. Counihan, Jr., Commander Naval Activities, Port Lyautey, Kenitra, Morocco." Official U.S. Navy photograph.

"Pictured above is United States Ambassador to Morocco, the Honorable Charles W. Yost, co-mingling with the large host of Moroccan, U.S. and foreign governmental officials, participating in the celebration marking the dedication of the new "International Library" presented by the U.S. Naval Base at Kenitra to the city officials of Kenitra, as part of a continuing program of "People to People" and "Community Projects." Official U.S. Navy photograph.

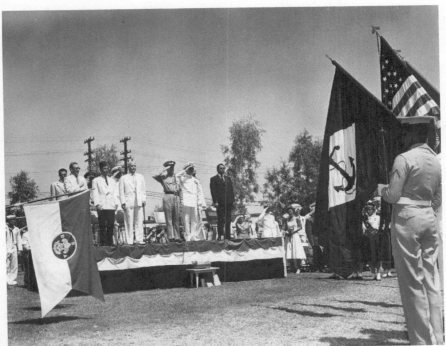

"With the colors massed in front of the reviewing stand, a salute is rendered by Captain John L. Counihan, Jr., Commander Naval Activities, Port Lyautey, Kenitra, Morocco; the Dutch Ambassador, the Honorable Goemans; the Pasha (Mayor of Kenitra), Excellency Abdelhamid El Alaoui; and Colonel S. Mandeville, Commanding Officer, Marine Barracks. The massing of the colors concluded the huge parade which was part of the of the gala 4th of July 1960 celebration held aboard the base and hosted by Commander Naval Activities as part of the continuing program of "people to People" and "Community Projects." The afternoon festivities consisting of an all-hands picnic followed the dedication of the new "International Library" in Kenitra, a gift of Naval Base authorities. The day was climaxed with a huge display of fireworks. Many Moroccan and foreign dignitaries were present throughout the day." Official U.S. Navy photograph.

Douglas E. Campbell

"Pictured above we see the new "Friendship Park" installed at the main entrance to the Naval Station, Port Lyautey, Kenitra, Morocco. Conceived and brought into being by Captain John L. Counihan, Jr., Commander Naval Activities, Port Lyautey, the "Friendship Park" represents a gesture of good will and a gift of beautification to the city of Kenitra. The above park was one of many community projects undertaken by the Naval Station during the past year (1960)." Official U.S. Navy photograph.

"Pictured above are two Quonset huts, part of ten Quonset huts given to the city of Kenitra for erection, renovation, painting and completion as school units. This gift of ten Quonset huts for increased school facilities for the Medina area of the city of Kenitra, was part of the continuing program of "People to People" and "Community Projects," as sponsored here by Captain John L. Counihan, Commander Naval Activities, Kenitra. In response to a request by the Pasha (Mayor of Kenitra) Alaoui, for Quonset huts, in order that his school program could be enlarged, the Naval Base surveyed ten Quonset huts, moved them to their new location, and renovated them. With the project completed, it is anticipated that the schools will be formally dedicated about the 1st of September 1960 in the presence of Naval and local Moroccan dignitaries." Official U.S. Navy photograph.

"Pictured above is Dr. Chattel, resident physician at the Canterac Hospital located in Kenitra, Morocco, inspecting a water distilling unit which was presented to the hospital by Naval Reserve Squadron 883 of Olathe, Kansas in 1960. Naval Reserve Squadrons deploy to Port Lyautey for annual training duty. This idea of training duty in the Mediterranean, and the presentation of a gift of good will to the Government of Morocco was the brain child of Captain John L. Counihan, Jr., Commander Naval Activities, Port Lyautey and has been in being now these past two years. All squadrons who come to Morocco for training bring gifts ranging from frozen bull semen, for the betterment of the cattle strain in Morocco, to powdered milk for the orphanage, and books for the "International Library" in Kenitra. All of these projects are part of a continuing program of President Eisenhower's "People to People" program. Official U.S. Navy photograph.

"Pictured above is the mammoth picture display, depicting "Friendship in Action," part of a huge display put on in the hangar on the Naval Station on "Friendship Day," 4 May 1960. In a continuing program of "People to People" and "Community Projects," "Friendship Day" was sponsored by Captain John L. Counihan, Commander Naval Activities, Kenitra, Morocco, as a gesture of good will and friendship. This successful event drew over 5,000 visitors, many of them school children who came aboard to witness this huge display and demonstrations of helicopter rescue, Navy firefighting and other static displays. The huge picture displayed above depicted Navy assistance and friendship in action during the Rharb Valley floods of the past winter and the Agadir earthquake of March 1960." Official U.S. Navy photograph.

"*Mrs. Mercedes C. Perry, wife of the Executive Officer of the Naval Air Station at Port Lyautey, and one of the members of the Officer's Wives Club Teaching Program, conducts her beginner's English class at the Takadoun School in Kenitra. The Moroccan students study Arabic and French in addition to English which is now being taught for the third consecutive year.*" *Official U.S. Navy photograph.*

Douglas E. Campbell

"A U.S. helicopter from the U.S. Naval Air Station, Port Lyautey, Kenitra, Morocco, is show above dropping food and supplies to stranded Moroccans during the Rharb Valley flooding (1958). During the course of the year, Commander Naval Activities, Captain John L. Counihan, Jr., is called upon to render assistance and aid in times of disaster. Above picture represents aid of this nature being rendered for the second year in a row when the Rharb valley flooded during a rainy season. Commander Naval Activities was called upon also to render aid during the Agadir earthquake which followed immediately after the Rharb Valley flooding." Official U.S. Navy photograph.

"Navy-Marine and Air Force players who participated in the football game at Kenitra's Municipal Stadium on "Orphan's Day" on December 4, 1959, hoist young Moroccan orphans on their shoulders at the end of their long thrill-packed day as guest of the U.S. Navy. Proceeds of the game went to the Societe Musulman de Bienfaisance, for the benefit of the local orphans." Official U.S. Navy photograph.

"The "Orphan's Day" football game held on December 4, 1959 at the Municipal Stadium in Kenitra attracted a large local crowd, many of whom had never seen a football game before. Among the dignitaries and officials were: (left to right) the Pasha's Khalifas (assistants), His Excellency Hadj Mohammed Lebbar (3rd left), and His Excellency Thami Serouillou; the Pasha of Kenitra (mayor), His Excellency Moulay Abdel Hamid el Alaoui; Captain John L. Counihan, Jr., Commander, U.S. Naval Activities; Captain Verne A. Jennings, Commanding Officer of the Naval Air Station, Port Lyautey; Mr. Abdel Rahman M'Kensi, local sports director; and Lieutenant Commander Leon H. Blair, Staff Liaison Officer."   Official U.S. Navy photograph.

In December 1961 CAPT Counihan was awarded the Legion of Merit for all the good work he did with the Moroccans, including integrating Moroccan students into Thomas Mack Wilhoite High School (see bolded section). Here is the Citation:

"The President of the United States of America takes pleasure in presenting the Legion of Merit to Captain John L. Counihan, Jr., United States Navy, for exceptionally meritorious conduct in the performance of outstanding services to the Government of the United States from December 1957 to August 1961 as Commander U.S. Naval Activities, Port Lyautey, Kenitra, Morocco. During this period, Captain Counihan has been highly successful in enhancing the prestige and stature of the United States through his contributions in the fields of international understanding and inter-Allied cooperation. Advocating and practicing closer relations with Moroccan and French peoples to the mutual

advantage of all, he has taken a strong personal interest in all aspects of these relationships, particularly in matters concerning children. **He has made possible the entry of selected Moroccan children into the dependents' school at Port Lyautey, thereby gaining the friendship and gratitude of both parents and children.** *He has projected the image of good neighbor and helpful friend for the United States. His program of friendship and mutual respect has been so successful that U.S. Naval Activities, Port Lyautey, was awarded the Freedoms Foundation George Washington Medal for Outstanding Achievement for 1960."*

The following six photos were provided by Linda Davis Maguire and covers the 1959-1960 school year. The first three were taken outside the Teen Club:

Left to right: Sue Scully and Laurie Thompson.

Left to right: John Ferguson, Billye Flint, Barbara McIntire and Kitty Hull.

Sue Scully.

That's the Teen Club I remember. I used to sit on those iron railings at the entrance. There was a couch inside to the right of the door... It was good to have this place to hang out!

Gary Skiff

Sue LeeMaster on right.

The school bus home to Sidi Yahia. Kitty Hull on the far left.

At Bouknadel Beach. From (l) to (r): standing is Sharon Foley and Joyce Barnes. Sitting are Billye Flint, Susan LeeMaster and me, Linda Davis.

The 1960 Yearbook

Administration: CAPT John L. Counihan, Jr., CAPT, USN (CO, Naval Activities); Verne A. Jennings, CAPT, USN (CO, NAS); John Augustine Donnelly, CDR, USN (Chairman, School Board); James E. Waldron, LCDR, USN (School Officer); Mart A. Murphy (Superintendent of Schools); Elwin B. Dell (Elementary School Principal); Brenizer L. Price (High School Principal).

Faculty & Staff: Faculty: Fred Davis; Guy T. Hagan; Bessie Mercer; Mark Mercer; Jawad Mughrabi; Anne Moussu; Virginia H. Reed; Mary V. Meyer; Gene R. Stebbins; Katherine E. Spears; Suzanne Thomas; and Carolyn Smith. **Staff:** Mrs. Margaret Willette (High School Secretary) and Mrs. Francis Wooldridge (Secretary to the Superintendent).

The 28 graduating Seniors of 1960: Franklin Camp Bacon (President); Robert R. Fish (Vice-President); J. Alexander Jakab (Secretary); Leila Ann Ryan (Treasurer); Lynn Kathleen Canfield; Patricia Katherine Thomas; Patricia Ann Ruhl; Anita Diane Jones; June Aldridge; Sandra Lynn 'Sandy' Boudrou; Jo Ann Watenpaugh; Evelyn Jeanne Badger; Dorothy Dell; Betty Jane Harvey; Kathleen Ann Steinke; Barbara A. Wilson; Frank D. Bowlby; Joseph Palen Perry; Karl Frederick Mohns; Gary Lee Kuykendall; Gerald Jones; Robert Davis; Wayne Smith; Neil Wray Hesse; Marvin Joel Ray; John Edward Bobe; Michael Augustus Murphy; and James Pembroke Emerson.

Class of 1961

1961 saw the Cold War continue to worsen with the USSR exploding some very large bombs during testing and then masterminding the building of the Berlin Wall - separating East from West Berlin. America sent a battle group to Germany and Americans and Russians glared at each other across the border. Due to this uncertainty many Americans built backyard fallout shelters in case of nuclear war. To make matters worse the Americans financed anti-Castro Cubans for an invasion at the Bay of Pigs which turned into a disaster. The Soviets put the first man in space on April 12th (Yuri Gagarin) followed by the US in May with Alan Shepard. Popular music included Chubby Checker's "Pony Time" and "Will You Love Me Tomorrow" by the Shirelles, and top movies included *West Side Story and The Parent Trap.* On February 26 Mohammed V, ibn Yusuf, sultan/King of Morocco, died at age 51; on March 3 his son, King Hassan II, ascended to the throne of Morocco and on August 30 the last Spanish troops left Morocco. King Hassan II saw significant political unrest and the ruthless government response earned the period the name "the years of lead." Hassan took personal control of the government as prime minister and named a new cabinet. Aided by an advisory council, he drew up a new constitution, which was approved overwhelmingly in a December 1962 referendum. Under its provisions, the king remained the central figure in the executive branch of the government, but legislative power was vested in a bicameral parliament, and an independent judiciary was guaranteed.

I Remember:

Just to kick off this chapter, I am Class of '61, I lived in Morocco from 1959 to 1962, living in town in Kenitra and later on base at Sidi Yahia. Lived in Bremerhaven, Germany before Morocco.

Wayne Lawson

I lived on Sidi Slimane from 59-61 and I am Class of '61.

John Quinn

Lived in Mekra Bel Ksiri, Rabat & Sidi Slimane from 1958-1960. Would have graduated with the class of 61.

Jim Archer

I was Class of '61 and lived in Kenitra, on the street between the clock and the train station less than a half block off (near the little park).

Melinda Platte McLaughlin

I was Class of 1961 and lived next to the NCO Club...by the way class of '61 how many of us left?

Daniel Gerald Hope

My family was stationed there from '58 to '61. I was in 4 & 5th grade at the school on the base. My dad was ADR1 Fred J Grulkey and he flew air crew with one of the VP squadrons, I think VP 23. I remember that fast pitch softball was his sport and he was quite a third baseman. My mother Lillian (Mike) Grulkey taught 1st grade at the elementary school. As a wide-eyed child of 8, I remember touching down at Port Lyautey in an R4-D (DC-3) from Rota, Spain after we had taken the ship from New York. My first flight! After the flight we went into the terminal for a "Wing Ding" milk shake. LOL. I suppose that stuck with me as I am a commercial, multi-engine pilot with over 13,000 hours. I got my DC-3 SIC license in October -- and still love a milk shake after a hop from time to time.

Wolf Grulkey

I was working on my family history, looking for military sites, and came across this website. My father was stationed at Sidi

Slimane 1959 – 1961. My younger brother was born there (or at least at the naval station). I remember going to school in Port Lyautey. We found a place to live in Kenitra and eventually moved into base housing at Sidi Slimane. We chased beetles thru the sand dunes and played tricks on our parents with chameleons! I rode a camel, an elephant and a donkey; my favorite memory is visiting Happy Valley and if anyone out there has any pictures, or knows where to get some, please let me know. My mother cleaned house once and got rid of all that stuff (that was before I got into genealogy!).

Cynthia Yingling-Hall

I arrived in Kenitra in July 1958. Believe I stayed in the Mamora Hotel just across the street from the fountain & geese. Lived about 2 km out Mohammad V Blvd toward Rabat. Graduated from TMW in 1961 and went state-side. Loved it there in Kenitra! I'm sitting on a camel saddle as I write this. Great people and times.

Jim Speed

Photo collage of the 1961-1962 years. Photo courtesy Carl Ferguson.

The 1961 Yearbook

Administration: CAPT John L. Counihan, Jr., CAPT, USN (CO, Naval Activities); James H. McCurtain, CAPT, USN (CO, NAS); John Augustine Donnelly, CDR, USN (School Board Officer); Quentin Wright (Superintendent, University of California); Brenizer

L. Price (High School Principal); Thomas A. Millar (Elementary School Principal).

Faculty & Staff: Faculty: Jessie Alexander; Mary Bailey; Daniel Joseph Bauman; Steven Bogden; Lester R. Bushue; Carol Holder; Gisele Catherine Jacquemart; Arthur J. T. Maroney; Jawad Mughrabi; Wilhelmina Rish Price; Virginia H. Reed; Katherine E. Spears; Paul William Standish; Suzanne C. Thomas; DeForest Tovey; and Bernice Eileen Wiese. **Staff:** Claire Tyson (High School Secretary); Colleen Frescoln (Elementary School Secretary).

The 28 graduating Seniors of 1961: Sara "Salli" de Saussure Davis (President); William Payne Wood, Jr. (Vice-President); Philanne "Toppy" Yould (Secretary); James Edward Adams (Treasurer); Harry Brener; John Joseph Carter; Nancy Catherine Clark; Clarice Damon; James Pembroke Emerson; Dennis M. Fatheree; Norman Robert Foley; Daniel Gerald Hope; Paula Ann Hubbard; Bobra Ann James; Darryll Wayne Lawson; Hammadi Mansour; Dave Alan McDonnell; Philip G. Milot; Charles James Nibley; James Brady Nolan; Judith Dawn Michell Perry; Marilyn Melinda Platte; David Walter Ross; Susan Andree Scully; James Gary Speed; Richard Fredet Spencer; Charles Everett Wills, III; and Patricia Ann Wood.

CLASS OF 1962

1962 saw the automobile continue to evolve as more compacts appeared and sold well in the US. The Cold War continued to worsen when the Russians placed ballistic missiles on Cuban soil just 90 miles away from the coast of Florida. President John F. Kennedy called the bluff by threatening war unless they were removed. They were removed but for a short time the world was on the brink of nuclear war and under the new term, MAD – or Mutually Assured Destruction. Afterwards President Kennedy set a goal of landing a man on the moon before the end of the decade and became more involved in politics in Southeast Asia by training South Vietnamese pilots. Folk music was evolving into protest music thanks to young artists like Bob Dylan and the birth of Surfing music by the Beach Boys grew in popularity. In England the Beatles record the single "Love Me Do". The new hit on TV for that year was "The Beverly Hillbillies" and the first of the James Bond movies, "Dr. No," was an instant success. Some of the other movies released included "Spartacus" and "El Cid". On January 23, Libya, Morocco, Algeria and Tunisia plan to form United Arab Maghreb; on October 9 warfare in trying to decide the Algerian-Moroccan boundary kills 130.

I Remember:

Hi from Karen Mitchell. We moved to Morocco in the summer of 1960 (It was Port Lyautey when we arrived and Kenitra when we left); lived in a hotel at first, then moved to a villa in town on Rue Mermose, owned by a Frenchman who was an amateur horticulturist - in the yard were 3 orange trees, 2 tangerine trees, 1 lemon tree and 1 grapefruit tree, as well as a new bed of grapes (ever seen a dog pucker up from sour grape? hysterical). After a year and a half in town, we moved into a Quonset "H" next door to the Marine HQ, when I was in my senior year. Graduated in 1962, then attended my first year of college at the University of Maryland Munich Branch while Dad finished out his 3rd year of duty with VR-24. We left Kenitra in the summer of 1963, when Dad received orders to Moffett Field in Mountain View, CA, and I went on to graduate from college at San Jose State.

Karen Mitchell, Class of 1962

Attended school from 1958 to 1961. I lived on the Sidi Yahia Communications Base with USMC Captain John Fridell's family for about a year then later, until my departure for Texas, with US Navy Commander Leonard Zaborski's family in a corner house with an upstairs in Kenitra. 1962 would have been my graduation year, but it happened at Aledo, Texas. Spent much time with the USMC Captain Jack Buckley family and their older son, Ronny (he would have been Class of '64), real fantastic people. One summer I hung around with the late Dennis Fatheree (R.I.P.) at the Sidi Slimane, US Air Base. Later I moved in with the Zaborski family. Bob Zaborski (R.I.P.) - Class 1964 - and I became like brothers. It was heartbreaking when I had to leave for the States. I owe much to these families and many other people involved in my "evolution" from the little orphan to a graduate from TWU, Fort Worth, Texas. My sojourn in Texas was again a conglomeration of good will, charitable people and their spirit of good heart and the Creed of the Optimist Club, especially the club at the Midtown Fort Worth and the McGlinchey family who provided me with loving family with all what a family means.

Ben Hasnaoui, or Mohamed Ben Laabdia Hasnaoui

Lived in Maroc 1958-1961. My dad was stationed in Sidi Slimane but we lived in Port Lyautey for all but about six months. Left in July 1961 and would have graduated with the Class of 1962.

John Fleming

My father, William E. Stanton LCDR ("Bill") and my mother Marion were stationed at the Port in the early 1960's. He flew C-130's around the European route as I remember. As a kid I attended the base school although we chose to live in town. Growing up in Morocco was a really rich experience for a kid and I have so many memories of playing golf at the base, hanging out at the exchange, and all the friends I had. I remember the wonderful local food, the hot winds that would blow through in the summer, the remarkable beaches, my Cub Scout uniform 'disappearing' off the clothesline several times, the first time my mother brought home snails to cook and they proceeded to escape all over the kitchen, taking the budda (sp?) gas tanks back for refill, learning French to talk to the kids in town, and my great teachers at the base school—Mrs. Cook was a stunner! Well sadly, my father passed away at the age of 48 leaving Marion to raise me from 16 out here in the San Francisco area. Marion had a great life until the age of 76 and passed away very peacefully in her home in Saratoga. Marion left behind myself and my wife (Midori) and our son (Mark) who recently graduated from Columbia. Not sure if anyone reading this will remember my parents, but certainly our time in Kenitra was filled with exciting times. I was watching a preview of Matt Damon's new movie about the Iraq war that is being filmed in Kenitra, which caused me to seek [the website] out. Thanks for taking the time to maintain it.

Bob Stanton

Who Remembers the Halsey Indoor Movie Theater?

The 2000 Reunion was held in Morocco and the alum attendees were allowed on the old Kenitra Naval Air Station/Naval Training Command. Here, Dottie Hull Sandoval stands in front of the original Indoor Theater and Radio Station. From the NAS Port Lyautey folks: "Originally rigged in 1948 by Gene Richardson as WNAA (Wired Naval Air Auxiliary) at 15 watts. "Gene Rich" (radio name) built this station on his own without Navy assistance. Then later boosted to 50 then 250 watts as (1484/1490/1512.5) WNAF, and later in 1956 AFRTS Kenitra 1 kW (Navy Broadcast Service) ["The Radio Voice of Morocco", heard as far away as London]."

Yep, this is where I was 11/22/1963, the day President Kennedy was assassinated, watching the movie *Can-Can*.

Billy Simpkins

I was there too and remember it as if it were yesterday.

Kathy Cox West

I saw *Love is a Many Splendored Thing*. Still like that movie. Remember who I was with and what I was feeling.

Gloria Kemery

I remember this stupid comedy-western called *Zachariah* which, as it turned out, was the cinematic debut for Don Johnson who later went on to play in Miami Vice. When the guy asked the gunslinger "Where'd ya learn to draw like that?" and the answer was "I learned to draw at home in my spare time"... well, it was a bad movie!! It was also a place where the school and others put on plays. My brother Tom was in *Oliver Twist* and got to say those immortal words to Mr. Bumble, bowl in hand to ask for seconds: "May I have some more?"

Doug Campbell

I remember several that I saw in the theater at Sidi which surprised the audience, such as *To Sir With Love* and *Shaft*.

Kathy Myers Strange

Went so often, sat on left side, midway down with the cool kids. Little kids, my youngest sister sat mid-section in first few rows as that is where they "belonged". I never once even went down the right aisle, somehow it was forbidden, maybe where the sailors sat? This was the Winter theater, as the outdoor theater was open in warmer weather. Saw *MASH* at that theater. Anyway, this tiny indoor theater was where live theater also took place. Went there every evening for months practicing for a live performance play written by a talented sailor. Had fun. I was surprised it was a Quonset hut with attached building that ran across the front of it. I think the end where the movie screen was and where the stage was, also was a build on. The front one had the restrooms and the back one had the stage, with dressing rooms and stage entrances. I remember analyzing the theater set-up as strange, but I don't think it came to me that it was a hut. If anyone remembers, we lived in a hut on base, while waiting for permanent housing. And our hut was so much shorter. This hut gave an airy feeling of height and the projectors booth was up a story. It felt like a movie theater to me.

Carla Golden Callaghan

I saw *The Graduate*. And then I think I was grounded, because I was too young.

Gina Mantlo

I saw *The Devil at 4 O'clock* with Frank Sinatra in this movie theatre.

Holly Myers Harder

I remember the movie theater with 5 cent bags of popcorn.

Jerry Counts

Every time I watch the movie *South Pacific*, I remember the Quonset hut movie theater where I first saw the movie.

Cynthia Yingling-Hall

At the Halsey the matinees were great - Star Trek, Mission Impossible and I think The Man from Uncle!!

Michele Fetterly

Oh, yes, I loved watch Star Trek and Mission Impossible. A great way to spend the afternoon, especially during the winter when we couldn't go to the beach.

Nancy Lukas-Slaoui

Who Remembers the Outdoor Movie Theater?

The outdoor theater was great, too! Saw *Jailhouse Rock* there and many others. Was there in 57-58 as a teenager. Spent lots of time in that swimming pool too.

Gary Skiff

Loved the outdoor theater there! Saw *PT-109.*

Dean A. Willis

They held USO shows at the Outdoor Theater ... I distinctly remember seeing The Doublemint Twins whom we all thought were hilarious.

Andrea Fleming Gast

My family would take blankets and pillows. It would get very cool to downright cold at night!

Brenda Cozad Nutt

I remember *Romeo and Juliet* at the outdoor theater.

Nola Fulkerson

The NTC Kenitra, Morocco, Outdoor or "Open Air" Movie Theater taken from a 35mm slide found at an Antique Mall!

The Outdoor Movie Theater with all the benches removed. Photo taken during the 2000 Reunion when the group was allowed to tour the base. Pictured is Alice Scully sitting in her favorite spot.

The 1962 Yearbook

Administration: CAPT James H. McCurtain, USN (NAS Base Commander); CAPT R. D. Cox (COMNAVACTS Commander); CDR John Augustine Donnelly, NAS Educational Officer; Mr. Quentin Wright (School Superintendent); CDR E. B. Faust (Chairman of the School Board); CDR Ray Miller (President, PTA); Mr. Brenizer L. Price (High School Principal); and Mr. Thomas A. Millar (Elementary School Principal).

Faculty & Staff: Faculty: Mary Bailey; Daniel Joseph Bauman; Lester R. Bushue; Ruth Carrington; Carol Holder; Gisele Catherine Jacquemart; Arthur J. T. Maroney; Jawad Mughrabi; Wilhelmina Rish Price; Paul William Standish; DeForest Tovey; and Bernice Eileen Wiese. **Staff:** Claire Tyson (High School Secretary); and Nancy Huppert (Elementary School Secretary).

The 28 graduating Seniors of 1962: Mariner Garnett Cox (President); Joan "Jody" Elizabeth Hawkins (Vice-President); Billye Blaine Flint (Secretary); Michael Richard Bush (Treasurer); Marjorie Lynne Adams; Thomas Van Atkins; Barry Wayne Barnett; Mustapha Chtaini; Thomas Kenneth DeNomme; John Augustine Donnelly, Jr.; William Lawrence Dunn; Carl Edwin Ferguson, Jr.;

Margaret "Peggy" Jean Froman; John Henry Fuhr, IV; Francis Stanley Hall; Sylvia Pat Hatcher; Rosalie Antoinette Laserre; Michael Williams Mays; Karen Leigh Mitchell; Melvin Bruce Ray; Donald Gaylord Rhodes; Jerry Allen Rogers; Robert Hugh Rogers, Jr.; Elizabeth Colleen Scanlan; Robert Leslie Simoneau; Robert Gary Tarwater; Margaret Anne Weld; and Dorren Fedrick Unger.

CLASS OF 1963

1963 witnessed the assassination of US President Kennedy which thrust Lyndon Johnson into the role of President. This was a difficult time to be President with the mounting troubles in Vietnam (the Viet Cong guerrillas had now killed 80 American advisors) and the continued campaign for civil rights by the black community. The push for Civil Rights caused violent clashes between blacks and whites, especially in the Southern States; the black Civil Rights leader Martin Luther King, Jr., was arrested in Alabama. Films included "The Birds" and "The Great Escape" and popular television programs included "The Virginian" and "Lassie". Ladies' fashion clothes and hairstyles included fur boots and towering hair-dos for evening wear. In world of music saw the beginning of Beatlemania after they released "I Want to Hold Your Hand/I Saw Her Standing There" and "Meet the Beatles". On October 14 there was another violent border conflict between Morocco and Algeria in the Tindouf area of south-western Algeria which had escalated into what is known as the Sand War. Afterwards, sensing stalemate and foreseeing more loss of lives, the conflict ended after Organization of African Unity mediation, with no territorial changes. A cease-fire was declared by both sides on October 30. On November 18 King Hassan II opens the 1st parliament in Morocco. On January 6, Philippe Perrin, later to become a Lieutenant Colonel and astronaut, was born in Meknes, Morocco. On August 21, Mohammed VI of Morocco (King of Morocco from 1999 to present), was born in Rabat. Of note was the death of Mohammed ibn al-Chattabi Abd el-Krim, Morocco opposition leader, on February 6. In May 1963, legislative elections took place for the first time, and the royalist coalition secured a small plurality of seats. However, following a period of political upheaval in June 1965, Hassan II assumed full legislative and executive powers under a "state of exception," which remained in effect until 1970.

I Remember:

My Dad, LCDR John D. Bernard was the Industrial Relations Officer from late 58 - to late 61...and I attended Thomas Mack Wilhoite from 8th grade to 10th grade... I would have been Class of '63. Dad took over from Leo Culjat whose daughter Dorothy left a post in 2003 here. Dad is still retired in Toledo Bend Texas [age 87] and has some smoking/asbestos related health problems...

My name is also John D. Bernard, 58, and my life at the Naval Air Station helped shape me into an instructor teaching at Tri-County Technical College in computing. Like everyone else I always wanted to go back stateside, but later realized that this was a fun, exciting three years of my life.

First, I need to thank the Shore Patrol guys who stopped me at night at a 4-way stop to tell me that my lights on the Lambretta were not on... They were not on because I had to roll the scooter down the hill [at age 12] to start it so my Dad would not know that I was joy riding his "go to work" vehicle... If they had asked me for a license or took me back to the house I would not be alive today.

Second, I would like to thank the VP-16 pilots who would fly me to Rota Spain in their P2Vs on Saturday mornings... AND for bringing me back... It was interesting to me because I would bike down to the terminal/flight room where the pilots went in and out, tell them that I was LCDR Bernard's son and beg for a ride to Rota... most said no, but there was always one... If my parents knew that I was out of the country for the day... again, I would not be alive today.

Third, there was Gallagher at the stables... for 50 cents he would saddle up the meanest Arabian Stallions for my brother Mike and I, and wish us good luck... we rarely made it out of the stable yard... as my horse would jump on Mike's horse or throw us though/over the fence... I think Gallagher had a sense of humor... he always offered us the brown horses but Mike and I would not have any part of it.

Fourth, and the Torrejon telephone operator... After climbing on the water tower at night by the base hospital, there was this lone, mysterious telephone. Picking up the receiver connected me to the Torrejon operator who would put me through to my friends who had gone back stateside or to my friends in Charleston, SC...

Most remember the Oasis, Johnny Horton's Battle of New Orleans on the Jukebox, the Teen Club, the inter-service football and baseball games, special services, etc... but the people make up life at a base, and the people were good people at Port Lyautey.

When Charlene Bratton shared the list with me of the Port Lyautey alums who have passed away, I was saddened to see Alice Scully's name there (she passed in 2011). She was personable, well liked, and will be dearly missed. Alice, Ron Buckley, and I had a connection in that we teamed up to sing at the 1960 TMW talent show... "Blue Moon"... Alice and Ron could sing... I could not. We practiced at Ron's Quarters where his Dad asked a Marine in his company to play the piano with us. This Marine was amazing as he played the piano by ear... you hum it, he could play it... Anyway, we nailed it.

John D. Bernard, EdD

I was Class of '63. We lived in Maroc from '60-'62 on the "red-top" circle in Sidi Slimane AFB.

David Verploegh

My sister, Kitty (Class of '64) and I followed Wayne Lawson's family from Bremerhaven, Germany, about a year after - '61 & '62. After our time in Kenitra we moved to Sidi Yahia and actually lived next door to Wayne. They were the sweet emotional teen years that are forever embedded in our memories. Jessie Allen and I even hosted a reunion here in Imperial Beach, CA, in 2001. I love the gatherings and have made it to almost all the reunions. A special thank you to all the younger group who have kept the fires burning.

Dottie Sandoval (Dorothy Hull)

Dottie Hull Sandoval asked me (Lynn Price Wallen, TMW class of '63) to write up my impressions of the TMW reunion held in Imperial Beach, CA, June 22-24, 2001, so here goes. In summary, it was one of the most intensely emotional experiences of my life! Many years ago, I can't remember how many, I began feeling sorry for myself that I would never be able to attend a high school reunion like "normal" people can. I guess we reach an age or stage in life when we begin thinking back, trying to recapture the feelings and experiences of youth, remembering the events and people and places that helped make us who we have become. For me that nostalgia centered largely on my high school years spent in Morocco. For my sophomore, junior, and senior years (1960-63), life centered on friends and teachers at Thomas Mack Wilhoite High School. What had become of them all? I felt very lucky that I had reconnected with a best friend from senior year, Lynn Kraighman Kramer, who had somehow found me through the Internet in 1997, but everyone else was lost to me forever. Or so I believed.

Last year Lynn attended a flower show at Epcot Center in Orlando and got to talking to a vendor who turned out to be a former faculty member of the Kenitra American High School (as TMW apparently had been renamed -- shame on whoever made that decision!). He told her about the TMW reunion taking place IN MOROCCO in two weeks, too soon for either of us to be part of it. That was the beginning of a year-long journey of discovery of the TMW network. For all my whining about the evils (read difficulties) of modern technology, I must now admit that the Internet has made it possible for me to recapture my past. Each week, it seems, we find another TMW alumna/alumnus added to Sandy Bartell's fabulous TMW webpage or Dennis Fatheree's magnificent email list.

Since I missed the Morocco reunion, I was thrilled when Dottie, Kitty and Jessie invited TMWs to Imperial Beach for another reunion. After 38 years, I would see classmates again. I had been corresponding by email with several of them over the past year, and our anticipation sharpened as June approached. I was probably even more excited than the others because I would get to see the tall, dark, handsome Midshipman who was my boyfriend (mostly by mail) for my last two years of high school and first two years of college.

The first event of the reunion was Friday, June 22, when everyone who had arrived gathered at Dottie's house before heading for a guided shopping trip (courtesy of Kitty Hull Daugherty) to Tijuana. I did not know some people because they were at TMW during earlier or later eras than I. But the ones I knew, I really knew! I mean, they still looked like themselves. You know what I mean. I don't know what I expected, but everyone was the same! Such fun! That meeting belongs to one of the five fingers on which I count the happiest occasions of my life. And things just got better as the weekend progressed.

Friday night everyone met at the San Diego dock to board the vessel *HORNBLOWER* for a dinner cruise around San Diego Bay. We took up 3 tables of 12 places each and enjoyed a good dinner and a beautiful sunset. Linda McCrerey (class of '66) and I sat together, and she was a blast -- was a freshman class officer with my little brother the year I was a senior. We spent a lot of the evening talking to Amine Hajji (class of '69) who was a Moroccan student in elementary school (I later found his photos in the '61, '62, & '63 SULTANs). He has a fascinating family history, is an engineer and is living in the U.S. now. Then the dancing began. The hit of the evening was definitely Dottie's husband, Roger, who was such a great dancer that lots of women wanted to dance with him (Linda and I were both brazen enough to ask him, so we were the lucky ones. Mostly he danced with his wife while the rest of us watched enviously). And I danced with my TMW beau for old times' sake, a sweet and poignant experience as the band played the last dance before docking.

Saturday was the really big day, emotionally. Dottie, Roger and Kitty hosted a fiesta in the Sandoval's backyard, and we all feasted on great Mexican food. Then each class in turn, beginning with Pat Le Fleur Jones ('56) and Suzanne Greksouk Kerry ('57), climbed the stairs to Dottie and Roger's upstairs deck, looked down at the assembled TMWs, and shared their memories of life in Morocco. Some of us were amazed to learn that the class of '56 had only 3 graduates, and their courses were by correspondence. But as each group spoke, we discovered that whether we were there in the 50s, 60s or 70s, our experiences were amazingly similar. Informal talks over the course of the weekend revealed similarities in some of our home lives that surprised us because we did not share them with each other when we were young (see the movie "The Great Santini" for some of these). I also heard some folks talking about the book "Military Brats" which explains why we did not talk about it at the time. For those of you who have seen photos but weren't there, the group photos of all of us in blue reunion t-shirts and caps were taken Saturday afternoon. My favorite photo was of me with my fellow classmates of '63, Dottie and Shirley Fatheree Faxon, both of whom are gorgeous and full of fun! Go class of '63 -- the BEST!!!!!

Saturday evening's event was the one I thought would be the coolest when I read the schedule before leaving home: a walk to the end of the Imperial Beach pier to watch the sunset and eat ice cream. So high schoolish! Such a throwback to the innocent fun our generation had as youth. An inspired idea for wholesome entertainment! I was looking forward to that pier walk most of all. But then Linda found a Tango club in San Diego and invited me to go with her, so I ducked out of the reunion and went dancing till midnight. If you've read my bio (which, in the tradition of a military upbringing, I dutifully wrote and submitted when Dottie told me to), you would not be surprised I chose to tango.

Sunday's farewell brunch was at Jessie Smith Allen's house (KAHS Class of 1972), and we all enjoyed another wonderful meal and the chance to hear more of Van Atkins' wit (he kept us laughing throughout the weekend). There was so much we didn't have time for -- didn't have time to talk to everyone as much as we wanted to, didn't have time to sing (Barry Barnett, please bring your guitar next time!), didn't have time to say proper goodbyes to all. The only way many of us were able to tear ourselves away to catch our planes was to extract promises to see each other at the next reunion (time and place undetermined). We are all painfully aware of the loss of two classmates, Marvin Hamlin and John Nibley (both class of '63) and of our popular history teacher, Mr. Maroney -- who were honored on a Memorial Board at Dottie's on Saturday -- and realize that the chance to reconnect with each other at a high school reunion is a special gift, made even more precious because we spent so many years thinking it would never happen to us.

Lynn Price Wallen

Graduated in 1963. In Morocco 61-63. Maiden name was Bourassa. Lived in Kenitra and on NAS in base housing.

Lyn Bunting

I rode the bus from Sidi Slimane Air Base to the navy base. It took 45 minutes to an hour twice a day. Quite a few of us played pinochle the whole ride, so the time whizzed by. We got adept at shuffling the 80-card deck in mid-air. I was there just the 1962-63 school year, but I really liked it. I see pictures of the buildings and base housing and it looks bleak now, but back then it seemed pretty. I'm trying to remember where Sidi Yahia was in relation to Kenitra, Port, and Sidi Slimane. When you are a teenager, those things don't matter.

Linda Newman Cox

Who Remembers When President Kennedy Was Shot?

I was in the Halsey [indoor movie theater] watching the movie *Can-Can*. After it was announced, the theater closed and we went home. My parents were having a dinner party and they got the message that the President had been shot just as guests started arriving. Daddy spent the rest of the night on the phone trying to find out what had happened. The dinner guests were clustered around the radio. It was a night I'll never forget. It was awful and Mom and Dad had the worst dinner party of their lives!

Kathy Cox West

I was at the Halsey watching the movie too...probably with Kathy Cox West (above). I remember everyone walking around in a fog. It was awful!

Cece Canton

My brother and I were at the Halsey watching *Can-Can* when the movie was stopped and an announcement came over the intercom saying President Kennedy had been shot. Everyone slowing filed out of the theater. We lived in Kenitra at the time and had to take the bus back and walk home. When we got home we told my Mom and she turned on the radio and woke my Dad who was asleep. He listened to the radio for few minutes, called his office (base security), got dressed and went into work. I don't remember much other than that.

Billy Simpkins

We lived off base; I was in first grade. We were at home and heard it on the radio. I don't think it was the base radio station as my great-aunt was living with us and she only spoke Spanish and French - no English. I have a feeling it was maybe Radio Luxembourg or a French station. I do remember that on the first school day after it happened, there was an assembly in a multi-purpose room of the elementary school.

Carmen Byrd Bohn

My parents were at the Halsey Theater. I was playing with friends in the front yard when neighbors started pouring out with the news that President Kennedy had been shot. My first impulse was to bike up to the theater with the news, but my parents and others came streaming home after the movie was stopped and the news shared. We listened to the radio (probably BBC) to get more details. For the next few days, the radio either had news or solemn music. The chapel held a memorial service and I was surprised at all the Moroccan dignitaries in attendance. It's strange to me that I can remember with such clarity the coverage of JFK's funeral and the shooting of Oswald but can't remember how I saw it since we didn't have television. Maybe it was newsreels at Halsey theater. I don't recall how many days of school was missed.

Bob Bull

I was at the Teen Club on the Main Base...They quickly got us on the bus and home to Bouk...

Jean Furlough

The 1963 Yearbook

Administration: CAPT R. E. Rau (NAS Base Commander); CAPT R. D. Cox (COMNAVACTS Commander); CDR R. H. Kallies (Education Officer); Mr. Quentin Wright (School Superintendent); CDR E. B. Faust (Chairman of the School Board); LCDR Hollis Goddard (President, PTA); and Mr. Earl F. Cartland (Schools Principal).

Faculty & Staff: Faculty: Mr. Lester R. Bushue; Mrs. Ruth Carrington; Mr. Jawad Mughrabi; Mr. Lawrence Daniels; Mr. George Samson; Mr. Paul William Standish; Mrs. Anne Samson; Mrs. Mary Strain; Mrs. Christine Mathis; Mrs. Wyona Byrd; Madame Christine Tuffery; and Bernice Eileen Wiese. **Staff:** Mrs. Nancy Huppert (School Secretary).

The 26 graduating Seniors of 1963: Johnnie "Tex" Warren Chalkey, III (President); Patricia Ann Keating (Vice-President); Constance "Connee" Dean (Secretary); Lynn Ellen Price (Treasurer); Assya M'chiche Alami; M'hamed Moati Amraoui; Samuel Edward Andrew; Ronald Gene Andrews; Anita Evelyn Anthony; Carol Anne Bart; Edward Charles Blackmon; Ellen Kaye Downes; Nora Jean Falls; Shirley Ann Fatheree; Judith Ann Hermanson; Carol Collins Howey; Barbara Lee Jacobs; Lynn Sharon Kraighman; Dennis Reno Porter; Richard Wayne Scribner; Constance Ann Riding; David Shermer; Martin John Steward; Gerald Theodore Fisher; Marvin Kurt Hamlin; and Armed Mrabti.

Class of 1964

1964 saw the war in Vietnam escalate when the US Congress officially authorized war against North Vietnam. More American servicemen were dying in this unwanted and unwinnable war. After three civil rights workers were murdered in Mississippi, President Johnson signed the Civil Rights Act of 1964. However, this did not stop the violence which continued to increase across many American cities. Lyndon Johnson was also returned to power after a landslide victory. This was also the year the Beatles took the world and America by storm and Beatlemania went into overdrive as they released a series of number one hits including "I Want to Hold Your Hand," and "All my Loving." Other British groups also found success including The Rolling Stones and The Animals. Together with the American talent of The Supremes and Bob Dylan, many say this was one of the greatest years for music in the last century. This year also saw one young loud talented boxer by the name of Cassius Clay win the Boxing World heavyweight championship from Sonny Liston. In Morocco, the births of two Moroccans would later make an impact on the literary and sports worlds – On May 7 the writer Mustapha Zerqti was born in Rabat and on November 13 the tennis player Ronald Agenor was also born on Rabat. Agenor made it to the French Open quarter-finals in 1989).

I Remember:

I was in Kenitra from '64 to '67 (8th, 9th, and 10th grade). Then moved to Hawaii, where I've been ever since! When you get to paradise, why leave? There's something funny that I recall from the spring of 1964. We were sophomores. We would go to Kenitra and buy these small corks that were used in the Moroccan equivalent to a cap gun. Each cork had inside it a small pellet of black power. We would buy bags of these corks and carefully pick them apart to retrieve the black powder pellets. The pellets were so volatile that if you just scratched one with your fingernail while you were picking apart the cork, it would explode, singeing your fingers. The goal was to accumulate a handful of the black powder pellets which we would then throw on the sidewalk or at each other to make popping and small explosion sounds. Yeah, I know, real nerdy. Darren Martin, Dennis Martin's younger brother, always used to carry a briefcase. Well, one spring morning when we were getting off the school bus Darren placed his briefcase on the sidewalk. It was really windy and the wind blew the suitcase over. It exploded! Apparently, he had spent all weekend picking apart corks and had a large bag of pellets in his briefcase. First period was Miss Birch's biology. The whole class was cracking up as Darren walked into the class with a smoking briefcase. He set it down on his desk and opened it up. A huge plume of smoke and ash rose from the briefcase as he pulled out his biology book which was charred and smoking. Funniest damn thing I ever saw!

As I said, my twin brother, Larry, and I attended TMW from September 1964 to June 1967 (8th, 9th and 10th grade). We lived in Kenitra and took a Navy bus to school. I was fortunate enough to attend the reunion in Rabat in 2000, and on the day we visited the base, the bus took the same route along the river, past the prison on the hill, to enter the base. That brought back a flood of memories. In fact, the entire trip was an experience I shall never forget. As I've described to my wife, the first day was a peak experience and each day after that got better! Like Colene, I reconnected with my classmates on the web, prior to the 1995 reunion in Greensboro, which I also attended. But unlike most of my classmates, I reconnected with my Moroccan friends a bit earlier.

This is a true story: in 1990, my wife and I moved to New York City so that she could complete per post-doctoral internship in psychology. One night, we were in Greenwich Village and I spotted a Moroccan restaurant. We went in and had dinner. We were the only customers in the place. After dinner, we lingered and chatted with our waiter. He asked me what I thought of Moroccan food and I explained to him that I was very familiar with it having lived in Kenitra. We talked some more, and as we became more comfortable with each other, I told him, "You know, this is will sound really stupid but I'll say it anyway. My best friend in Morocco was Amine Hajji and I've often wondered what happened to him. Do you know him, by chance?"

The waiter paused, smiled and said, "He's my cousin!" And I said, "Right, I'm from out of town and you're from New York and you're telling me you're related to a guy I went to school with twenty-five years ago!" He laughed and insisted it was true. Amine had gone to college in the United States and settled here. The waiter said he didn't have his phone number but told me the City where he lived and where he worked. The next day, I called the company and within a minute had Amine on the phone! Of course, that led to our two families getting together a year later, and then in 2000, I stayed at Amine's parents' home in Rabat after the reunion! The internet may be the facilitator, but there's nothing like taking a risk and talking to someone!

From my experience of attending the 2000 reunion in Rabat, nothing has changed. I was on a bus that had been chartered to take the alumni from the airport to our hotel. The bus driver started to get frustrated with a truck in front of him, so he pulled out to pass, only to discover a much larger truck heading right for us! His natural response was to swing all the way over onto the left shoulder and execute the passing maneuver, seemingly oblivious to all the pedestrians who were jumping out of the way! I was sitting in the front seat behind the driver at the time, and I'm not sure if anyone else on the bus even noticed. We were all so excited to be there but were quite tired from the overnight flight from New York.

Lee Sichter

I lived in Kenitra with my two sisters Melissa (in the 7th and 8th I believe..., recently passed) and Melinda, a senior..., class of 61..., now going by McLaughlin. I just realized, I should have let her write that..., dang. I was in the 9th and 10th grades. Our surname was Platte and they called me Butch. Those were among the most fantastic, wonderful years of my life..., '60-'62. Had I stayed I would have been the class of '64. I managed to do that in Charleston, South Carolina, and that was another amazing ride..., a beautiful, charming and fun city. I finished at an incredible school called St. Andrews High..., not religious. These days they mostly

call me Sherwood. I love the time of our shared lives in Morocco...,
I really do.

Sherwood Platte Duane

Graduated from TMW in 1964; was in Morocco from 1962-
1964; lived in Kenitra for a year then Sidi Yahia base.

Donna Wilcox

Who Remembers Their Favorite Snack Food?

French bread with cheese and salami. I also loved chocolate
covered peanuts.

Everette Dotson

In Morocco it was fresh French bread and cheese!

Kathy Myers Strange

French Bread, Cheese and Moroccan Wine! I also loved Red
Cream Soda from the machine at the Teen Club.

Karen Ruth Butler

Loved those Oasis French Fries drenched in gravy. Not a
vending machine snack but I sure snacked on that more than
anything else I can remember!

Doug Campbell

How I would love to have some of that hot bread and creamy
cheese!

JeanMarie Sample

French bread and donuts at the beach.

Marguerite Golden Bright

French fries and fresh French bread in Morocco. Fresh potato
chips and cheese when traveling to Madrid, Spain

Tony Collins

Rice and salted gravy at the Oasis.

Leslie Jones

Soft ice cream cones at the Oasis.

Sandy White Bartell

Moon Pie and Honey Buns from the Commissary and, of course, Brochettes.

Michele Fetterly

Oranges from the Medina. I can still smell and taste them. I also loved the fries at the Oasis. And Brochettes!

Patti Gay Hartzell

The small egg rolls at the Chinese restaurant in Rabat and my dear Fatima, Mina's, cous cous.

Joan Ellen Bernard

Warm French bread and beach donuts with the harshly grained sugar on top.... I'm sure some of the crunch was sand! Ha, ha!

Nancy Lukas-Slaoui

Making chocolate chip cookies during slumber parties. Dependent young teenager.

Pam Mazzara Kohel

The 1964 Yearbook

Administration: CAPT R. E. Rau (NAS Base Commander); CAPT R. D. Cox (COMNAVACTS Commander); CAPT R. S. Downes (Commander, NCS); CDR R. H. Kallies (Education Officer); CDR F. J. Gisko (President, PTA); Mr. R. W. Hostrop (High School Principal); and Mr. Earl F. Cartland (Elementary School Principal).

Faculty & Staff: Faculty: Faculty: Mr. Claude Berard; Mr. Daniel Bridge; Mr. Lawrence Daniels; Miss Mary Koch; Mr. Ted Johnson; Mrs. Arlene H. Liddy; Mrs. Christine Mathis; Mr. Jawad Mughrabi; Mr. Claus Sadlier; Mrs. Anne Samson; Mr. George Samson; Mr. John Winton. **Staff:** Mrs. Evers (Elementary School Secretary).

The 18 graduating Seniors of 1964: Dale L. Roberts (President); Ronald Lee Jackson (Vice-President); Judith "Judy" Dawn Tripp (Secretary); Bruno Frank Niewinski, II (Treasurer); William

Crawford Barr; Raymon Dahl Canton; Barbara Alice Evans; Patricia Elaine Halstead; Bertha Adale Hammond; Lucie Reynolds Hardester; Patrick Hugh Hargis; Barbara Christina Hermanson; Mohamed Ikhlef; Abdellah Amid Salah; Crystal Annette Smith; Peggy Joyce Warren; Nora Lynn Watts; and Donna Marie Wilcox.

Class of 1965

1965 saw the war in Vietnam continue to worsen as more Americans die in the unpopular war; the Anti-War movement grows and on November 13th some 35,000 march on Washington as a protest against the war. There is also civil unrest with rioting, looting and arson in Los Angeles. This was also the first year in which mandated health warnings appeared on packs of cigarettes. The latest craze in kid's toys was the Super Ball and the Skate Board. Fashions also changed as women's skirts got much shorter and men's hair grew longer. The word Hypertext is created to describe linking in early computer systems and computer networking. The St. Louis Arch is completed and the Beatles release four new albums including "Help". Unrest is also growing in Morocco – on March 23 the Moroccan army shoot into a crowd of demonstrators, killing about 100. On June 7 King Hassan suspends Morocco's Constitution. On October 28/29, Mehdi Am "Ben" Barka, Moroccan socialist leader, was kidnapped and murdered in Paris. On November 12 a general strike was called for all Moroccans against the murder of Ben Barka. Meanwhile, another Moroccan tennis star, Guy Forget, was born on January 4.

I Remember:

I lived on base from '60-'63 in the corner house across the street from the elementary school. My neighbor across the street was that fox, Cece Canton and her family. Her two older brothers were very dear friends. Would have been in the class of '65 had we stayed.

Patrick Foley

I remember the Summer of 1962, when Dad came home with his new orders. We were anticipating the return to our home town of Jacksonville. "Morocco ?? Wait!! Isn't that in Africa?" We survived the initial shock and prepared for our adventure. A few months later we were headed to Norfolk. Our '59 Ford was dropped off, and we were on our way in an old C-118 aircraft with fueling stops in Newfoundland & Azores. We arrived at NAS Port Lyautey Air Ops terminal. A few introductions with our sponsors and soon we were unpacking our few items in Mamora Hotel. The hotel was bare basics with a small room, sink, shared toilet down the hall, no food service (the restaurant had been closed for months), no dressers, no tables, but a beautiful pool. Initially, the only food that we ate off base were Coca Colas (in a large liter bottle that tasted somewhat like American coke) and delicious 3-foot-long baguettes from the French bakery. By the second week, our express shipment was delivered. Mom would buy the supper ingredients at the commissary each day using the bus service and heat up the meal on the newly arrived hot plate. The room couldn't handle the added electrical load of the hot plate, so she did all the heating in the dark. Three weeks later we were upgraded to nicer rooms with a table, dressers, better electrical wiring and our own toilets. I started to make friends in the hotel and life didn't seem so bad. The sights and sounds were still alien to me; the women covered from head to foot, the call to prayer, the donkeys in town carrying firewood, language that I couldn't understand, scary drivers, no television, and absolutely no drinking of the local water. Little did I know that the next 3 to 4 years were to produce so many fantastic memories.

After 2 months in the hotel, Dad found a villa in town and we moved to a great house in Kenitra. A little grocery shop was across the street. Our house was surrounded by a tall wall with cut glass on top, and several fruit trees were in the courtyard. The French landlady was nice, but no English and our French poor. Our furniture was unloaded, and we were "home".

I remember that 9th grade in high school was horrible. I just didn't fit in. I was getting low grades which I never experienced in my previous 8 grades. Five of us "newbies" had 2 classes without any text books. The teachers were running off smelly mimeograph sheets every day for our studying and homework. The parents were called in and told that we'd soon be dropped from the class if the textbooks didn't arrive. Mom sent a letter to her sister and books were "expedited" over to us. Expedited meant 2 to 3 weeks. Mail typically took 10 days either direction. The Danish ship *Groenlund* brought in most of our supplies. I gradually started to fit in at school. Things were much better later when Sidi Slimane shut down and the school became a smaller community.

I became mobile with my bicycle. One bike ride was with Mike Frye and Michael Cumm. We headed south through the neighborhoods of Kenitra and then in the open country. We had pedaled a long way and we came upon a school with some zillion kids outside on both sides of the road. We stopped way short and contemplated our next move. We didn't want to backtrack but were unsure how the kids would react to us here "in the boondocks." We decided to build up a head of speed and jet past them before they could react with taunts or whatever. The plan worked; we heard a lot of noise as we passed by - either Arabic cheering or jeering. It might have been laughter since as soon as we sped out of sight, we reached a dead-in and had to go back. That day we traveled over 30 miles seeing a water buffalo and lots of donkeys, driving past the lake near the beach, resting at Plage Mehdia, exploring the jetties and the WWII gun turrets, and ending up at home without any parent knowing where we were.

Our next move was on to the base on February 18, 1963, near the elementary school. We had the middle unit of a 3-unit building. With the bedrooms upstairs, it was a comfortable home. Life became much easier with access to "everything" (but still no TV). In June we even got a telephone (phone number "276"). I enjoyed golf, Teen Club, the Oasis, bowling, baseball, tennis, handball, shooting baskets, pinochle, free movies, swimming, and lots of playing with the kids in our combined backyard made by the 7 buildings around the circle. A short walk or bike ride and I could be anywhere.

I remember the rumors that were rampant throughout 1963 about everyone's future. Several outfits departed, and our on-base community became a bit smaller. Dad was dreading orders to Rota or Naples. The Moroccans were moving on board and taking over many of the buildings near the high school. The school needed to be relocated. With the transfer of Fleet Intelligence, their building became available. The last departing personnel left in December 1963 and work started soon after to prepare the building for the HS new term. The new building welcomed classes on 6 January 1964. All the academic classes were in the one building. The Marine parade grounds across the street provided plenty of area for phys ed and special events. Another building adjacent to the parade grounds was used as a locker room. Life was good.

I remember the base being turned over to the Moroccans on January 6, 1964. It didn't affect us much other than the front gate was closed to American traffic, and we were told to stay out of the Moroccan areas. The back gate became our access to Kenitra and the beach.

I also remember the flood of January 1963 that left thousands homeless. It kept the off-base kids at home. The Sebou River was over its banks and sending dead livestock and etc. out to sea. The base helicopter was kept busy plucking people off their rooftops. September 1963 brought the Algerian – Moroccan War over disputed Saharan Desert. No impact to us but travel into town was restricted. March 1964 gave us a scare. My friends and I were playing pinochle when the earth tremor hit. We were certain that the hot water heater was getting ready to blow and we ran outside. Then we surmised it was a small earthquake.

When it comes to remembering high school, I remember those High School trips. One of my first trips was the journalism class overnight trip to Tangier. I think the purpose was to visit the Voice of America station, but it was more fun than that. Mom and Dad provided one of the 4 cars, and I think I was in the backseat with Kathy Meehan and Rose Hanna; two girls I always enjoyed being around. Others were on the trip, but the only one I recall is Cecil Byrd. On the way home, we came across camels and stopped for pictures and rides. I have home movies (very short) of Kathy, Rose, Cecil and me riding them. Unfortunately, home movies from the 60's were hit and miss, and these were mostly "miss."

During my Sophomore year the coach took the baseball team down to Casablanca to play the Nouasseur teams. The Air Force brats were a lot better than us, but we eventually got them kicked out of Morocco.

During my Senior year we went to Spain for basketball games. We took a bus (and ferry) to Rota, Seville and Madrid. The players were put up by families of the players. I recall spending time at the respective high schools being introduced and being bored sitting in their classes. In Madrid, a few of us skipped school and played golf. We finished too late to meet up with our host players and I ended up hitching to the family's house off base. Boy was the father mad. After the Madrid game, coach arranged for us to return to Rota by train. It was a thousand times better than the long bus ride to Madrid. One of the players (not to mention names but it was Pete Tenney) apparently had some bad food and each burp or fart was suffocating. Thank goodness for trains. At Rota we played a tournament with the same 3 teams and we came in second, much to everyone's surprise. Steve Blackmon and Cecil Byrd were the two key players. Our bus ride home was uneventful except the ferry ride across the Strait of Gibraltar was a bit rough. At Kenitra we were greeted by much of the school and parents. Quite a homecoming.

Other memorable trips: I joined Mark Stokes, John Razi, and I think Danny Broussard for a trip to Ifrane. Mark and I went skiing and then tried to hitchhike back to our hotel with our skies. We weren't having much luck and started throwing snowballs at the cars that passed us by. We apparently hit one, since the car stopped and started to back up. We jumped into the woods and decided that it was better to just thumb and hope. It worked. Two French girls picked us up and took us back to the hotel. We thought that we struck it rich, but they let us out and sped away. The four of us took a crowded bus back to Rabat. I'm still embarrassed at my ignorance. We packed some bread, oranges or something like that. We started eating as we became hungry or maybe bored. Many of the passengers glared at us. Who knew eating on a bus was frowned upon. At sunset, the bus pulled over at a roadside stand and everyone hurried off to eat. It was Ramadan! I felt bad but still managed to buy a camel skewer from the roadside stand and have some real food.

Ifrane was the favorite place for my family to go camping. There was a grassy area about 100 feet off a side road and next to a babbling mountain fed stream. We would have an occasional visitor, usually a teenage goat herder and never had any problem with the locals. The only negative that I recall was our trip way south in which my brother Steve convinced Dad to take a shortcut clearly marked on his map. The road turned out to a decent road until the payment gave way to dirt with loose sand in areas where we had to get out to lighten the 1959 Ford monster and push. Water became an issue. We stopped to take pictures of the three boys (Steve, David and I) on a desert sand dune. After 4 hours and 54 miles, we reached a paved road. It lead us into a town with very narrow streets, veiled women fully covered, donkeys and general mayhem as much as can be imagined as the Moroccans stared at and the young kids ran after this huge white car. As we left the town, one old man threw a rock at us. A short while later we reached civilizations and stopped at a hotel for much needed Coke and bottled water. That trip showed us lots of camels along the road and in the fields; also dirt devils.

Our senior trip was wonderful. We took the ferry to Malaga, Spain, followed by a short road trip to Torrelimos to the Carihuela hotel. I recall the sunbathing at the pool, the bullfight and dining / sangria in town. Thanks to Steve Robb for preserving the memories with photographs that I think most of us still have today. Six of us recreated the one photograph at our 50th reunion.

Senior trip was paid in part by the seniors selling pizza and hotdogs for lunch at the high school. We also had a few car washes, and I peddled coffee at the high school for adult night courses.

I remember that the schools and base emphasized that rabies was a severe threat and to avoid all animals. At the time Morocco was experiencing a rabies epidemic. We were shown a film on a child with rabies. I'm certain that in today's environment, a school would be sued for subjecting children to such horrors. Therefore, I was very aware of and avoided dogs on my many travels. A young boy in our neighborhood contracted rabies and died. He had recently attended a birthday party and all the birthday goers had to undergo the painful series of shots in the stomach. Before I knew better, Richard Evans and I would go frog hunting with our BB guns at night in the area between housing area and the Sebou River. We were found by the Shore Patrol (sans guns which we hid when we saw their headlights). They sent us home. A few nights later a pack of jackals came close to the housing area with their incessant yapping and howling. We decided that maybe these night walks weren't such a good idea.

Shore Patrol seem to encounter students often, but I guess they handled us with kids gloves. One night, Steve Blackmon and

I were on our scooters with passengers on the back and we went screaming down the road along the Sebou River. Sure enough, the Shore Patrol caught us and brought back to the Officer of the Day. He let us off with a warning. Another time about 10 of us snuck into the building housing the high school lockers to play, I think, "lights out soccer." Someone spotted the Shore Patrol coming into the building and we quickly hid. We all thought our hiding spots were decent until the Shore Patrol turned on the lights. We stuck out like sore thumbs. We were rounded up, names taken and released. Thank goodness for the Teen Club or we'd been in trouble all the time.

The EM Club received permission to sell popcorn at Halsey Theater. Dale Roberts and I were hired. He took the weekdays (he had a social life) and I took the weekends (I only wished for a social life). My social life was Teen Club and the movies. At Halsey, it seemed like most of the high school kids occupied the front left-hand side of the theater. I recall kids (or me) arriving late and trying to find an empty seat with the theater being pitch black at times. I'd rather arrive early. I always felt honored to stand up for the playing of the National Anthem. My popcorn sales did well and later, they trusted me with the "Roach Coach." I had never driven a stick shift and had to learn quickly how to double shift a cantankerous old truck to get it to the Outdoor Theater. Weekends were always busy with hotdogs, popcorn, ice cream and similar stuff. I also worked at the library for 50 cents an hour. After graduation Cecil Byrd and I worked alongside the sailors in the warehouse doing some offloading but mostly doing inventory. The sailors introduced me to the concept that a broken beer case allowed a few of the intact beer bottles to be broken as well but only after the beer was consumed. I tried but never could stomach a hot beer.

My older brother Steve bought a Lambretta 150cc motor scooter when we moved into the villa. He later drove it from Kenitra to the college campus at Munich, Germany visiting much of Europe. Upon his return home during the summer of 1964, he opted to attend the University of Florida and I bought his scooter. I had it repainted from mainly red to mainly maroon. Mobility with the bicycle was great, but the scooter made it phenomenal. My Lambretta was my commute to school, to work, to wherever on the base and to the beach. I made my only trip to Sidi Yahia when

Jeannie Peebles needed a ride after school. I felt like king of the road with a pretty girl behind me and cruising along the countryside. However, the drive back was lonely and a bit nervous. The summer after graduation I had a trip to an offsite recreational area with sailor friends. I recall too much wine and being sicker than a dog. The next morning, on the way home the two of us maxed the scooter out at about 61 mph. The same sailor later convinced me to try the Kenitra night life. The place he picked (a brothel) wasn't very appealing and we headed to Rabat instead. We basically drove past some unsavory areas without stopping and we started homeward. We stopped at a resort (I think at Plage des Nations) and had a couple drinks. We made a cold drive midnight home with no nasty consequences.

As to be expected, families were leaving with their new orders and the sendoff at the base terminal became a social affair from time to time. Mark Stokes, Jeannie Peebles, Crystal Smith and I received a decent sendoff when we left for Munich in August 1965.

I returned once more to Kenitra over Christmas and then, 35 years later, for the 2000 reunion in Rabat. A bus trip to the base was arranged and it was fantastic to see the old stomping grounds again. We were treated like royalty by the Moroccan base personnel.

Bob Bull

I arrived in Port Lyautey all the way across the world from Portsmouth, Virginia, to begin two of the most memorable years of my life. Who knows how that experience shaped my life forever. My family was very committed to faith, the church and the concept of being a missionary. Every weekend we would pack up our Rambler station wagon with everything you could imagine from the commissary and head to a missionary family somewhere in Morocco.

We travelled all over Morocco, places probably not even on the map. We brought missionary families things they had probably not had in years. This was my mother and father's ministry. I remember Agadir and other very remote sites. I also remember our basketball team at school travelling all over Morocco to play basketball at Moroccan schools on their courts that had the oblique foul lines. Boy, were those rough and tumble brawls. There was no concept of how to play without fouling. It was a full contact sport. I remember we tried to played with technique and finesse but a few minutes into the games we decided if they wanted to foul we would show "them" how to foul. LOL.

I remember trips to the beach and into the medina and how you could look around and see no one out in town and stop to repair my scooter or check something and all of a sudden look up and realize there were fifty people all around you out of nowhere.

I remember sculling and crewing on the Sebou River at sunrise in the morning with my trainer Monsieur Noel when the river was smooth as glass and the mist sometimes showed in the morning. I remember our training sessions in the afternoons three days a week and the smelly bodies and my rowing partners changing and putting back on the same woolen clothes after working out. Deodorant? What is that?

I remember the reaction we had to men and boys holding hands out of basic simple friendship and how that freaked us out. LOL. I remember the trips to Gibraltar and the basketball games at all the military bases in Spain.

I used to life guard at the pool where I was also a short order cook. I also ran the canteen truck and sold popcorn at the movie theatre. I also worked stocking in the PX. Lots of the older kids ended up going to college after graduating from Wilhoite at University of Maryland in Munich I think.

I remember when we tried to play basketball again the Navy and Marines on base we got killed. Those guys were phenomenal. We didn't have a prayer but with fast pitch softball, we did not do so badly. We were quick and ended up having a great bunting offense. Of course we had to import a fast pitch pitcher though.

And then there were all the motor bikes....fast fast fast. Me of course had a slow Lambretta scooter. I used to be friends with Karen and Sandy Hansen. Captain Hansen was base commander at one point and Colonel Canton was the head of the Marines. Robbie and Irving were on the basketball team. My secret crush back then was Anne Durgee. Met her again after so many years when we had our little reunion here in DC back in 2000.

Cecil Byrd

I was a dependent at Port Lyautey from May 1958 until October 1961. My father was a pilot in VR-24 (W.G. "Porky" Hatfield) . I attended school through the 8th grade there, so would have been Class of '65. Lots of hours spent at the Teen Club. Lived in town for the first year and a half. Had a good time and good experiences. I suppose most military members from this time period are deceased or nearly so. There are a lot of us dependents who were there during this time period and we are in our 60s-70s now. Port Lyautey was my favorite place to live as a dependent. It was a great time to be a high school age dependent because there was much to do and learn. I yearn for those days and have never lived anywhere that I liked better. I played baseball, basketball, ran track, and participated in every sporting event available. We went to the European World Series of baseball in 1958 and came in third place. While there, we were able to visit the World's Fair in Brussels. I also fell in love in Port Lyautey, with a cute girl in my class. I shall not name her because she would likely not remember me. Bob Hope came to put on a show one of the years we were there. What a great showman and what a troupe of characters he brought with him. Good looking gals! (I hope that's not politically incorrect to mention...) Those were some of the best days for the Navy and our country. I can't get in sync with some of the modern people's thinking. Well, enough of my rambling. Those days remain in my memory forever.

Mike Hatfield

Prom 1965. Left to right: Patty Dilucido, Bud Davis, Cece Canton and Pete Tenney.

The 1965 Yearbook

Administration: CAPT B. McLaughlin (NAF Base Commander); CAPT J. B. Hansen (XO, NAF); and Mr. G. A. Lyons (Principal).

Faculty & Staff: Faculty: Mr. Claude Berard; Miss Marie Roepke; Mrs. Barbara S. Plomondon; Miss Monice LaRay Somers; Mr. Raymond Fontenot; Mrs. Arlene H. Liddy; Miss Lula C. Faulkner; and Mr. Albert G. Stephenson. **Staff:** Mrs. Wanda Oeser (School Secretary).

The 19 graduating Seniors of 1965: Robert James Bull (President); Kathleen Agnes Meehan (Vice-President); Jean Bates Peebles (Secretary); Mark L. Stokes (Treasurer); Georgette Assouline; Daniel Phillip Broussard; Jean Marta Busbee; Cecil Curtis Byrd; Michael Edward Davis; Patricia Teresa Dilucido; Karen Hansen; Mohamed Ikhlef; Joseph Fleming; Mohamed Joudar; Marcia Rae O'Neal; Ahmed M'Rabet; Stephen D. Robb; Adbellah Amid; and Beverly Ann Still.

CLASS OF 1966

1966 saw inflation grow as part of the effect to fund the war in Vietnam. Both the US and USSR continued in their space race to see who would be the first to land a man on the moon. Race riots continued to increase across cities in America and National Guard troops were needed to maintain law and order. The fashions in both America and UK came from a small well-known street in London (Carnaby Street) part of the swinging London scene, both women and men wore patterned pants and flowered shirts and boots, shoes and even caps utilized the plastic and vinyl for a wet shiny look. The most popular groups included the Beach Boys with *Pet Sounds*, the Rolling Stones with *Under my Thumb* and the Beatles with *Revolver* and *Yesterday and Today*.

I Remember:

I was in Kenitra (lived on base, across the street from Cece Canton) from '63-'65. Would have been in the class of '66, but Dad was being transferred back to the States mid-way through my senior year, and the rules were such that I had to go to an Air Force Boarding School in Dreux, France. Would have much preferred to stay in Maroc, but that's another story.

Got to re-unite with Cece in Arlington in the summer of '66 and then again in '71 in Coronado. She still had (and reportedly still has) an infectious zest for life! We've recently re-connected via Bob Bull (class of '65) and my older (by a year) sister, Karen; I hope to visit Cece in Coronado in January.

I live in northeastern Utah - 45 miles south of Wyoming and 30 miles west of Colorado. I was brought to the hinterlands by the Ute

Indian Tribe, for which I worked as a lawyer for 10 years before realizing that, while I loved practicing law, I despised most lawyers. (My apologies if you are a rare, honest lawyer.) Conveniently, my mother and younger (by 9.5 years) sister, Sue, became seriously ill about the time I got fed up with fighting with lying lawyers, so I spent time between northeastern Utah and Austin (where Mom and Dad retired), trying as best I could to spend winters in Texas (because it's colder than a well-digger's butt where I live) and summers in Utah (where there's no humidity, mountains and red-rock arches) taking care of them. I also found the second love of my life (after working for Indians): rescuing and re-homing homeless dogs.

I haven't heard much from our classmates over the years. The last I heard, Steve Blackmon was the principal at a high school in San Marcos (I think), TX, but that was at least a decade ago. The Bloom brothers' parents retired in Tampa, but I don't remember hearing what the "boys" ended up doing.

A year ago I was diagnosed with kidney cancer that has metastasized to my lungs. I'm incredibly lucky: although there is no cure for metastatic kidney cancer, there are several treatments that have proven successful in postponing the disease's progression. I'm responding well to one of those treatments and - again being lucky - have few, all very manageable side effects. So, like most of the folks reading this, I'm expecting to die of something other than the dreaded incurable cancer!

My best to all former Sultans!

Sandy Barr Hansen

NOTE: Sandy passed away since writing this piece.

I was Class of '66. We lived in base housing '60-'63. I attended 6th, 7th, 8th & 1/2 of 9th grade. Lived next to the White girls around the corner from Cheryl Ann Terry (who I've been trying to find) & just a few blocks from the PX. Baptized in the base swimming pool where I was on the synchronized swim team; in Church choir; my Mom was the Girl Scout leader. Lots of memories of wild scooter rides & sneaking to my Fatima's during quarantines.

Gloria (Outland) Kemery

We lived on Port Lyautey from '60-'65...a long time due to the fact that my Dad grew up in Casa and spoke 8 languages fluently, all dialects of Arabic. But, of course, my teenage life was much more important. We started out in the duplexes down from the hospital near the PX, then the next row down across from Pat Foley, then Captain's Hill...wow, was that one fun! I loved Morocco and grew up there.....sort of, with all the fun on base. I had a VERY hard time acclimating to the States...no TV my entire teenage life going to my Senior year in Arlington, VA. I hated it...the weather, the cliques, lonely time! My family, or parts of it, went back in '72 after my Dad retired from Marines and lived in Rabat. He was in private business with AMG & the Moroccan govt. Brother John lived in Casa with his family and I went over to live in Rabat, with my daughter, in '76 for 2 years. Class of '66.

Cece Canton

My name is Anne (Durgee in high school) Lusk. I left the middle of my junior year in the end of 1964, so I would have been Class of 1966. When I was a Freshman, we were in a school building near the pool. By the time I was a Junior, we had moved to the school building opposite the parade ground. I know in the transition that many of the areas on base became off limits to us because those sections were being given to the Moroccans. For instance, we could no longer use the pool. In the second school building, we no longer walked to the Oasis but were able to get food in the school building. There also was a teen center but I don't recall if that was accessible after the move and the base transfer. I moved to Rabat in '62 as my father was a chemical engineer building a chemical plant in Morocco. My parents sent me to TMW, rather than the girls' French school, and I rode the hour-long bus ride with everyone from Rabat to Kenitra. We lived in a house near the American Embassy in Rabat.

Anne Lusk

I remember arriving in Morocco in June of 1965, checking into a hotel (don't remember the name) and falling into bed from an exhausting flight over. I awoke to what I thought was a fight going on outside my window. I jumped up only to discover two ladies covered head to toe in djellabas laughing and dickering with a tradesman for wares that he had on his donkey's back. He wore a filthy djellaba and a red fez and had a mouth full of gold. We had an indoctrination that day on base. My dad worked at Bouknadel, the transmitter site and was RMC James Hatcher. We were told that for all intents and purposes we were not actually in Morocco; that is, the Navy wasn't. Which after much explaining meant that we were there as trainers to the Moroccans who co-owned our bases and were in transition to take over. So, no uniforms off base, no flying of the flag and no talking about what my dad did while there.

After a week at the unnamed hotel my dad decided that we were going to live in Kenitra and not on base unless required to. He was a great lover of other places, people and cultures and wanted us to always live on the economy wherever Uncle Sam sent us. We ate their food, celebrated their holidays, and were always to be the antithesis of the "ugly American."

So, the hunt for a house began. Meanwhile, we moved to the Mamora where we had two bedrooms and a kitchenette and my mom did what she always did when we moved anywhere, began making where we were, home. She got us on a schedule, assigned chores and responsibilities and we all began to explore this fascinating place!

Down the street to the right as you exited I found a dressmaker's shop with a beautiful wedding gown in the window. I was standing at the window admiring the intricacy of the beading when the owner came out in a hurry and almost knocked me down. He was a Spaniard by descent and French by birth. He was very apologetic and when he realized I was American began to speak in broken English and we exchanged names. His was Vincent Mari and he had lived in Morocco most of his life when his French Foreign Legion father had moved the family there in the 40's on assignment. Thus began a friendship that opened up many doors to the French people in town.

I spent a lot of time that summer getting to know Vincent and his family. One night my family was invited to the Mari's home for dinner. We arrived and found a beautiful Spanish Doña with 7 sons ranging in age from 50's to 20's. Her husband had died years before and they had remained in Morocco. That night was magical. Their house was lovely, with a beautiful courtyard in the back and a long table set up under a grape arbor hanging full of little green soon to turn to red grapes. There were lights in the trees and Moroccan lanterns everywhere. And the smells, oh the smells! For dinner there were mussels in garlic wine sauce with fresh crusty French bread to sop up the liquid. The next course was artichokes with lemon garlic aioli. Of course they had to teach us how to eat the leaves and scrape them across our teeth to get the succulent meat and how to cut it open and discard the choke and discover the wonderful heart. We laughed the evening away, as we enjoyed pigeon tagine and couscous and sweet red wine that "Mama Mari" made herself from the very grape arbor we were dining under. After dinner the chair and tables were moved and the soft music was turned up and we danced the night away. At some point during all this, a new son came home from his job as a pharmacy assistant and joined the party. That was the night this 17-year-old girl fell in love. Tony was his name, he was 23 and drop dead gorgeous! He ate in the kitchen and joined us after his respite and walked straight over and asked me to dance. We danced the rest of the time together. His younger brother tried breaking in once or twice and was told, "NO!"

School started, we were in an apartment on Rue de Zem Zem, and suddenly I was thrown back into an American High School setting after a summer of dates at local bars, the theater, the opera and a fairy tale life that I never dreamed I'd experience. I found my 12th grade year a bore! I wasn't into the stable set, or the teen town set, I was much more mature than all that...said tongue in cheek. So, my memories are totally different from everyone else's. I had those same type of memories from our tour in Trinidad, WI. My memories were much more about the Moroccan experience which has stayed with me all through the years.

Since we were in town, we of course had a Fatima. Her name was Khadijah and she took me everywhere. We went early to the Medina and Souk to buy food for the day. I was always mesmerized by the sights and sounds and oh my, the smells. She bartered and I learned to do the same, pretty well. We would stop by the little kiosk that sold makeup and she would look at it all. I tried to get her to buy some and she was shocked that I would suggest such a thing, but I could tell she had dreams of putting on the beautiful colors in the pretty little pots. I was also learning a little Arabic and had fun trying it out with her help.

I still spent a good bit of time at Vincent's and my mom had started having him make our clothes as well.

Bonnie Arey

This photo is dated 22 December 1966 and was a Christmas Party at "The Haven Orphanage" in Azrou, Marrakech, Morocco. It was a Christian orphanage sponsored by the Base Church through the military Commanders. Many of the TMW students brought boxes of gifts, food, and clothes for them. Wonderful memories, with some of my best friends. — identified in the photo are students David Aiken, Hunter English and Dean A. Willis (second row behind Santa).

Bob Bennett

The 1966 Yearbook

Administration: CAPT L. E. Darby (CO, USNAVCOMSTA & CO, USNTC); CAPT J. B. Hansen (Chief of Staff, USNTC); Mr. A. B. Chandler (Superintendent of Schools and Elementary School Principal); Ernest M. Morgan (High School Principal).

Faculty & Staff: Faculty: Miss Mary Holler; Miss Gale Barnes; Mrs. Mary Eide; Miss Carol Thornton; Miss Kathy Lewis; Mrs. Nancy Speck; Mrs. Evelyn McKenna; Mrs. Marjorie R. Poe; Mr.

Albert G. Stephenson; Mr. Patrick Gillen. **Staff:** Mrs. Louise Morgan (Secretary).

The 24 graduating Seniors of 1966: Douglas Baillie Roberts (President); Karel August Rudolf "Rudy" van Haeften (Vice-President); Barbara Diane Cox (Secretary-Treasurer); Abla Amin; Georgette Assauline; Sandra Louise Barr; Lynn Norfleet Carney; Mary Elizabeth Glass; Mansour Guessous; Rose Marie Hanna; Ellsworth Hugh Hargis; Elizabeth Ann Hatcher; Linda Gail Ison; Mohamed Joudar; Abdelhai Laabi; Alexander Phillipe Laurent; John Alison Madewell; Stephen Dennis Martin; Jacqueline Rae McGraw; Mark Sigmund Mohns; William Livingston Moseley; Christine Dale Schroeder; Madonna Edna Smith; and Delores Marie Still.

CLASS OF 1967

1967 saw an increase of American troops in Vietnam – now at 475,000 - while the number of protesters at peace rallies against the war also increased. The professional boxer Muhammad Ali (formerly known as Cassius Clay) was stripped of his boxing world championship for refusing to be inducted into the US Army. In the Middle-East, Israel went to war with Syria, Egypt and Jordan in the Six Day War and when it was over Israel controlled and occupied more territory than before the war. Once again in the hot summer, cities throughout America exploded in rioting and looting - the worst being in Detroit on July 23rd where 7,000 National Guard troops were bought in to restore law and order on the streets. In England a new type of model became a fashion sensation by the name of Twiggy and miniskirts continued to get shorter and even more popular with a short-lived fashion being paper clothing. Also during this year new discotheques and singles bars appeared across cities around the world and the Beatles continued to reign supreme with the release of "Sgt. Pepper's Lonely Heart Club Band" album. This was the year coined "The Summer of Love" when young teenagers got friendly and smoked pot and grooved to the music of The Grateful Dead, Jefferson Airplane and The Byrds. The movie industry moved with the times and produced movies that would appeal to this younger audience including "The Graduate," Bonnie and Clyde" and "Cool Hand Luke". TV shows included "The Fugitive" and "The Monkees" and color television sets become popular as the cost came down and more programs were filmed in color. Two Moroccan births of note in 1967: Khalid Skah was born on January 29 in Midelt and went on to become a 5K and 10K runner; Moulay Brahim Boutayeb was born on August 15 in

Khemisset and went on to win gold at the 1988 Summer Olympics in the 10K run.

I Remember:

I was a teacher of several subjects depending on the year: English, social studies, art, and humanities. The years were fall of 1967 through spring of 1973. I lived on the base in Kenitra and in Kenitra on Rue Amir ben El Ass across from the Boomer family.

David Loren Bass

I was Class of '67 and lived at Sidi Yahia from 64-66. The McQuagge and Franks family shared a duplex on the base.

Charlene Franks Shook

I came to Kenitra (on base) in the spring of '66. Found my way to the radio station that summer. I have great memories of being in Morocco with all of you. I was Class of '67. I spent some time in the Navy after graduation and even a longer time working with the FAA. I'm now retired living in St. Augustine.

David Aiken

I came to Le Maroc the last of '65 (kicking & screaming) - no, I know, no military brat would do that. I was living in Orange Park, FL, and didn't want to leave my friends. We lived in the Hotel Mamora (Kenitra) for about 3 months before getting base housing in Kenitra. It took me perhaps 2 weeks to fall in love with Morocco. I was sad to leave May of '67. I had wonderful friends there. I'll never forget the smell, sights and people.

Brenda Cozad Nutt

I was Jackie Earnhardt and I was in school from 1966 and graduated in 1967. We lived off base for several months in this neat villa near the back entrance of the base. We then moved to Sidi Yahia where my dad worked--he was the chief in charge of the EM Club. Long bus ride to school each day, but a good time to visit with friends and do homework. After graduation I moved to North Carolina for college. I loved the famous hamburgers from the Oasis. I can still remember the smell of them cooking and the jukebox playing "Reach out I'll Be there". Anybody else remember that?

Jackie Earnhardt Manns

The Oasis Snack Bar where they served Jackie's hamburgers and the best French fries smothered in gravy.

My father, Troy C. Beavers, was a career Naval Aviator and between 1959 & 1961 he was stationed at Port Lyautey in Operations SQ. We lived on base and I went to the 6th and 7th grades at Thomas Mack Wilhoite High School, so I would have been Class of 1967. I still have "The Sultan" yearbooks. I have many good memories of this time and found Morocco fascinating. I have never returned but often wish I could.

Mary Alice Beavers Jackson

My father served with the US Air Force at base outside Kenitra/Port Lyautey in 1966-1967. My sister and I attended High School on base. We lived off base. My father and I joined the Kenitra Bowmen Archery Club and I practically lived in the clubhouse. I enjoyed the Fleet Club and live music and knew many Navy & Marine servicemen. My father, a WWII veteran knew the trouble they could get into, so there was plenty of beer and home-cooked meals and a spot on the floor or rooftop patio for them to sleep. I got in a street brawl along with three Marines one night. My folks encouraged the single servicemen to stay at our house when they had a weekend pass. We didn't have much money and it was a warm evening so we decided to hike the three or four miles from the Fleet Club to Bir Rami II where we lived. A group of Moroccans started following us and got on our heels asking for "dirhams". The odds were 3 or 4 to 1. One of them made the mistake of trying to grab a wristwatch off one of the Marine's arm. The fight was on. Knowing if someone got hurt badly there would be huge trouble, the Marines would dodge a swing, then shove the guy to the ground then do a foot sweep on the next one, shove a third into a wall. Hooting and laughing the whole time. In ten seconds it was over. We jogged for a few blocks right down the middle of the street. Then we started singing "Yellow Submarine" except "the big green machine" was substituted for the original words. We filed into my folk's house like nothing happened. I am still in touch with several guys from Maroc and we exchange emails weekly. I would like to communicate with some of my archery buddies from that time. Tony Cavazos, Jake? Grimsley, Bob Storey, Wolfe, Pat Patterson, Marzak, Dan? I used to hang out in the Oasis and listen to the juke box and see a different movie each night. My father was M/SGT Raymond Sutton.

Bryce Sutton

We lived there from the fall of '64 to the spring of '67. We lived on base the whole time. My Dad got the house the old administrator vacated when he was rotated to another assignment. Working permanently for DOD overseas we did that quite often since, like the diplomatic corps, we all knew each other. Our house was on the circle 2 houses down from the Chief's Club. We lived next to the Lyons whose Dad was the other administrator on base.

Lew Chandler

The 1967 Yearbook

Administration: CAPT Frank R. More, USN (Base Commander); CDR Roger A. Bisbee, USN (School's Officer); CDR Donald C. Staley, USN (Chief Staff Officer); LTCOL Charles F. Bunnell,

USMC (PTA President); Michael A. Fay (Supervisory Principal) and Mr. David W. Twohy (Principal).

Faculty & Staff: Faculty: Mrs. Gale Bass; Miss Gail Bristol; Miss Janet Kissel; Mr. Steven Motta; Mr. John Bennett; Mr. Gerald Ludwig; Miss Brenda Burch; Mrs. Nancy Speck; Miss Inez Bliven; Miss Lilly Garcia; Miss Ethel Melton. **Staff:** Mrs. Evelyn Paulson; Mr. Dave Horne; Miss Renate Phillips; Miss Bonnie Sutton and Miss Jackie Earnhardt.

The 14 graduating Seniors of 1967: Michael R. Kampfe (President); Jacqueline "Jackie" Earnhardt (Vice-President); Christine S. Naprstek (Secretary); Bonnie M. Sutton (Treasurer); David A. Aiken; Brenda G. Cozad; Mariam T. Dorros; Catherine M. Hargreaves; David C. Horne; Kathleen G. Moore; Barbara E. Patterson; Lewis A. Richardson; Ong-In Shin; and Billy R. Walton.

CLASS OF 1968

1968 saw the continued rise in both the European and American marketplaces of Japanese imported cars and other goods - troubling the governments of UK and USA as they worried about industries in their own countries being affected and the jobs being lost. On 4 April 1968 the Reverend Martin Luther King, Jr., was assassinated; Robert Kennedy was mortally wounded when he is shot by Sirhan Sirhan. The peace movement continued to grow as more and more Americans turned against the war in Vietnam. Again, 1968 saw more race riots occurring throughout cities in America. The music scene was once again set by the "Beatles" and the "Rolling Stones", and fashion flirted with see through blouses; midi and maxi skirts joined the Mini Skirt as part of the fashion trends. There was an influenza pandemic in Hong Kong and the first Black Power salute is seen on television worldwide during an Olympics medal ceremony.

I Remember:

I lived in Morocco from 1963 to 1966, 7th through 10th grades. We were veterans of the Astor Hotel. and if anyone remembers the villa right around the corner from the Astor on Rue Moulay de Abderahmane with the two blue goldfish ponds, that was us. After about a year in Kenitra we moved on base to Sidi Yahia, where we lived until we left Morocco.

Andrea Fleming Gast - Class of '68, but graduated stateside

I graduated from TMWHS in '68. I lived in Sidi from February 12, 1966, to August 3, 1968. Made many wonderful friends there and this was my favorite place I lived as a military (Navy) brat. It would be interesting to go back sometime but even more fun if we all could reunite together someday as a class (classes) again! Here's a blast from the past... I've heard of or been involved in some mischievous fun on base as a dependent. Our friendships were close and most of us were involved in something we laugh at now.

So now you have me reminiscing about my magical life in Morocco, so as the beat goes on....

On a cold evening in January, 1966, over the dinner table, my three brothers, Jim, Don, Tommy and I were told about our next move. We were leaving Frankfurt, Germany and on to Dad's next duty station. We were accustomed to moving every few years as we had done so all our lives during Dad's 30 years in the Navy and this was the only life we knew. I was turning "Sweet 16" at the end of the month and a few weeks later I was packing to go on my next adventure, AFRICA!

Africa, I imagined, was on another planet or close to it. I had only seen it in the movies and Tarzan pretty much summed up where we would be living, swinging from trees in the jungle full of slithering snakes and monkeys eating lots of bananas. Our resources were limited to the high school library and, of course, the Encyclopedia Britannica, which our family still owns today. We learned what we could about this mysterious country. We were quickly reassured life would not be in the jungle but closer to a desert. Ok, I thought, camels were much better.

Suitcases were piled high on the roof of our white Ford station wagon with the six of us inside and anything else we could fit in there, trusting Dad knew where he was taking us. I never questioned his decisions. I remember seeing the Rock of Gibraltar behind us in the distance from the ferry as we approached Tangier, AFRICA. It was nothing close to what I had imagined when we reached shore again. The beautiful people, the colors, the amazing buildings, palm trees, the transportation, the dress, the spicy aromas, and of course, lots of donkeys, single-humped camels. It was all different than anything I had seen before. The weather was a welcome change from the chilling cold in Frankfurt, Germany, we had left behind and noticeably so traveling south toward Casablanca and toward our final destination. I already loved this country!

Arriving at the home of Earl & Nancy Loop, our sponsors in Kenitra, we were greeted warmly and the excitement grew. Kenitra was one interesting city, just waiting to be explored and my two brothers, Jim and Don, were eager to get started. Dad gave each of us a dollar and Mr. Loop explained the short walk to the Medina, an outdoor market full of colorful clothing, scarves, leather goods, silver and gold jewelry, shiny brass, colorful fruits, and ohhhhh the spices. The fragrance of the grilled brochettes filled the air, luring us to the homemade street carts, wanting to taste them. I was totally captivated as we wandered through the streets, soaking in the experience of the whole culture. Music played in the distance. It was mystical and romantic. I returned with a huge grocery bag full of juicy ripe oranges to share with my family. I paid a dollar for them. We were taken to our temporary housing and unpacked, knowing this would be our home until base housing became available for us in a little city called Sidi Yahia. Mom and Dad took us to register for school at Thomas Mack Wilhoite High School. It was a small school compared to Frankfurt and classes were in session so we didn't get to see any kids. It was Friday, February 12th and the Principal, Mr. Morgan, told us there was a school dance that night. Later that afternoon two cute guys were at our villa door. Lewie Richardson and George Phillips introduced themselves and came in to invite Jim and me to the Valentine Dance that night. I don't remember why we didn't go, but we didn't. They stayed awhile and visited. It was good to know at least two cute guys at our new school the first day.

I didn't realize it then but at 16, I was just beginning one of the best milestones of my life and to this day I can say those were the happiest days of my years growing up. My world was small and friends quickly became family. It was special. The school was small and everyone knew everyone. There were three bases, Kenitra NTC was the main base, Sidi Yahia NCS was about 30 miles from Kenitra and there was also another base called Bouknadel RTF, all virtually connecting themselves to each other, not too far from the Mediterranean Sea and the Atlantic Ocean. We were scattered between all three bases and going to school in Kenitra. Years later I learned Sidi's large antenna field outside the base was a receiving station, and my Dad, Lenwood O. Gay, was closely connected to NSA in Fort Meade, Maryland. We never knew what Dad did. He was sworn to secrecy and honored that until the day he died on February 24, 2017. He is still my only hero.

Our weekday 30-minute bus rides to and from school were so much fun. There were always men riding donkeys on the side of the road, with their wives walking, with bundles of sticks on their backs. The shanty hand-built homes blended into the landscapes and it was evident these people really worked hard for what little they had. This was probably my first real lesson on gratitude. The countryside was sparsely dotted with scrubby trees as well as palm trees and sandy terrain. Women were completely covered except their eyes and hands. The culture was so much different than ours. We were never allowed to fly the American flag on base and military uniforms were to never be worn off base.

Years later I found out we were not really there, according to the military (We were a secret base). We spent a lot of time on the bus doing our homework, singing, catching up on everyone's day and making plans for the evening or the weekend which usually included our hangout, the Teen Club, at the back of the base in a Quonset hut complete with a jukebox, a pool table and of plenty room to dance. I always sat in the back with my friends. When I think of the school bus though, I always think of Sue McQuagge. She is the only one from Sidi who mastered that eyelash curler without pulling out her lashes. She would spend her half hour bumpy morning ride talking and laughing as she put all her makeup on and, believe it or not, curled her eyelashes without ripping them off her eyelids. We were all amazed with her steady composure. On the way home she spent less time taking her makeup off as her parents wouldn't allow her to wear makeup. That's just what we did...and secrets back then were closely guarded. Always fun times on that old grey school bus.

I did take my own skip day once with Debbie Cannon. It was the day Kathy and Tom Sutton were flying back to the States and they were leaving that morning from the airport on Kenitra base, just a short walk from the school. After riding the bus to school, Debbie and I rendezvoused and never walked into the school, sneaking our way around the building and hiking to the airport to see our friends for the last time. The morning was beautiful, the sun was bright and we were all crying and hugging. Then as we turned around, there was Mr. Morgan, our principal, standing there watching us with his arms folded in front of him. BUSTED! He motioned for us to come over and told us to come straight to his office when we returned to school. We watched Kathy and Tom leave and hiked back to the dreaded sentence we were about to be delivered. He made us call our parents and tell them what happened and that we were caught. That was more than enough sentence to me because I knew that meant I was grounded for 30 days before I even made that call. I believe Mr. Morgan thought that was sentence enough and dismissed us to class, marking us as an inexcusable tardiness for the day.

Then there was the famous Sidi water tower! I had heard about the brave ones who conquered the top and how "dangerous" it was. I later learned the danger was trying not to get caught. It was a calculated plan to make sure we had enough "Watchers" and "Climbers." It was a practiced timing and everyone had to be paying attention. The water tower was at the back of the base, close to the teen club which gave us cover if in danger of getting caught. The teen club lights were on, music was playing and someone timed the patrol truck as he made his rounds around the perimeter of the base. After a few practice rounds and a lot of guts and nerves, we staged for the climb. As the truck passed with his spotlight always shining along the fence and then up the tower, he turned the corner on his way to the other side of the base. There were about 6-8 climbers and being the brave one I was, I was second to last to climb just before George Cornelson. From the top we could see everything! It was like climbing Mount Everest. I felt like I should beat my chest like Tarzan but knew to keep very quiet! We got the signal the patrol truck was coming towards the back of the base again and everyone scurried their way down. I guess there were too many of us because he was almost around the corner and I had only made it about halfway down and George was above me. George suggested we should climb back up and lay flat on the front grated deck so the light wouldn't hit us. We did just that. The patrol car stopped and he got out, walking toward the tower, approaching the lucky group who made it safely down. I couldn't hear the conversation but I could hear my heart beating. I knew if I got caught I would be grounded for the rest of my life. Shining his flashlight up to the tower, he climbed back into his truck and continued his rounds. To this day I'm not sure if he knew George and I were up there or not, but I would like to believe he did, since he was just a few years older than we were. He let us have our thrill. I never climbed that tower again. I'm certain it took a few years off my life.

Music at our school dances was provided by either our Velvet Voiced DJ Dave or our favorite famous local band, "Sidi Limits." Although the band's name always stayed the same, the players rotated as the military seemed to dictate who was available and whose father was once again transferred on to another duty station. The band was always great through the years. My brother Jim played with them. I think of them when I hear "Wild Thing", "House of the Rising Sun", "Satisfaction", "California Dreamin", "Paint it Black", "Red Rubber Ball", "Sounds of Silence"' and more. When they weren't playing we would pull out our reel-to-reel hand-held tape player (we all owned one) and play songs recorded from records we shared with each other as well as songs the base radio station played manned by of course, our great DJ, Dave Aiken. "Sidi Limits" also filled in for a singer and dancer who appeared in several movies in the 60's, Candy Johnson. When she arrived, her band, The Exciters, quit on her. "Sidi Limits" stepped up to the plate as she sang to the troops at the club. You may remember her in the Beach Party movies, the one who shimmied her tassels hanging from her short dresses. We all got together and made her dinner at our home. It was pretty exciting to sit and talk with her.

We were all easily amused and I have heard, but only witnessed a few, stories as they were whispered through the halls of school. I do hope someone tells the story of the donkey brought on base in Sidi one night and tied to a tree in Captain's front yard. Another story was about a handful of high school guys jumping the fence of the Sidi base pool late at night and were caught in their skivvies only to be marched, carrying their dry clothes in their arms, to an adult party most parents were attending at the home of one of the intruder's parents. And there was the story of Paul Lopes coming home one night after a bit too many "spirits" only to wake up in the morning with his beautiful shiny Beetle haircut locks shaved completely off. He wore a hat to school for a long time. Paul was a great sport and truly earned the title of "Chrome Dome." We had a choice of movie theatres in Sidi, either the inside theater between the small bowling alley and library or the outdoor theatre just past the base pool. Both were fun and movies were free. My brother Jim worked at the popcorn stand at the outdoor theatre. I remember Sue McQuagge taught me how to smoke in the indoor movie theatre after school. Cigarettes were 20 cents a pack. We would each insert a dime into the cigarette machine and share the pack. We took turns taking the pack to our homes as we both would have been in big trouble if caught with them. Jackie Earnhardt and I landed our first job at the base exchange as cashiers which gave us first pick of any new clothing arriving. I spent my entire paycheck on clothes my junior/senior year. I also enjoyed the cute sailors and marines coming through my line on payday. I wasn't allowed to legally date a military man until I turned 18 but I admit I snuck out and met a few at the movies. I was pretty sure my Dad checked out every guy I dated before I got an all clear permission. We had several chaperoned parties at our house, and some included those cute guys. I only had my heart broken once while in high school. I fought for him and lost. We remain friends to this day.

We didn't have much but we did make the best of what we did have in our wardrobes. Some of us made an honest attempt to be creative with a sewing machine, and some even braver wore our own creations. Some of us ordered our dresses from the Sears and Roebuck catalogue, some bought clothes at the base exchange, and some even found beautiful clothes on the economy. No matter how we looked at it, we all had a huge wardrobe because we shared our clothes with each other. My "go to" closet was owned by my best friend, Bert Schuessler aka Bobbie Bridges. She always had the cutest dresses. Clothes and shoes were not a trend setter as I remember. Our senior graduation photo proved that. Three of us were wearing the exact same white shoes in the front row, probably purchased from the base exchange. There was never any competition on who had the best threads. We seemed to share everything. I remember Michelle Fuselier, who later married Johnny Hanna, had come to school wearing a beautiful fall hairpiece. It was wonderful and I really wanted one as well! She helped me pick the color and style of mine and we both were so excited anticipating the arrival of mine. I recall it costing $10.00, big money back then. I welcomed the change and long straight hair was my dream since I was born with lots of locks of curls. Today I'm happy with my curls as they have faded into grey and easier to manage since I live near Wrightsville Beach, NC. I call it my beach look and in the morning when I wake up, it's all over the place. I just look in the mirror and say to myself, 'well I worked all night to get it to look like this', run my fingers through it, and go on with my day. Simple has always worked better for me.

During the summer we spent most of our time at the Sidi base pool. It was always hot, sometimes we had temps go into the 130's, Siroccos I think they were called. The sweltering heat was somewhat bearable because of the lack of humidity. The occasional days when the wind was just right we had the smell of the paper mill across the street from the Sidi base. The pool was the only place to keep cool since we didn't have air conditioning. We all had wonderful dark tans. We were carefree and happy. There was always music coming through the jukebox, water splashing and laughter, the scent of baby oil laced with iodine to speed up our tans and towels clustered close together on the grass so we would not miss bits of conversations between each other. When I hear "Dancing in the Streets" I always think of Mariam Dorros. She played it a lot and danced to that song all the time. I remember one morning I received a phone call (our phone number was 347) from the lifeguard, who I thought was cute but always had a girlfriend, one right after the other. He asked me to come to the pool and spend the day with him. That was my very first official phone call date ever. I washed my hair and quickly rolled it into large curlers to make it straight and pretty. I nervously sat under a plastic cap with hot air blowing through the tube to dry it. I threw on my yellow bikini and made my way to the pool. I knew Lewie well but we were always just friends. I had no idea why this pool visit made me so nervous but it did. We were alone and he asked me if I wanted to help him clean the bottom of the pool before it opened. He strapped some weights around my waist and put an air tube in my mouth and coaxed me into the deep... That was the beginning of my first serious relationship. He drove a car and I was not allowed to ride in it with him, EVER! One evening I was called out by my parents because someone told Mom I was "parking" with Lewie at the end of the road by the teen club and the windows were steamy. Shocked at the accusation, I couldn't convince Mom and Dad it wasn't me. I was grounded, again, for 30 days. A few days later Lewie broke up with me and I later realized it was this "Other Woman" I was blamed and grounded for. That was the first time my heart was broken. We all have stories like that from our times in Morocco and there were always those "Other Girl Stories" which to this day we talk about and laugh of our naive days in Morocco. I remain friends with Lewie and his wife and we still laugh as I refer to her as the "other woman." She asked me jokingly if I wanted him back and I reluctantly answered no.

School was fun. I made my first dress in Home Ec. and actually wore it. I never had to dissect a frog or learn the Constitution. I never liked math and proved it with my report card. I loved Art and Mr. Bass showed me how to embrace it. I was very social and loved my classmates. I was Junior Class Treasurer and Senior Class Secretary. I was also High School Sweetheart my senior year. As the years passed I have never forgotten the walks to the Oasis for french fries at lunch, our Teen Club trip to Efran seeing snow for the first time in awhile, slumber parties, high school games and plays, Faberge cologne, silver ID bracelets, Friday nights to La Cage nightclub, hay rides to the beach with the Teen Club...oh that's another story. I guess I can tell the Teen Club Hay Ride story now since I'm too old to be grounded. We all went to the beach one night as a Teen Club hay ride event. It was chaperoned, but not too closely, by Mr and Mrs. Smith. We each paired up and bought a bottle of wine to share. I think we spent a quarter each on a 50-cent bottle of wine. I paired up with George Cornelson although he didn't like wine and this was my first try. I drank the whole bottle myself and had to empty my tiny tanks. A few of us wandered out looking for a little girl's room. All we could find was a stinky dugout area on the side of a hill with wooden sides and door. The floor was a makeshift toilet we had to stand and squat, trying to hit the hole in the ground. As I squatted a huge dog began barking over my head. There was no roof, just the black sky with stars, and the head of a huge dog illuminated by the moonlight looking like it was ready to jump down on me. It scared the dickens out of me as I darted out of that outhouse and ran back towards the beach with Becky Garrett and a few other gals, explaining what happened along the way. I decided the ocean was the better choice. A few minutes later my brother Jim was swimming out to rescue me. He asked what I was doing as I was already over my head. I said I was swimming back to the United States. He brought me in and saved my life. I was lucky that I was spending the night with Becky. I was told it took a couple of guys to sneak me into her house and upstairs to her room. That night I swore off wine. It was my last in Morocco and I knew I was the luckiest gal in Morocco since I returned to school Monday morning with a full head of hair, escaping the female title of 'Chrome Dome' Paul Lopes earned and held forever. We were so carefree back then. I didn't do drugs, heck, I really didn't know about drugs, we were so protected. I heard later some explored more than wine and truthfully we were all just trying to grow up.

Fifteen students from Thomas Mack Wilhoite Junior-Senior High School were selected to participate in the American Music Festival in Seville, Spain in May of 1968. Out of fifteen students, Johnny Hanna and I were the only chosen seniors to go. Thirteen underclassmen joined us as well. It was a fun trip, and each of us stayed at various homes of other students from Seville American Junior-Senior High School. The festival was held Saturday, May 18, 1968. There were four schools involved, Madrid Jr./Sr. HS, David Glasgow Farragut Jr./Sr. HS, Seville American Jr./Sr. HS as well as our school making it a huge event. While we were all singing and playing instruments in the Theatre Lope De Vega in Spain, our senior classmates were back in Africa orchestrating an event of their own. I never understood why they didn't wait until Johnny and I returned but the entire senior class secretly planned their own Senior Skip Day, scheduled for Monday, May 20, 1968. There were 27 unexcused absentees (15 were seniors) and 15 excused Spain trip absentees (Johnny and I being the only seniors). By the time Johnny and I returned the news was funny to us except that Mr. Gundacker announced over the intercom, since the senior class took an illegal skip day, the Senior prom was cancelled. Days later it was reinstated but certainly gave us a scare. The Prom was held in the Bab Es Samaa Room of the Rabat Hilton Hotel at 7:30 on Sunday, May 26th 1968. Donn Colee was my prom date, a DJ at the radio station, and in the Navy. We still keep in contact with each other. A few days after we returned there was a history test. We all promised to study while we were on our trip but speaking for myself, I never opened a book. When I walked into class, I think Miss Maddox was subbing that day. I realized it was a written essay and I had not a clue what to write. Wanting to look busy, I made my plea by writing an essay about my (educational) trip to Seville Spain, why I didn't have any time to study, and I wanted a second chance to take the test after I had a chance to study. I was the first one to turn in my essay and the teacher read it and started laughing. She got up and walked out of the room putting me in charge of the class as they were writing their own essays. A few minutes later I saw her out in the hallway with Mr. Gundacker and she motioned to me to step out there. I knew I was going to be suspended by him and grounded by my parents, regretting every word I wrote on my essay. They both laughed and gave me another chance. I passed the essay the second time I took it. I was relieved to find out teachers were human and do have a sense of humor! I wonder if Miss Maddox remembers that.

There were several students attending our school from other countries. Maria Benkirane was from Morocco and a fun friend to have. She told me her family was somehow related to King Hassan (he was her uncle or something). She invited me to spend the weekend at her home in Rabat. This was my first experience staying off base with a foreign family. Her home was fascinating. The floors and walls were white tile and it was cool in there, considering how hot Morocco got. The vibrant accent hues stayed consistent with the bright colors of Morocco. We entered through the kitchen door greeted by cooks busily preparing dinner for that evening. It smelled wonderful in there. Some words were exchanged, nothing I understood, but Maria and I sat at the table sipping on a glass of Moroccan mint tea eating fruits and chatting between each other. A few minutes later a lady walked over from the stove and handed Maria a ball of sticky golden taffy like substance. I thought it was candy or some kind of treat. Maria explained to me that it was made of honey and oranges and cooked down to that consistency to remove the hair off her legs. "ARE YOU KIDDING ME?" I thought. I wanted to eat the stuff! They laughed and kept coaxing me to spread it on my legs, ripping it off rewarding me with smooth hairless legs. I never came to terms with spreading that perfectly delicious candy on my legs. It smelled wonderful. To this day I use a razor on the few precious hairs I have still growing.

Dinner that night was the most amazing food experience I had in Morocco. We entered a room with huge pillows on the floor, surrounding a table in the center, filled with the most amazing spread of food ever! Salads, Couscous, flatbreads all heaping in vibrant colored clay bowls. The only thing I was really familiar with was the mint tea and there were two ways to drink it. Either with a hunk of sugar tucked between my bottom lip and gum, sipping the hot tea through the sugar, or drinking it straight from the glass, already heavily sweetened. Either was, it was always sweet.

Although they showed me the proper way to eat Couscous, (with my right hand) they were kind enough to offer me a spoon, which I eagerly accepted. The desserts were delicious. There are no language barriers over a table filled with food. Smiles and Ummmmm's of approval was all we needed, sandwiched with lots of satisfying smiles. To this day, Moroccan food has been my go to favorite food ever!

It was the evening of Monday, June 10th, 1968, 6:30 PM. The number-one hit song was "Mrs. Robinson" by Simon and Garfunkel. Our President was Lyndon B. Johnson, the nation was mourning the death of Robert Kennedy and the Vietnam war was active with bombs falling over Saigon, a war I am still to this day trying to wrap my head around. I still have my POW bracelet many of us ordered that year. Mine reads CAPT. DOUGLAS CONDIT 11-26-67. Our senior class of seventeen, who attended Thomas Mack Wilhoite High School/Kenitra American High School were in our caps and gowns, sitting on the stage of the Kenitra NTC Base Outdoor theatre on this beautiful evening. I sat in the front row watching my classmates approach the podium one by one as their names were called to receive their hard-earned diplomas. My name wasn't called and there I stood with my classmates, the only one without a diploma in my hands. I truly thought I hadn't graduated with my class and was too embarrassed to remind them they forgot mine. As our school principal, Mr. Gundacker, approached the podium to call on the Chaplain Lt. W. G. Blank, to deliver the benediction and I sank back in my folding chair, looking for an inconspicuous exit from the stage. A long pause filled the stage as Captain Feaster rustled with the papers on the podium making room for the Chaplain he said, "I know how much Pat Gay has been sweating her English grade," glancing over at me with a serious look on his face. I was horrified he was going to announce I was the only one on stage who had to repeat her senior year again. He picked up his papers and said, "Well look what I found up here. It's a diploma for Pat Gay." He asked me to please come forward to receive my diploma. I'm not sure which was more embarrassing, not receiving my diploma with my classmates, being singled out to receive my diploma by Captain Feaster or opening it and noticing it was blank inside! Upon further investigation, I discovered they had covered my original diploma with a blank piece of paper making it look like it truly was a blank diploma. I'm not sure how many teachers were involved but it was a joke they played on me for always having a really important reason to get an excuse to leave many of my classes during the school year. I never had the opportunity to thank my wonderful teachers for the best prank that ever happened to me. It was the mother of all pranks back then, a true "Gotcha". My parents knew about it before hand as Mr. Gundacker asked them for permission to pull it off days earlier. Our class motto was "The future is not in the hands of fate but in yours". I was so grateful that diploma was finally in my hands. I still laugh to myself when I hear the words "High School Diploma". We all celebrated with our families and guests at a reception at NTC Officer's Club after the ceremony.

I met my future husband at the pool in Sidi, the summer of 1968 when my parents went to Germany to pick up their new Mercedes. He was in the Navy and we were married May 20, 1970, in Glen Burnie, MD. I left Morocco in August of 1968. On the day I left Morocco, I was truly sad, leaving my friends and my then-boyfriend behind as well. We went to Algeciras, Spain and boarded the USS *Constitution* on August 3, 1968. I shared cabin #446 with Holly Kannenberg, who happened to be returning to the States the same time. We all had so much fun and the only time I ever saw my parents on that week-long voyage was at dinner. A friend had asked me to call him when I returned to New York and it was then I realized I actually needed money and I didn't even know how to use a pay phone. I hadn't seen one since I was in the 7th grade. I had to dial "O" to ask for her help and she talked me through it and put the call through for me. Life was simple and different in Morocco than in the States. I didn't know it then but I had just left the best times and the best friends of my life on the other side of the pond, never to return again.

It was hard returning to the States then. There was no school for me to return to, no friends to reunite with, no real memories to pick back up on. It was lonely. I really wanted to be an airline stewardess but I went straight from Morocco to cosmetology school, worked awhile, then got married in 1970. I didn't like doing hair so I went into cake decorating, became a professional cake decorator, putting my creativity, Mr. Bass assured me I had, into a profitable living, designing wedding cakes, working with brokerage companies and teaching others how to be creative as well. It was a fun career.

One constant we had in our lives was that we had each other. We took care of each other like sisters and brothers. There was never any class rivalry, we all hung around as a close group. My parents taught us to never judge anyone by their looks, color or what they had. I learned to look inside the souls and discovered the unique beauty in each person. We never questioned friendships, we just were. We got there when we did and left when we had to. The military controlled all our friends and if we were lucky, we got a few years at the most, with each other before we moved along to another station with our Dads to make new ones. Over the years some of us stayed in touch with each other. Life in the military was not like that of many who live in the States as civilians. Our friends were special and we never "Grew up" with a best friend or two. We didn't make plans about how we were going to grow up and get married and our babies were going to be best friends and live in the same town for the rest of our lives. Nothing like that. Our friends are all over the world. Just like the dandelion blowing in the wind, we land where we are and set our roots, temporary as they may be, and then off to another place, wherever the wind takes us, wherever the military places our Dad. And we survived. We don't have much baggage, we have beautiful memories to embrace. We laugh and cry and make random "I was just thinking about you" phone calls. We visit each other when we can and attend class reunions, which are great. Then we cry again as we part ways...again. I still to this day, find it hard to get too attached to new friends. I allowed the military to teach me this and, to this day, a lot of my dearest friends are those that I "tried to grow up with" in Morocco. That nomad blood still flows through my veins.

Living as a Navy Brat gave me the beautiful opportunity to travel and see so much of the world others have yet to see. I began my life on January 30, 1950, in San Juan, Puerto Rico, born at El Morro Castle. I was the first of 4 (definitely the favorite daughter) followed by my three brothers, Jim, Don and Tom Gay. My mother, Rosa Lee Gay, took great care of us through the years as we were able to go with my Dad, CTCM Lenwood O. Gay, to the many duty stations throughout his naval career. His duty stations took us to Bremerhaven Germany, Istanbul Turkey, Fort Meade Maryland (NSA), Zweibruecken Germany, Frankfurt Germany, Sidi Yahia Morocco, and finally back to Fort Meade Maryland where Dad spent his last years of his career as the first

Senior Enlisted Advisor to Admiral Noel Gayler at NSA. Today his portrait hangs on the walls of the entryway of NSA in Fort Meade. All of his overseas duty assignments allowed us to spend our vacations together traveling to see many European surrounding countries, camping, and taking in their history and beauty. I do believe we saw every beautiful European country there is. One of my most memorable visits was to the Berlin Wall with the Girl Scouts. I knew then, at that early age, just how special that was.

Thanks to Facebook, many of us have reunited and its easy to catch up on our daily lives. I attended some fantastic reunions, the largest and most special was the 1992 Greensboro, NC, reunion as it was the first for most of us. There was also a small reunion in Virginia and another in Florida. We did have a small reunion here in Wilmington, Wrightsville Beach, NC in the fall of 2011. We had so much fun and I can't wait to reunite with those, as well as others, again.

My memories remain etched deep in my heart, and there isn't a day goes by that I don't wish we could all go back to those innocent, beautiful times in our lives and relive them once again, oh but I do, often, in my memories. It remains the most magical time of my life!

As Sonny and Cher would sing,

"The Beat Goes On"....

The beat goes on, the beat goes on
Drums keep pounding a rhythm to the brain
La de da de de, la de da de da

Charleston was once the rage, uh huh
History has turned the page, uh huh
The mini skirts, the current thing, uh huh
Teenybopper is our newborn king, uh huh

And the beat goes on, the beat goes on
Drums keep pounding a rhythm to the brain
La de da de de, la de da de da

The grocery store's the super mart, uh huh
Little girls still break their hearts, uh huh
And men still keep on marching off to war
Electrically they keep a baseball score

And the beat goes on, the beat goes on
Drums keep pounding a rhythm to the brain
La de da de de, la de da de da

Grandmas sit in chairs and reminisce
Boys keep chasing girls to get a kiss
The cars keep going faster all the time
Bums still cry, "Hey buddy, have you got a dime?"

And the beat goes on, the beat goes on
Drums keep pounding a rhythm to the brain
La de da de de, la de da de da

And the beat goes on, yes, the beat goes on
And the beat goes on, and the beat goes on
The beat goes on, and the beat goes on

"The Beat Goes On"....

Patricia Anne Gay Hartzell

A few other guys and I (Air Force dependents) got picked up by the MPs at Sidi Slimane on several occasions. Looking back on it now I realize the MPs must have had a good laugh at our expense and really treated us good except they always made our parents come to the jailhouse to pick us up. Most of us turned out OK and kept out of trouble after we rotated. I don't imagine it's as boring on bases these days. Looking back at it now all of the enlisted men such as those MPs were really young but seemed older to me because of the uniforms and discipline. At 15/16 us guys were just trying to be cool with our low slung Levis and ducktail haircuts!

Jon Thorium Piercy

Lived in Kenitra from 1962 to 1964. Would have been Class of 1968 had we stayed.

Holly (Myers) Harder

I was at Sidi Yahia from 1964 to 1966 and lived on base the entire tour. Class of '68.

Mitchell Franks

I was there from '63 - '65 (8th, 9th, and a few months of 10th grade). I would have been Class of '68. I think we started out in the Astor Hotel and then the 2nd floor of a house owned by "John" and his family until we moved onto Kenitra base. We lived in the townhouses. Dale and Billy Roberts were just down the hill and the Bulls were around the corner. Andrea Fleming Gast one of my first pals at school along with Sue Brown. Later, Kathy Hargis was my best bud.

Christine Miskinis Marshall

Lived in a hotel for a couple months and the rest on the base at Bouk. I went to high school at Thomas Mack Wilhoite from 1964-1967 & would have been Class of 1968. I like to find out info on what happened to my old friends. My stepfather was stationed on Bouknadel & was in the Marine Corps. Anybody from that era? God Bless.

Lloyd H. ONeil

Arrived in Country summer of '66. Lived in town (Kenitra) just down the street from the Paulson Family. Mrs. Paulson was the School Secretary, '67-'68. Then to USNR(T) Bouknadel where I shared the Base confines with Bonnie Hatcher, Cindy Baker, Chris and Paula Raines, Paul Lopes, Lloyd ONeil and B. Jacobsen. Loved going to "La Plage" (Bouk Beach). Myself and Lloyd would take the morning 0800 bus and come back on the 1700, burnt to a crisp. Bottle of wine, 100 francs, stick of French Bread, fifty francs. Needless to say, had some "high" times at the "Beach." I remember the "pizzas" from the Oasis. Simply great. Pepperoni, cheese and sauce and the "oil" from the pepperoni. In addition, the "meatball" sandwich, ... to die for. Really good, right after school just B4 catching the bus back to Bouknadel. Would always end up having to give a "bite" of my meatball sub to Chris Raines. Always. So funny. Really liked Chris Raines. She and her sister Paula. Her Dad at that time ran the little Transmitter Site, i.e. Bouknadel. I remember several songs off that Oasis jukebox. Quite often playing any one of them as you entered: Psychotic Reaction, Hold On I'm Comin', The Mighty Quinn, Manfred Man; Reach Out, Workin' In A Coal Mine, Respect, Aretha Franklin, Downtown, Petula Clark. Really did enjoy The Oasis. Had the same sort of facility at Bouknadel, but smaller, jukebox, shuffle board, short order grill for the usual including the prized little pizzas. Yeah, ... nice, the music, the food, Chris Raines & Paula, Paul Lopes, everything and everyone else.

George Cornelson

Spent 2 years in Morocco, Kenitra & Sidi Yahia 66-68 coming from Key West. Returned to Key West in '68 and stayed. With the exception of 2 years in Germany 75-76, Army time. Lewis Richardson KAHS class of '67 is my brother-in-law. Good to see you all.

Robert Goodreau

The majority of graduation ceremonies were held at the base Outdoor Theater. Here is an example of Graduation 1968 – the first year that TMWHS was changed to KAHS:

What year did TMWHS become KAHS?

So, some history here: prior to the first Graduating Class of 1956 the school was simply called "Navy 214." In 1956 the entire school system, from Grades 1-12, was basically working off of correspondence courses with monitors located in Quonset huts. It was in 1956 that it became known as "Thomas Mack Wilhoite Schools" (plural) because grades 1-12 were all in the same place. The term "Thomas Mack Wilhoite Schools" continued through the end of the 1962 school year as evidenced by the difference shown between the 1962 and 1963 Yearbooks.

In 1963, when the student body at TMW outgrew their school space the Base Administration split it into two schools - the Thomas Mack Wilhoite Elementary School was for Grades 1-6 and the Thomas Mack Wilhoite High School was Grades 7-12.

1964 was the first year that the high school moved into the building across from the Parade Grounds. It is shown prominently for the first time in the 1964 yearbook with the name TMW High School. The official name of the high school, Thomas Mack

Wilhoite, stayed that way through 1967 (the Thomas Mack Wilhoite Elementary School never changed its name). Brenda Cozad Nutt explains: "My 1967 diploma has 'Thomas Mack Wilhoite American/European High School'. Teacher David Loren Bass had the best explanation. He commented that he arrived to teach in the fall of 1967 and the name was already KAHS. He thought that 'was to reflect the diversification of the schools in the European District by using local names'. Which would mean that the name was changed during the summer of 1967."

The 1968 yearbook was the first yearbook showing "KAHS." Kathy Myers Strange corroborates this: "When I ended the '66-'67 school year it had not changed from TMW. We left August 4th. On my return in '71 it had changed." But change is hard sometimes. Patti Gay Hartzell remembers: "We called it TMW when I graduated in '68. I was surprised the actual name was changed." Yet the photos of the 1968 Graduation Ceremony at the Outdoor Theater clearly display the change.

Deborah Robin Kafir corroborates the confusion as well: "We got there in '67 and it was called both names depending on who was talking. I am burning a few remaining brain cells here, but it had to do with renaming schools around the world to identify them as "American" to justify funding. I was on the *Sirocco* staff and I believe there was an article about it, but it might have been in the base newsletter."

The 1968 Yearbook

Administration: CAPT E. B. Abrams, USN (CO USNTC); CAPT Ernest M. Cadenas, USN (School Board's Officer); Mr. Michael A. Fay (Supervisory Principal) and Mr. George G. Gundacker (Principal).

Faculty & Staff: Faculty: Mr. David Loren Bass; Mrs. Doris Chula; Mr. Norman Chula; Miss Nancy J. Gatewood; Mr. Don Larson; Miss Judy Maddox; Mr. Frederic Meyer; Mr. Steven Motta; Miss Janice Taylor; and Mrs. Alice Whipple. **Staff:** Mrs. Evelyn Paulson (School Secretary).

The 18 graduating Seniors of 1968: Ahmet Acet (President); Michelle Fuselier (Vice-President); Patricia Gay (Secretary); Ruth Amar (Treasurer); Nadia Alami; Wail Bengelloun; Maria Benkirane;

George Cornelson; Patricia Davis; Hala El-Behbety; Johnny Hanna; Amelia Knox; Azedine Kozemane; Tahar Meddoun; Mohamed M'Rabet; Roberta Schuessler; Linda Slaughter; Wanda Vitalic

CLASS OF 1969

1969 saw, on July 20th, one of mankind's crowning achievements when American astronaut Neil Armstrong became the first human to set foot on the Moon and uttered the immortal words "That's one small step for man, one giant leap for mankind." Opposition to the war continued to increase with more and more attending anti-war demonstrations and demanding that the US withdraw from Vietnam. The music came from groups including the Doors, Led Zeppelin, Janis Joplin and the Beatles and the most famous music festival of modern times, Woodstock, took place on a New York farm on August 15th to 17th with more than 400,000 avid music fans attending to see the Who, Jimi Hendrix, Crosby Stills Nash and Young, Richie Havens, Arlo Guthrie, Jefferson Airplane, Joe Cocker, Joan Baez, the Grateful Dead, Country Joe & The Fish, Creedence Clearwater Revival and other live performances. Fashions reflected the anti-war sentiment with military jackets adorned with peace signs, and other trends including long unkempt wild hair and headbands. In Morocco, on June 30, Spain ceded Ifni to Morocco. Although the Spanish enclave of Ifni in the south became part of the new state of Morocco in 1969, other Spanish possessions in the north, including Ceuta, Melilla and Plaza de Soberanía, remained under Spanish control, with Morocco viewing them as occupied territory.

In 1969 the 7th graders put on the play "You, the Jury." This novel play allowed the audience to act as the jury and vote whether Barbara Scott on trial for the murder of Chester Arthur Brant was innocent or guilty. From left to right: Charles Whitbeck, Bruce Fairchild, Ben Kenyon, Jeff Fairchild, Elaine Davis and Keith Bennett.

I Remember:

We were teachers from 1969-1971, Spanish, Civics, Social Studies and Bob coached, taught PE, Health, Science. Our first child was born in May 1971 there. We lived in Mehdia Beach at the far end of the second row of villas.

Mary Zamora and Bob Thompson

I was there from 11/1969 - 8/1971. Lived off-base in a villa. Was married at the time to a Navy guy who worked at Sidi's receiver site. I loved living in Kenitra. They got their independence from France in 1956. I taught at Thomas Mack Wilhoite School. Had 36 kids and white scorpions on the playground. When returning to the States took a cut in pay. Hey, was thrilled to have a teaching job. Some days ....especially on a Friday, we had a "ropeyarn"! Hence, I was a Navy-wife!! Hubby loved the NCO club and going downtown. Went to the Marche in Kenitra and visited the Marche in Medina WITH OUR FATIMA (never took French). Read a lot 'cause no TV or phone. Phone was at a store connected to the villa. Called many times to substitute teach and sweated where was hubby after he had duty. But there was a decent library at NCS along with exchange, commissary, beauty parlor, and I forget what else!!!! Took the bus from Kenitra to base for one dirham. So am giving you folks a Navy wife's prospective.

Harriet Sutherland

My brother Lee and I (Class of '69) lived in Kenitra on Mustafa Rafi and attended TMW from 1964-1967 (8th, 9th and 10th grade). We lived in a hotel for the first couple of months and at the same time when George and Renate Phillips lived there when they arrived in Morocco. Andrea [Fleming Gast], you were our first friend that summer when we arrived, living around the corner.

Larry Sichter

My Father was in USAID. Lived in Rabat, first arriving in '59 staying first in Agdal and then down the hill from the Embassy, until we moved to Mali in '61. Attended Rabat American school when it first opened until I left (the first time) in late '61. We returned in '66, again living in Rabat, this time in Suissi. Lost touch with everyone after I returned Stateside, from the U, of Maryland - Munich and joined the Navy in '71. Just recently made contact with y'all - so many memories! Wow... We were attached to the US Embassy in Rabat, starting in 1960. I went to High School in Port Lyautey back in 1965, graduating in 1969. Plenty of great memories of the base and the great bunch of guys there. So much so, I enlisted in the Navy in 1970 and then got posted to Davisville, RI. Love history and am reading everything I can find about Port Lyautey from operation Goalpost to the NTC closing in the mid '70s. Can still remember the royal blue French fighter planes on the runway and adjoining tarmac on the east access road when I first arrived and then later the Moroccan F-5 jets steep inclined take-offs just outside the school building's windows. Of course we can't forget our own airport terminal with the MATS aircraft just outside the passenger fencing. I can still smell the overstuffed brown chairs & couches in the waiting area! (must have sat there too long...). Can still see the Moroccan personnel around their barracks, down the hill from our BEQs and the Hospital but this side of the Acey Duecy CPO Club. I remember the Moroccan officers shopping in our PX, sorta exercising their 'base privileges'. And, I remember the total lack of our flying Old Glory, looking instead at the green star on a red flag.

Andy (Andre) Milot

I went to TMW from '64 through '67; would have been Class of '69. It was a wonderful time of my life and a real growing experience!!

Renate (Phillips) Macomber-Colbath

I was Class of '69. We lived in Morocco from November 1961 to August of 1963. Lived off base in a villa about a block from the Mayor's house in Kenitra, and then moved on base. We lived in a townhouse about a half-block from TMW elementary school. I have three brothers: Tom, Lawrence and Terry. My father's squadron VR-24 was transferred to Rota, Spain; so that's where we went after living in Port Lyautey.

Sandy Lyle

My father (Bernie Price) was the High School Principal for three years (1959 -1962) at Port Lyautey. My mother (Wilhelmina Price) was an English teacher. My sisters, Cynthia and Bonnie also attended school at Port Lyautey. I was in Kenitra from 1960 - 1963. I would have been in the class of '69. We lived on base at Kenitra. I had cousins (the Byrd family) that lived at Sidi Yahia at the same time. My fourth-grade class picture of Mrs. Cook's class is on my Facebook page. I played with Harold Ashe near the Chief's Club. I think Harold's mom was from Hawaii. I'm still in love with Debra Sydlowski.

Leland Price

I was in Kenitra from 1960 to 1963. I was in the Class of 69. We lived in town for a bit and then on base at Kenitra. You would remember me as Peggie Schwartz. Our Fatima was one of my fave people/memories from Kenitra. She was a sweet dear person also, I miss her. I remember how the storks used to nest on top of our chimney, drove my dad nuts. LOL!

Chessie Roberts

Although Cece Canton was from an earlier class year, her memories of her Fatima fit in well right here:

When I went back to visit our Fatima from Port Lyautey, Zora, in 1976, in her same little place outside of the base, she served us mint tea and gazelle horns. She was blind and hugged and cried with me...I looked around that little house and saw on the wall a purse that I had given her when I was a teen. I almost lost it seeing that one. She raised my sister Jeanne, who was 6 months old when we got there. She was my confidant....what we could understand from each other..ha! She always hid things from dad for me and told him off in Arabic when he started yelling at us kids. They had some wars, and she got him to back off many times. I could catch a lot of the words...loved that part! My mighty diplomat father brought down by our Fatima!! He would never touch her in front of us.

Cece Canton

(Note: Below is a reprint originally published on Clifford Smith's website)

September, 1965. A young boy encounters a situation that is to bring many changes to him, physically and emotionally. After enjoying the experience of getting a passport and being inoculated for diseases that I didn't know still existed (or ever existed, in some cases), I entered a new world; a new world that was to bring me through the perils of puberty and culture clash.

After being met at the Kenitra Naval Air Station terminal by our "sponsor", we were taken to the hotel we were to call home for a month or so, in the heart of the Arabic city adjoining the base. We were instructed what not to eat or drink, where not to go, what not to do, and who to stay away from. An interesting introduction to our new home, Morocco. This was going to be the last time I saw our flag except in the classrooms, in official parades which had to be accompanied by the Moroccan flag, and at the Embassy in Rabat. While living in the hotel in town, I was able to familiarize myself with the 'lay of the land' and identify points of interest (from my perspective). Once in our place on base, freedoms were granted by my folks and I proceeded to make a few of those interesting places regular haunts.

Being right on the coast, the best beaches, I found, were right down the road between Kenitra and Rabat. Since motorbikes, bicycles and animals are primary modes of transportation, no licenses were required to operate them. Thus, my first legal motorized vehicle, a Peugeot motorbike. Can you say "Freedom!"? All that was required was to pay the annual road tax. This became an issue later.

The beach became home, but you can only be in the sun and surf just so long. There was school, the Teen Clubs . . . ahhhh, yes, the Teen Clubs. There were 3, one on each base. At Kenitra was the Air Base, at Bouknadel (Boo-k-na-del) was the Transmitter Site and Sidi Yahia (Cidy-i-e-ah) was the Receiver Site. These sites were for tropospheric scatter radio for those anthropologists out there. The term may be so old nobody knows what it means anymore. The Teen Clubs had pool tables, record players, ping-pong tables, and other attractive items for the kids between 13 and 19. On the weekends, we had dances. Until we got a band together, the record player was the source of our tunes. But that wasn't going to be left that way for long.

A few of the guys at Sidi Yahia and Kenitra got together and formed the "Sidi Limits". (Now you're getting closer to why I use the nickname City Slicker.) I was the bass player and drummer and I have a story about In-A-Gadda-Da-Vida, but I'll save that for another time (Yes, the long version.). We rotated which Teen Club we played at, so every month on the same weekend, we were playing at the same base. If my memory serves me right, the 1st weekend of the month was Kenitra, followed by Bouknadel then Sidi Yahia on the 3rd weekend. We had the last weekend off if there was one that month. It was a living blast. As they said back then, "It was far-out, man!" After a while back in the States, I picked up a Reader's Digest and saw a small article about the Sidi Limits. I was famous!

The motorbike opened other doors, too. With the freedom and the wheels, I was able to get around all sorts of places. One of these places were "The Cliffs". When they built the base, they used a section near the shore as fill dirt for the developed areas. This left the cliffs ranging from 20 to 40 feet tall. Indigenous to this area were hawks who took over the cliffs, Black Hawks and European, or Brown, Hawks. It was one of the latter that I obtained from a nest. I raised this hatchling to full growth. It was hilarious to see and hear when the little devil wanted someone to open the door to let him in. Screeching and pecking at the door. No matter where I went, he was with me. We had a special bond... a brotherhood.

I would leave on my motorbike and Screech (an appropriate name, don't you think?) would chase me and land on my shoulder. We would ride for miles and he would lean into the wind and stay right there. Occasionally he would take off and fly for a while but would land and continue the trip as a passenger. We were inseparable. Once, when we went to visit a Moroccan friend, Screech went with me. After we left, so did the Moroccan family, permanently. How was I to know it was considered bad luck if a hawk comes into a house. Nonetheless, we stayed together. On the last day I was in Morocco, I let Screech go. I had been weaning him from me slowly as I knew when we were leaving. We drove to Rabat to get our plane. I had a homemade ID tag on Screech, and from the airplane window, I saw him sitting on the nearby fence. (Get out those Kleenex now.)

My family had wheels, too. So did some of my father's co-workers. With those wheels we traveled even more. Almost every weekend we would take day trips to see things, from Volubilis the Roman ruins, to the Jacqueline Kennedy villa south of Marrakech. We traveled from Tangier & Te´touan in the north where Spanish is the secondary language, west to the Sahara, the mother of the Sirocs (the hottest, sandiest, wind storm that you could imagine), to the Casbah in Casablanca (of movie fame, if you are old enough to remember or watch the late show), and the Royal Palace in Rabat. Fantasia's were the most fun.

Fantasias were gatherings of people to attend the mosque of their ancestors. This could be termed a very large family reunion. The festival had various activities, and all participants were set up in tents. Tents to live in and tents that housed their entire business inventory. It was an instant city. There were belly-dancers, horse riding competitions, various games of soccer (football there), and other activities. It was non-stop, until sun-down, that is. The food was absolutely out of this world. There is no better eating anywhere in the world than at these fantasias, but you didn't want to ask what it was you were eating. There were fantasias taking place periodically everywhere. When one family's fantasia was over, the next week someone else's was beginning.

Visiting local residents was one of our favorite activities, as this was customary with our American friends as well. The Moroccans, however, took this as a particular honor and set up a banquet for us. A multi-course meal was served to us.

- Rosewater hand-bath
- Sweet biscuits
- Mint tea
- Cous Cous – a wheat-germ piled on a large dish with meat and vegetables placed on top — this was the vegetable dish
- More mint tea
- Tajine (Ta-gene) – Meat swimming in a broth containing almonds, boiled eggs, & raisins — this was the meat dish
- More mint tea
- Oranges marinated in cinnamon and sugar
- More mint tea
- Sugar Cookies
- More mint tea

All this food was served in a common dish that was also used in the cooking. Except for the Cous-Cous, all the food was eaten by hand, no utensils. Spoons were provided for the Cous-Cous because we were Americans. The Moroccans ate the Cous-Cous by hand, rolling a small amount into a ball and using the thumb to push it into the mouth. The Tajine was eaten with bread held between the fingers, pinching off pieces of the meat. The bread was also used to sop the broth and pick up the items in the broth. The meats used in the dishes could be anything living in the area. One host's dog was never seen after we visited them. Hmmmmm. Another time the host assured us that camel was a delicacy.

As visiting the locals was a favorite pastime, once we went to visit one friend. They had a nice 3-story villa. We went to the roof to look out across the city and I noticed there was a young girl looking out from a room on the roof. Being the introvert that I am (ha ha), I went over and began talking to her. I went into her room and we talked for a very long time, mixing English, Spanish, French, and Arabic (Berber) so we could communicate. After a time, some very concerned Moroccans entered and asked me to join them downstairs. I noticed the grandfather and the father in heated discussion, but I could not understand what they were saying, but they joined us for the continuance of the festivities. I was to learn later that Grandpa was insisting that I marry his granddaughter since I had spoiled her and that we were both of marrying age. (At age 13 for me and 12 for her – Marrying age?) I had committed the following taboos:

- I had seen a girl of marrying age without her veil;
- I had been with a single girl without a chaperon;
- I had physical contact with a single girl of marrying age;
- I had indicated my desire to have her as my wife (by not verbally declaring the opposite).

How was I to know that the girl had silently consented to be the wife of a rich American boy? It is a good thing the father convinced the grandfather that I was just a stupid American! Phew, got out of that one!

But trouble seemed to follow me. I was driving my motorbike around town one fine day. I was stopped by the Gendarmes (pr. – John-darms) who are the local constabulary (police, for short). They confiscated my motorbike because I had not paid the road taxes. Bummer. I had to walk most of the way back home. When I contacted my Dad at work, he asked one of his Moroccan co-workers what could be done about it. We were to find out in a short while after this incident that this friend was a high muckety-muck in the Moroccan government, answering directly to the King. Well, this friend took us down to "City Hall". When we arrived, there was a line of folks at least a ¼-of-a-mile long, all going to retrieve their bikes, motorbikes, donkey-carts, etc. There had to be almost 2,500 people in this line – I swear! Our friend, Mohammed Ben-Kaffa, took us to the front of the line, started informing the city officials just how fast he wanted my motorbike located and brought to us, and he wanted the required tax stamps to be in place for all required taxes. I've never seen so many people rush around like that. Within 10 minutes my motorbike was in my possession again, complete with tax stamps. I was I-M-P-R-E-S-S-E-D!!! It took me longer to wait for the darned bus than it took him to locate my motorbike amongst the thousands they had confiscated that week.

As I had mentioned, the Moroccan friend was a government official. After the incident we checked to see who he was and found out. Then it hit us, every time we went on a sight-seeing trip, no matter where we were, there was always someone there willing to guard our vehicle. We never lost not one single item out of or off our car. This was quite a feat as Americans were not always welcomed with open arms. But a volunteer guard was always there to assist. Shortly before our permanent departure, we found out that those guards were there at Mohammed Ben-Kaffa's orders. We always tipped them well as we thought this was a regular occurrence. When other Americans had their cars vandalized, stripped, or otherwise damaged, it became clear to us that we had a protector.

All this was well and good, and, for the most part, all went very smoothly for us and we really enjoyed the stay. You see, the bases that were there were considered Moroccan military training bases. All American military personnel were "instructors". That is why we were not allowed to fly "Old Glory" except indoors or special events. This arrangement came to be a critical issue. Do you remember the Israeli "6-Day War"? Well, it happened during our stay in Morocco. The bases were sealed and nobody (and I mean nobody) could enter or exit the bases. All American personnel and their families that were living in town were ordered to come to the base and they were housed in the school, the gym, in barracks, and anywhere else they could find room. Quadruple guards were placed on the perimeter fence and gates. There was an announcement that the King of Jordan, the King of Syria, and the King of Egypt had declared that all American bases in any Arabic country be bombed as we were allies of Israel. The King of Morocco stated publicly that there were no American military bases in his country, only Moroccan training facilities with American instructors. Boy was I glad someone had the foresight to make that kind of arrangement. I then became a true believer in diplomacy. After a couple weeks after the war was over, we were allowed to again return to the status-quo. The atmosphere was different for a little while and we were shunned by the Moroccans to a certain extent, but that eased and all was normal again.

It was more of the beach, the Teen Clubs, the *Sidi Limits*, Screech and so on. Life was good. And I was enjoying every minute of it. But, as with Adam and Eve, paradise was lost. We had to leave. The U.S. Government had other plans for my family. So back home to the good ole USA.

Did I tell you we didn't have TV at all in Morocco? After 2 years over there and no TV, it was another culture shock to return to Star

Trek, Space 1999, Lost in Space and other hi-tech shows. Yes, there had been a culture shock twice. But the hardest one to deal with was the one when we returned. I was no longer able to drive anything. I had a curfew. And I was not able to travel around the countryside alone. After all I was in the USA. But, to this day, I yearn for the time when I can return and look up my almost-bride-to-be.

Cliff Smith

The 1969 Yearbook

Administration: CAPT E. B. Abrams, USN (Base Commander); LT Daniel S. Robertson, USN (School's Officer); Mr. M. Prince (Supervisory Principal) and Mr. Ernest M. Morgan (Principal).

Faculty & Staff: Faculty: Mrs. Karen Bachmann; Mr. David Loren Bass; Mrs. Betty Lou Cummins; Miss Nancy J. Gatewood; Mr. Burton "Burt" I. Gloor; Miss Judy Maddox; Mr. Frederic Meyer; Mr. Keith Radi; Miss Carmencita Suero; Mrs. Frank Swindle; and Miss Janice Taylor. **Staff:** Mrs. Linda L. Gunberg.

The 20 graduating Seniors of 1969: Amine Hajji (President); Donald Eugene Long (Vice-President); Janice Kay Feaster (Secretary/Treasurer); Safwan Bengelloun; Jack Kenneth Carr; Evelyn Elaine Davis; Maxine F. Fetterly; Patrick Leo Garvey; Penny Lee Gillen; Judith Lee Glover; William Henning Jacobsen; Benjamin Clarence Kenyon; Barbara Kotakis; Carol Ann Lacy; Rita Dolores Landis; Andre "Andy" Victor Milot; Abdelkrim M'Rabet; Joseph Y. Ruff; Charles Irvin Whitbeck; and Raymond Alan Yates.

Class of 1970

1970 saw music continue to make significant impact with the largest ever rock festival held on the Isle of Wight with 600,000 people attending, including some of the biggest names in music including Jimi Hendrix and The Who. This is also the year the Concord makes its first supersonic flight. Another significant change was that the age of voting was lowered to 18 from 21 in the US. Thor Heyerdahl departed Morocco and crossed the Atlantic Ocean on the raft *Ra II*. He arrived in Barbados 57 days later, on July 12. Moroccan footballer Noureddine Naybet was born in Casablanca on February 10; Prince Moulay Rachid of Morocco was born June 20. King Hassan was being pressured to rid the bases of Americans as reflected in this declassified State Department Intelligence Note written by their Bureau of Intelligence and Research (RAFN-4) entitled "Morocco, Kenitra and the King" dated November 3, 1970:

"Since the evacuation of Wheelus airbase in June 1970, the sole American military facilities remaining in the Arab world are in Morocco: the US Navy Training Command at Kenitra and sensitive communications installations at nearby Bouknadel and Sidi Yahia. A king's word rather than any written treaty guarantees their existence. In 1963, when the US evacuated the military bases it had occupied in Morocco, King Hassan orally assured President Kennedy that these facilities could remain indefinitely; he repeated this oral assurance to President Johnson in 1967. Both sentimental and political reasons appear to lie behind the King's commitment. This, however, may increasingly be eroded by anti-US pressures and by his own excessive efforts to utilize the existence of the bases as a lever for obtaining greater US aid and support.

Royal Sentiment. King Hassan's personal feelings towards the US cannot be accurately measured. We do know, however, that they go back to a memorable boyhood experience: his presence at the 1943 meeting at Casablanca between his father, Mohammed V and President Roosevelt.

Since then, Hassan has placed considerable value on friendship with the US, probably reflecting a continuing sense of personal gratitude to the first major Western power that expressed favorable interest in Moroccan independence. In addition, the king probably retains favorable memories of his contacts with American personnel at Kenitra while he was Crown Prince in the late 1950's: he, his brother, and sisters got to know Americans there and learned to rely on US facilities for luxury goods and on base officials for various personal and political services.

A Convenient Option. Hassan has also developed important political reasons to cultivate the US. His "American option" has become a means to many ends. On different occasions he has been able to use the US as counterweight in various dealings: with his domestic opposition, hostile neighbors (notably Algeria), ex-colonial power France, and the USSR. His trip to Washington in 1963, for example, enabled him to draw an implied US stamp of approval for the controversial constitutional system he installed at that time. Similarly, he played up Moroccan-US ties during the four-year period, 1965-69, when the French withdrew their ambassador and suspended economic assistance.

From the outset Hassan apparently recognized that his US option, to be credible, required a continuing and visible US interest in close relations with Morocco. While Hassan probably appreciated the element of disinterest in US diplomatic friendship for Morocco--in contrast to the French whose designs he considered neo-colonialist--he also seemed to have realized it could well lead to declining US attentiveness. Hassan therefore looked to the US military for support and sought White House attention, skillfully trying to establish a personal relationship with each new president.

To place his US insurance policy on a more secure basis, he assured President Kennedy in 1963 that the Kenitra facilities could remain. Three years later, he attempted to carry his "special relationship" with the US a step further. Hassan's domestic problems in 1966 were formidable; drought had caused a severe shortfall in farm production and the political parties were chafing under a state of emergency rule imposed the previous year. Moreover, Morocco was at odds with its North African neighbors as well as Spain and France, and the king was under military pressure to counter the Algerian threat with an arms buildup. In a deftly orchestrated campaign (including a visit to Moscow and bilateral talks with the US), Hassan laid the groundwork for his proposition in January 1967, that Morocco and the US conclude a formal mutual security arrangement. His proposal met with rebuff by US officials, but Hassan nevertheless reassured President Johnson, during a visit to Washington in February 1967, that the US could continue using the Kenitra facilities.

Advantages to Hassan Outweigh Drawbacks. The arrangements on Kenitra have provided Hassan with considerable leverage to help ensure a continuing flow of US military aid and economic assistance. It has enabled him to prevent a gradual phase-down in US aid levels that had been planned as a consequence of the 1963 evacuation. Instead he was able to count on substantial US support in later years. Overall, through fiscal year 1969, Morocco has received, since 1953, about $66.2 million under the military assistance program and an additional $692.4 million in US economic aid ($56.2 and $292.5 million, respectively, since FY 1963).

Over the past seven years, Hassan has thus parlayed the US stake in Kenitra into concrete political and economic advantages for his regime. These benefits give Hassan, if anything, a greater stake than Washington in a continued US military presence. Moreover, he has thus far succeeded in neutralizing the political drawbacks in the arrangements. Foreign criticism from radical Arab quarters, notably Algeria during the June 1967 war, has not deterred him from maintaining this apparent anachronism in the Arab world--nor has it barred him from active participation in Arab councils and diplomatic campaigns. At home he has been able to sidestep the potentially embarrassing question of whether the US military facilities constitute an infringement of Moroccan sovereignty. By placing Moroccan flags over the three installations, Moroccan military insignia on the uniforms of US personnel, and a sizeable Moroccan military presence at the Kenitra base, Hassan has been able to marshal supporting evidence for his claim that the three bases are legally--and genuinely--Moroccan. (Moroccan military and civilian officials and, to a considerable extent, educated Moroccans in general, are aware of the continuing US military presence at these installations--although not the details of their activities). Indeed, at a press conference in July Hassan baldly asserted that even Soviet party leader Brezhnev had acknowledged the bases to be Moroccan. His credibility appears to remain intact even though the Moroccan opposition press, echoing news despatches on the Symington sub-committee hearings, has recently begun for the first time to question the US military presence. His defense of the status quo serves to tie his past verbal assurances even closer to his power and prestige.

Facilities May Be Caught Between Hassan's Enemies and His Own Expectations. Notwithstanding this royal support, the US military facilities in Morocco face an uncertain future and may be increasingly subject to royal pressure. The Moroccan monarch appears in a paradoxical situation. On the one hand, his present determination to preserve the US presence leaves him increasingly vulnerable to the tides of popular opinion. Another rapid rise in Middle East tensions could compromise the US facilities, and a renewed outbreak of Arab/Israeli hostilities almost certainly would do so. Furthermore, Hassan's uncompromising stance toward his domestic opposition is likely to drive the political opposition, desperately searching for ways to embarrass and harass the regime, to intensify its attacks on the US presence. Moreover, organized labor is likely to join the attack since the authorities on October 1 ordered the Moroccan workers (over 750) employed at US facilities on the three installations to disaffiliate from the country's largest trade union.

On the other hand, the growing number of dissatisfactions Morocco finds in its bilateral relations with the US, including the prospects of declining American economic and military assistance, will probably cause Hassan once again to attempt to use the bases as leverage against the US. That the regime has thus far permitted the opposition press to publish articles critical of Kenitra--while Morocco seizes newspaper issues and arrests journalists for articles on numerous other subjects--suggests that Hassan may already have opened such a campaign. If the American response is unsatisfactory to Hassan, he may well put additional pressure on the US by increasing Moroccan controls over the bases."

What the Intel Note failed to mention was the possibility of an attempt on the King's life. In 1971 and 1972 KAHS students and their families experienced two failed coup d'états against the King. The impacts of those attempts are reflected in the 1972 Chapter under the heading "Who Remembers the Attempted Assassinations of King Hassan II in 1971 and 1972?"

I Remember:

My twin, Andrea Stampley, and I attended 10th and 11th grade at KAHS (1967-69). We lived in Rabat. I met my future husband, Ned Garvey, at a party at Gary Snell's house the summer of 1968. I was sitting on a sofa beside Andre Milot when Ned and his brother, Pat, walked in. The buzz was that two cute guys from the States had arrived! My sister and I left Morocco for Mississippi, where we spent our senior year in the Delta while our father went to Vietnam. Wow, coming back to the States and our first civilian existence was the culture shock! We watched Neil Armstrong's walk on the moon on our grandmother's TV our first day back.

Angela Garvey, Class of 1970

My family arrived in Morocco from Fort Monroe, Virginia, in July 1967. We lived in Rabat, about a block from the U.S. Embassy in what we believe was the only "pink-washed" house in town! We took the bus to KAHS, an hour each way, so the bus rides provided times to chat and get to know the rest of the Rabat group. We left in July 1969, just before our senior year, so I would have been Class of 1970. My husband, Dave Carr, arrived in January 1968, from Atsugi, Japan, and lived in Sidi Yahia. His family (including brother Jack, who graduated in 1969) also departed in the summer of 1969, returning to the state of Washington. Dave and I were out of touch for 36 years, reconnected in 2004, and married in May of 2006.

Andrea Stampley

I arrived in Morocco in the summer of 1967 and attended 10th & 11th grades; left in August 1969 when my Dad retired, so I would have been class of '70. We lived first on a street with 10 houses, then up on Captain's Hill behind the amphitheater and chapel. Had a hard time calling Mr. Bass 'David'... old habits die hard!!! Graduated high school in AZ and Arizona State University in '74 then one year in Colorado, and southern California ever since. I located Judy Maddox on Facebook, she taught Spanish and music... her married name is Spivey...

Susan Fairchild Barry

I was Class of '70. I was born and raised in Rabat (Quartier L'Aoufir or Aviation). Two years after my family had moved to Salé, I got a scholarship to attend KAHS as a junior in !969. It was so interesting to see that 25% of alumni were international. 1969 & 1970 were two great years of challenge for me.

Brahim Benhim

We lived in Rabat from 68-70, graduated in 70.

Ned Garvey

An article entitled "*Navy's Low Profile in Morocco*" and written by Michael Miner appeared in the April 15 1970 edition of the St. Louis Post-Dispatch:

(Kenitra, Morocco). "You don't normally ask a Marine guard where he buys his suits. And you do not normally consider the United States Navy a bastion of reticence. Ask an ordinary Public Information Office what its command mission is and the answer is as snappy as a salute: We Sail to Serve! We Fuel the Fleet!

But the U.S. Navy Training Command here plays it cool, very low profile. "It's so low it's not apparent," Cmdr. Myles Vayo, head of the Public Information Office, said. "We're the only public relations office in the Navy that doesn't publish any information about itself."

The Navy's problem is a simple one. It wants to be liked. In Morocco the need is political. As Arab friends go, Morocco is one.

So the Navy speaks softly and carries basketballs instead of big sticks. The American flag does not fly at Kenitra or at the two small communications stations at nearby Sidi Yahia and Sidi Bouknadel.

The 700 Navy men stationed here are forbidden to wear uniforms off the bases. Even when Capt. E. M. Cadenas wants to drive over to either Sidi he first has to change into civvies.

There are many young Americans in Morocco. However, the sailors are easy to spot because they're wearing bell-bottoms. Also, their hair is cut short and their shirts are pressed. Their conversation is Beckettesque.

"Low Profile..." explained Mike Wade, a communications technician, "...it's the same as though we're not here. We're here. You'll never see a fight. Well, yeah, you will. You won't see it often. Everybody fights on base."

Someone said King Hassan II was not supposed to know the Americans were here. "Sure the King knows," Wade said. But the King doesn't make speeches about it. "The people here in Kenitra are very pro-American," Wade said. "And when we go up to Tangiers we're just tourists."

"We had to fly here in civilian clothes. It's against Moroccan rules to travel commercial transport in uniform. There are some strange laws. I saw in Marrakech, it's illegal to carry an ice cream cone on Sunday afternoon."

The base looks like an American town, with stores and an American Express office for a bank. It was a Naval Air Station, now it is officially a Moroccan Air Force base, with the U.S. Navy present only to provide instruction on the Northrup F-5 jet plane.

At the main gate were several uniformed Moroccans and Marine Sgt. Michael Giles, who sat in his own small guardhouse smoking a pipe and reading a book.

Giles was on duty, and he felt constrained from saying anything of interest, but his appearance deserves mention. He was wearing a cuffless black, pin-striped suit; a wide-collar deep-orange shirt with blue stripes; a matching tie; rectangular silver cufflinks, and dark brown boots.

"Best-dressed Marine on base," said Roland Gotreux, a machinist's mate, who had driven up in a jeep to do something about this journalist in an old Army jacket with missing buttons.

The most radical departure from Navy practice has been turning the Shore Patrol into plains-clothes cops. In Kenitra, the rumbling old bos'n—stomach sloshing inside his wide, white belt, billyclub bouncing off his hip—wears white-on-white shirts and over-the-calf socks. He sits at a quiet table in the Fleet Club and thinks about the Old Navy.

Kenitrans are not inclined to accept the official word that the Americans in their midsts are here only as advisers. Local thinking falls into three schools: that the Americans have a naval air base in the city and Morocco has nothing; that American and Moroccan bases exist side by side; or that an American base has been camouflaged as a Moroccan base.

Capt. Robert E. Hawthorne, military attaché in Rabat, said there is no reason to suspect duplicity.

"The U.S. has no say about what goes on in Kenitra," Hawthorne said. "The U.S. gave up the base in 1963 in anticipation of a possible request by Morocco to get out. They were grateful and we've maintained good relationships."

Hawthorne said that King Hassan II has things under control and "the people are satisfied and hopeful." He said, "There are rumors all over Morocco" but they should be "soft-pedaled."

What sort of rumors are these?

An entrepreneur in Tangiers said he was paying a 1-franc tax imposed by the "Moroccan Liberation Movement" on each purchase of pot.

Driving north from Kenitra with a Moroccan official, I asked: "Is the King popular?"

"The King is unpopular."

"Why?"

"Capitalist." We passed a huddle of shanties, some with roofs. "The poverty." A group of little children ran into the road and scattered like geese before the automobile. "The children are not in schools" "Why?" "No schools."

U.S. sailors at Kenitra and Sidi Yahia field basketball teams which go on goodwill trips throughout Morocco. The games are demanding. "The way they play it here, it's more like soccer than basketball," one Sidi player said, "I want to lose my temper, and I look at all the Moroccans sitting out there and I hold my temper. I say to myself, wait till we get them on our court."

Sidi recently made a trip to Oujda, on the Algerian frontier. By American standards it was a disaster, yet a good weekend's work under the diplomatic point system. Sidi lost both games and a warmup jacket."

Four from the Class of 1970, from left to right, April McSwain Allen, Toni D'Agostino, Juanita Reyes Cornette and Kathy Gleason. Photo courtesy Juanita Cornette, taken at the TMW-KAHS 1992 Reunion in Greensboro, NC.

What Was Your Favorite Form of Transportation?

My form of transportation - my freedom - was my little 49.9cc Flandria. If it was under 50cc you didn't need a license plate. Paul Collins (Class of '72) could bore out the cylinder and push it to probably 55cc! It was the only vehicle I owned besides lawn mowers where you had to add oil into the gas tank and hope you got the mixture right! Went everywhere with that machine - Mehdia Beach, Rabat once, all over Kenitra and nearly every road on base...

Doug Campbell

I had a 1967 Honda C-110 in Sidi 75-78.

Clifford Smith

I remember that bike! I walked a lot in Morocco, and stateside. The base bus took me off base and to the other bases. The local bus took me to Rabat. I rode with other people too, of course. Gotta tell you, there was just no other experience like riding a hot bus with chickens on it!!! :)) And Oh My Gosh, how could I forget all those crazy Fiat taxis!!!!

Kathy Myers Strange

I remember your bike. My parents have pics of my moped, but they are in a storage room. I remember seeing your bike at the usual hot spots; pool, theater, Oasis, HS, etc. I tried every trick to eke out HP, but a 50cc can only do so much especially with a centrifugal clutch. I was envious of you guys with gears.

David Neumann

I went everywhere in one of these.

Bonnie Arey Fowler

When I graduated from HS I was able to upgrade to a Honda 350CL Scrambler for my college transportation. We had moved to Arizona, so most of the time it was great except for those 30-degree winter mornings. I would have been the envy of HS if I had it in Morocco.

David Neumann

Scott Devers, Nathan Adkinson and I had Itoms....purchased in Naples....good looking but not very fast.

Patrick Foley

Flandrias were sold in the Exchange, but never remember the Itoms but they pretty good-looking bikes (check out pic). They too were only 50cc, so you can't expect much more than 5HP without a lot of modifications.

David Neumann

I never did get motorcycles out of my system, so I currently ride this 1997 Honda Valkyrie 1500cc with about 100HP. No problems on hills now.

David Neumann

I am still riding :)

Clifford Smith

Peugeot bike...boy's version. The best-balanced bike I have ever had! I had the girl's version, but the boy's was better, of course...the extra bar. There was also a green Peugeot motor bike for my brothers.

Cece Canton

Peugeot bicycles were great. Cece, John and I argued all the time over who had the best bike. I got the motorbike very late in my stay in Maroc...sold it in Seattle in 1966.

Patrick Foley

I found this pic of a 1974 Peugeot moped. Since they look a lot like a Flandria moped, I'm not sure if this is what I rode around on. Whatever it was, it sure beat walking.

David Neumann

We had both...2 bikes and a motorbike. It looked at lot like that one, David, but in the early 60's. Pat, my bike was the best...ha! What fun that place was!

Cece Canton

Larry Yeo drove a 150cc Lambretta in an ugly green color like shown. I think his was a 1968 SX model. Where would we be without our transportation?!

Doug Campbell

My form of transportation was walking, unless some nice soul gave me a ride! :) I'd forgotten what a yucky lime green color Larry's bike was.

Kathy Myers Strange

The color of Larry's Lambretta reminded me of getting hit by the flocks of yellow butterflies along with an assortment of other bugs including ones with stingers or pointy legs. I was in the Exchange one day when Gary Smith came in with a swollen eye; he explained a bee had gotten under his goggles. My windshield comes off easily on my Honda Valkyrie, but I leave it on during the summer unless I've got an urge to get clobbered.

David Neumann

Dean Willis on his Flandria.

I had a Flandria while attending KAHS.

Mark Roberts

I had two Flandrias when I was there. Great memories!

Patrick Senf

Had a Harley 125. Ride a 2013 Wide Glide now.

Tony Collins

We had a group that would rent mopeds and go all over. With Mom I did the souk, the eye doctor and salon. With Zorra our Fatima we went to movies, her home and the non-tourist places. Dad drove us all over on vacations.

Gloria Kemery

Wow! I found a picture of a Honda SS50e like I had in Rabat!

Mike McSwain

The 1970 Yearbook

Administration: CAPT Ernest M. Cadenas (Commanding Officer, USNTC); LT Daniel S. Robertson (Schools Officer); Ernest M. Morgan (Principal).

Faculty & Staff: Faculty: David L. Bass; Sondra Einfeldt; Carolyn K. Duckworth; Judith L. Freeman; Martha M. Howard; Linda L. Gunberg; Burton I. Gloor; Nancy J. Gatewood; Rachel I. Jacoby; Courtlandt C. Kauffman; Michael T. Meats; Mary-Jo Morris; Robert E. Thompson; Arthur Stoeberl; Mary L. Thompson; Brenda K. Travis. **Staff:** Linda Rollins; Steve Shirar.

The 27 graduating Seniors of 1970: Thomas J. Jimmerson (President); Gary E. Snell (Vice-President); Diane Marie Ermogeni (Secretary); Sharam Kamali-Nafar (Treasurer); Theron James Abbott; Najet Alami; Idris Assed; Khalid Benchekroun; Brahim Benhim; Paula Grace Chestnut; Basim Clor; Toni Ann D'Agostino; Burley P. Fuselier, Jr.; Edward J. Garvey; Ruth Ann Gillen; Kathy

Ann Gleason; Lawrence Harrison Hope; April L. McSwain; Marilyn Jean Moore; Russell Patrick Neunsinger; Bruce Newman; Juanita Reyes; Kyle M. Ruch; Cynthia Jacquelyn Ryan; Abdelsam Tazi; James H. Weltch; and James V. Wright.

CLASS OF 1971

1971 saw what well could mark the start of the digital age when the microprocessor was invented. We also saw the use of more and more of the transistor technology in use in things like hand-held calculators which although are still very expensive over time will drop in price and increase in function. It is also the first year North Sea Oil production begins in Norway. One other major change is the change to Decimalization in the UK and Ireland on February 15th. The birth of Greenpeace signaled a need to question how we manage the resources entrusted to us and a means of organized questioning of governments around the world. On July 10, an assassination attempt on King Hassan II of Morocco failed; 101 were killed including Moroccan general Mohamed Madbouh. The Moroccan footballer Mustapha Hadji was born on November 16.

I Remember:

I arrived in late June 1969 and left April 1970. I would have been Class of 1971. We lived in Kenitra near the train station.

Debra Kay

The two years (1965-1967) we spent living on the base at Kenitra bring back so many memories... I would have been Class of 1971. I remember learning to play pool at the Teen Club. The outdoor movie theater. Sights and smells of the souk in Tangier. Mint tea in the Casbah in Rabat overlooking the harbor of Sale. The snow-capped Atlas Mountains towering over the palm trees and pink walls of Marrakech. Riding the weekend bus to Bouknadel Beach and drinking rum and coke on the hotel terrace (I was 13!). Learning to ski at Oukaimeden. Dancing to the Sidi

Limits. Riding motorbikes to Mehdia Beach and exploring the old fort there. The "Kenitra Bullet"... Each year at Christmas the Carneys at the Teen Club would organize a toy drive for Moroccan orphans. We would ride to Ifrane on a Navy bus where a British ex-pat couple ran an orphanage for about 20 kids. It was in an old stone farmhouse surrounded by a few acres of vegetable gardens and a pen for wild boars (I think we had one for dinner). The kids were so excited to receive the presents and show us around the farm. After spending the day there, exhausted, we slept on the bus ride back.

I have to tell you some stories, proving that military kids grow up so fast as they move around the world and soak up different cultures! I was 12 years old when we arrived at the base in Kenitra in 1965. Our house was 1/2-block from the PX and the park where the "Kenitra Bullet" (a 1940's vintage bus) made hourly runs into town. We often went to ogle new Peugeot and Flandria motorbikes and, of course, buy fireworks. The bus stop in town was in front of an enlisted bar where we learned that the bartenders were not opposed to serving beer to a 12-year-old. They also had a cigarette machine where you could get a four pack for 1 Dirham. On summer weekends we often took the special services bus to Bouknadel Beach. After exploring the rocks and playing in the surf we would have a rum and coke on the hotel patio before the bus picked us up.

During this time, I peddled my bike all over the base delivering the *Stars and Stripes*. Every two weeks, on payday, I collected for the paper. A few customers were sailors in the barracks and always a challenge to find on payday. One customer, Carpicki, a wise guy from New Jersey, could always be found at the craps game held in the pool room between the barracks. I knew nothing of the game but was often persuaded to bet my pay on Carpicki's roll of the dice. Here I am at 12 years old playing craps with sailors. Vice came early for this young man.

In the spring of 1967, my Mother signed my sister and I up to go on a trip to Marrakesh to attend a Berber music and dancing show held in a Roman amphitheater. The special services bus was half-filled with families and the other half with sailors and marines. The hotel in Marrakesh was woefully unprepared for our arrival and didn't have enough rooms. My Mom, sister and I along with another mother/daughter combo were assigned to a single room with 2 beds and a couch. This was a serious affront to my 13-year-old masculinity and I protested most vociferously to my mom who relented and went back to the concierge with me. 'Why certainly" the desk clerk assured us "there is plenty of room in the dormitory." My masculinity restored, we went to the show which was fantastic and returned to the hotel where I moved my belongings to the dormitory. It was a long room with three single beds and 20 sailors and marines. I was allocated 1/3 of a single bed with 2 sailors. Later that night the floor would be covered in drunken bodies and one guy slept in the bathtub.

The hotel was shaped like a square doughnut with a pool and open bar in the middle. At night, gates secured the first-floor access to the bar but the designers never considered the ingenuity of 20 thirsty sailors and marines. When I got to the room they had stripped the sheets off the 3 beds and were busily knotting them together to make 2 ropes to reach 3 floors down to the pool area. Armed with pillowcases, they emptied the bar of any and all alcoholic beverages, then climbed back up to the room. Debauchery ensued. A few of us were on the balcony and were hailed by an elderly German maintenance worker kittycorner from our room. With little prompting 3 of us climbed over the balconies to play cards and share our ill-gotten booze. When we got back to the room (it must have been after 2 AM) it was deserted! We found a disoriented sailor in the hall who informed us that two local prostitutes were open for business in the Navy bus. The two sailors I was with rushed out and found the bus parked on a side street with a long line of sailors and marines outside the front door. Several sailors I knew offered me cuts in line. Hey, I was only 13! My Dad would kill me! I barely remembered climbing into my 1/3 of the bed.

A few days later my father questioned me about the incident, knowing I was involved but not accusing me. I denied everything. The Navy made good on all the damages to the hotel!

Dean Willis

We lived in a villa in Kenitra during November '67, then on base (Kenitra) from December '67 to May '70. I would have been Class of 1971.

Ken Schubert

I arrived in Morocco when I was 14, at the beginning of the summer in 1968. During the Vietnam War. I remember staying in Kenitra in a hotel until we could move onto the base. I ate Grape-Nuts cereal three times a day because I hated the hotel food. I had my first scooter ride that summer. A Moroccan man told me to stop running around barefooted. When school started, I loved the school lunch truck because I could buy BBQ potato chips and Dr. Pepper every day for the entire 3 years I was there. BJ Gleason and I hitch-hiked to the beach almost every day in the summer. We bought donuts from a vendor roaming through the sand. His feet were like bark. We never used sunscreen. We met Conrad Hilton at the beach. Our school counselor took us for a ride in his Mercedes. BJ and I bought clothes from the market in Rabat and sold them to a store in the US. I had a crush on the base DJ. Our song was Stairway to Heaven. The summer between my Junior and Senior year I was allowed to retake Algebra because we had an amazing school secretary who felt sorry for me. Mark Ellinger was my boyfriend and took me to our Senior prom. Because of Mark, I learned that boys could be kind, funny and total gentlemen. French and yearbook were my other favorites because I loved the teachers and they made me feel there was more to school that might be useful later. Chorus was great too. My Dad was the base hospital administrator and also a Church of Christ preacher. I never went to a dance until Prom. In spite of all my non-academic interests, I graduated 4 out of 12—a stat that I used to get admitted to college. I was the first and only college graduate in the entire Dixon family for many years. I credit the teachers and staff at our school for ALL of it. And having a best friend who was smart and kept me accountable. And there were angels too.

Nola Dixon Fulkerson

I went to grade school there '61 - '64 and back again to attend KAHS, graduating in 1971. My baby sister was born there in October 1970. I enlisted in the Navy there in 1971 and retired as an AOC. Great times there at MAMAS and some of the other bars. Cheese, olives and Heineken, great combo.

Joe Yeo

Memories of the 1971 Junior-Senior Prom. As was tradition, the Junior Class spent the year raising money through candy bar sales, booths at base fairs, car washes, etc., to pay for the Prom, knowing that the following year the Junior Class would be doing to the same for them! Proms were usually held in Rabat with many of us heading to La Cage afterwards to dance the night away.

From left to right – five from the Class of 1971 at the Prom – Jack Desrocher, Bill Bradley, Mark Ellinger, Farley Snell and Greg Davis.

Mark Ellinger with his date Nola Dixon (who was also the 1971 Prom Queen) holding a bouquet of roses at the Prom.

I remember looking back on those days of hitchhiking there and how stupidly trusting I was and how different life is these days. And the market in Kenitra had the best oranges ever, and there was a little cafe with the best pommes frites ever, and mint tea I make can never hold a candle to the Moroccan mint tea. The croissants at the Hotel Mamora, the beignets from the camel man at Mehdia, how spoiled we were to have a Fatima, a gardener, sometimes a driver, and the free outdoor movies in the summer. I often slept outside on a Moroccan sheepskin rug, unbelieving how bright and plentiful were the stars, and how crisp the fall nights were. There are no bad memories. I remember it as truly magical in every way. Russell Young and and Chris Allam - they could have their own comedy show! Farley Snell running for class president, national honor society induction, the cute little motorized bikes ("scooters") and using one to help Jack Desrocher deliver newspapers while he was on vacation somewhere. And a sweet couple, Claudia from Brazil and Doug from the US...and Soon Mi Shin from Korea, along with our wonderful classmates from the Mid East...wonderful dear people, all. And my dear friend Nola, talented and beautiful with a heart of pure gold. I was, and am, so lucky, so blessed!

Barbara "BJ" Gleason Ford

The 1971 Prom – surrounded by students and teachers, Doug Smith (Class of 1972, looking skyward) is dancing with Class of 1972 Stephanie Staupe.

Who Remembers the Attempted Assassinations of King Hassan II in 1971 and 1972?

The 1971 Moroccan coup attempt was an unsuccessful attempt by rebel military leaders to assassinate King Hassan II of Morocco on 10 July 1971, the day of his forty-second birthday. Lieutenant-colonel M'hamed Ababou, under the orders of General Mohamed Medbouh, were the two main instigators of the attack on Hassan II's summer palace in Skhirat on the Atlantic coast, about 12 miles south of Rabat. Many invited guests were Americans who were playing golf on the King's golf course when paratroopers dropped from the sky, firing their weapons. No immediate action was taken, thinking it was part of the King's birthday celebration – until the paratroopers opened fire on the crowd. The main motive for the attempted coup was the unveiling of several occurrences of corruption inside the Moroccan government and royal family. The 1972 Moroccan coup attempt was another unsuccessful attempt to assassinate King Hassan II on 16 August 1972. The attempted coup d'état occurred in Morocco when a rebel faction within the Moroccan military attempted to shoot down an aircraft carrying the Moroccan king, Hassan II. The attempt was orchestrated by General Mohamed Oufkir, a close advisor to King Hassan. He was assisted by Mohamed Amekrane, commander of the Moroccan air force base at Kenitra. On August 16, four Northrop F-5 jets, acting on Oufkir's orders, intercepted Hassan's Boeing 727 as it returned from France. Reportedly, King Hassan grabbed the radio and told the rebel pilots, "Stop firing! The tyrant is dead!" Fooled, the rebel pilots broke off their attack and the King landed safely at Rabat airport. Our Kenitra Air Base, where most of the rebellious Air Force officers were based, was surrounded and hundreds arrested. We were told to stay indoors and close the curtains. Oufkir was found dead of multiple gunshot wounds later on 16 August, ostensibly from suicide. Many of his relatives were imprisoned, not being released until 1991, speculated to be because of international criticism for possible human rights abuses. General Amekrane fled to Gibraltar after the coup's failure; he failed to receive asylum and was extradited back to Morocco where he was executed by firing squad.

The U.S. Ambassador at the time was Stuart W. Rockwell, father of KAHS student Steve Rockwell. Mr. Rockwell attended that birthday party for King Hassan II. "Rockwell was strolling toward Hassan," *Time* magazine reported, "when he saw a guest in front of him topple to the floor, blood gushing from his leg." The king and his 500 guests faced gunfire and grenade explosions. According to *Time*, 92 people died in the attack, which lasted more than two hours — including the Belgian ambassador, Marcel Dupret — before the coup was put down by loyalist troops. Mr. Rockwell spent two hours lying in the dirt at gunpoint that day but suffered only a sprained thumb. He continued serving as ambassador until 1973 and retired in 1979 as the State Department's deputy chief of protocol. Ambassador Rockwell died March 12, 2011, at the age of 94.

In his own words, as recorded by the Association for Diplomatic Studies & Training: "This was the King's annual celebration of his birthday, which took place at his summer palace south of Rabat, between Rabat and Casablanca, at Skhirat. It usually involved all the notables of the realm and all the chiefs of foreign diplomatic missions. It was a stag party, and everybody was very informally dressed in sports clothes, and there were opportunities for golf and tennis and swimming and clay pigeon shooting, but mainly for a huge banquet at mid-day in this summer palace. It was a very sportive affair, supposed to be, until just as we were about to go in to sit down to lunch, we heard these sort of popping sounds, and somebody said, "Oh, the King has arranged fireworks for us this year." And until people started to fall with blood pouring out of them, we realized that the palace was being attacked, and the King's entourage, especially the military members, rushed out to defend it and were cut down. The rest of us were trapped inside or out on the golf course or wherever we might be. We were lying on our faces outside the palace until the King was uncovered by the cadets who were left in charge, and as soon as the [cadets determined that the king was not being attacked by nefarious forces but, actually, by the cadets themselves], they laid down their arms and everything returned to normal. It was very strange. I mean, there we were [with our faces in the dirt] with all our limousines parked down in the parking lot. Although the Belgian ambassador had been shot dead and the Syrian was wounded, we all went back to Rabat, and the countryside seemed perfectly normal. People were selling fish by the roadside, there were swimmers at the beaches. It was hard to believe that this bloody event, which must have cost the lives of about 130 people, had occurred only two hours or so ago."

U.S. Ambassador to Morocco Stuart W. Rockwell

My Dad worked with USAID improving wheat conditions in many of the Moroccan cities. We visited the Sahara, Fez, Marrakech among others. We stayed at Holiday Inns and Ramada's which now seem like a well-deserved vacation! It was on one of those trips that the coup was taking place, unknown to us. There were no cell phones then, and it wasn't until after we got our mail at the local annex in Rabat that we noticed what seemed odd ... downtown was practically deserted. When we got home we realized what was happening. We got a call from the Embassy advising us to stay indoors. We lived in Sousi (sp) which had a golf course; it was one of the ones the King golfed at. It would not be until later that I realized the extreme danger we were exposed to. Yet we were blessed to have gotten home.

Carmen Hedges (Carmen Acosta)

I remember, my dad had duty that day and he ended up being the senior officer on base, everyone above him was golfing with the king. He just followed protocol and it worked out, everyone came back safe.

Charlene Golden Coke

I remember. I was looking forward to going to the outdoor theater that night and of course it was closed. Teenagers and their priorities!

Gloria Ford Hammons

I remember the one in '72. I was in the Tour Hassan Hotel, and heard the jets' machine gun fire.

Mike Flanagan

I remember closing all the drapes and shutting off all the lights in '72.

Steve Staupe

I remember them both! We were living close to the train station in '71, which became very active. We had to move on base at Sidi soon after.

Kathy Myers Strange

I remember. Dad was Officer-of-the-Day. We did not see him for days.

> *Carla Golden Callaghan*

Yes.... it was scary... didn't see dad for days.

> *Stacey Moen*

We arrived in Morocco on the very day and moment of the second coup attempt. We spent 3 hours on the Rabat airport runway in an Air France plane with no AC while they sorted things out. Welcome to Morocco.

> *Jerry Counts*

I believe my dad got there right after it happened.

> *James Carter*

I remember. We were in Rabat - saw the soldiers marching prisoners in front of our hotel. We had just arrived a week or so before - didn't understand French or Arabic. Complete chaos - we were at the beach when it started; had to hide in the dark. Machine gun fire all night and our hotel was hit. Soldiers came to every room to see if we were hiding dissidents. Our sponsors got us out the next day. Scary intro to Morocco. We were there for 3 attempts during the time we lived there.

> *Sheila Bright Roberts*

I was at the Hotel Mamora in Kenitra - we were still waiting to get base housing at NTC. Military families at the hotel were told not to venture outside until the coup was over. Many of our dads were on standby at or close to the base including mine.

> *Robert Oberkehr*

I remember. My dad was invited to the king's golf birthday celebration and was captured with other officers from the base.

> *Nancy Lukas-Slaoui*

First one occurred 2 weeks after we arrived. Sat in the Embassy hotel with a "go" bag ready to evacuate. Two more after that. You are so right about the scary intro to Maroc! But, our family loved all four precious years we had there. Best years of our lives as a family I think.

JeanMarie Sample

It is permanently etched in my memory! I think it was the first time I was truly scared for my safety but when I got home, my parents were at the club and didn't seemed concerned at all...could have been the vodka talking.

Laura Koepke

I can remember standing on our roof watching the jets attacking the palace on one of the several attempts. Dad said they were celebrating the King's birthday.

Tony Collins

No but was there when they fought for their independence from France. We had friends in the government, so had a machine guard at our house 24 hours a day. It sort of intimidated the boys. LOL. We lived at the beach and had to go through a barricade with armed soldiers to get to town and had to bribe them both ways.

Sharon Grandy Vinson

I was in Paris, traveling with a friend, and read about it in the paper. I went to the US Embassy to ask if my family was ok...turned out they were, but like others have posted, my dad was taken prisoner and at least one in his group was shot...and I remember my mother telling me after the fact that our Moroccan neighbor was arrested for a role he played in it.

Barbara Ford

Nancy's Dad was talking about it a couple of weeks ago. I believe he was playing golf. Also, they took his clothes.

Cheryl Woodward

Yes, that's right. We kids were listening to Grand Funk Railroad in the sun room, and my dad came home beat up and wearing his underpants and someone's torn t-shirt. We were shocked. My mom came out of the back bedroom, took one look at my dad and said, "John, what kind of birthday party was this, anyway?" "Damn it, Winnie," he said, "there's been a coup d'état!"

Well, that was the end of the hanging out/listening to music party. Everyone went home and soon after that we had to get our suitcases ready for a possible evacuation.

Nancy Lukas-Slaoui

I was there in '59 and '60, lived in Kenitra, and felt completely safe. Never had a clue there would be trouble like this.

Barbara Gentry

It was still very safe. The Moroccans watched out for the Americans!

Kathy Myers Strange

Should have been in Rabat where the shit was happening. My parents had gone to Rota and I was alone with the dog when Armed Forces put a chalk letter "A" on the outside gate post. I dug in and hunkered down in the woodshed for a day and a half...me and the dog. Ya, I remember.

Brian Piantadosi

My family was there for both coupes, but I just remember hunkering down in the house until they were over. My Dad was the USAF liaison officer, so he was gone for several days during each one but to this day he's never told us much about what he did during those times. He knew all the pilots in the 2nd coup, so he was sad they all were executed publicly but since they didn't take out the king that was the consequences. It's interesting to hear you guy's stories and some of your parents had a rough time. We were only there in Kenitra for 2 years and it was good times for the most part, so I hated to leave. My dad was not down at the flight line at the time of the coup and he only helped maintain the F-5s, so he couldn't be tied to it but I believe the USAF wanted my dad out of there for our safety. You couldn't ever claim Morocco wasn't exciting.

David Neumann

After the second coup I worked at the NTC airstrip. KAHS had a vocational program. Instead of a class or two, you could work somewhere on the base for a couple hours on school days. I started in the motor pool but the local employees thought it was funny giving me all the dirty, hard work. I got word that I could work with the "Crash Crew" at the airport instead. We played pool when not practicing putting out enflamed planes. We had to set up on the runway every time a plane landed or took off. Very cool experience as a 16-year-old. I never gave it a thought that it might not be a good place to be if the stuff hit the fan again. Anyone ever work there or remember the "Crash Crew" truck parked on the runway when planes landed or took off?

Jerry Counts

There were a few in the 60's. One where all the generals were executed...friends of my Dad.

Cece Canton

I remember a couple of times we were supposed to be confined to the base 60-63.

Gloria Kemery

I was out shopping with a classmate when the 1972 coup happened. When I got back to our home in Rabat, I learned that the jets had strafed the king's palace right over our house! We lived only about a mile away from the palace. My parents, brother, and our three house staff fled down to the coal cellar and stayed there until it was over. All I heard later was that there had been an attempted coup d'état on the king's life. At that time, I didn't understand the repercussions for the people who had been involved in planning and carrying out the attempt; I think my parents shielded me and my brother from that information. Decades later, I read a very raw and powerful memoir by Malika Oufkir, the daughter of General Mohamed Oufkir, one of the main players in the coup. The general was executed and Malika and her family spent the next 20 years in a Moroccan jail out in the desert. If you get a chance, read it. The title is, "Stolen Lives: Twenty Years in a Desert Jail." It really made me realize the lucky and privileged lives most of us led during our years in Morocco.

Sandy (White) Bartell

Because my father also worked at the golf course, his Moroccan co-worker and friend could translate, which was an advantage. He also was wearing a yellow sweater which later proved to be an advantage as the officers/leaders of the coup attempt also wore yellow. As the cadets and soldiers came running down the hill towards the golfers they were yelling and being directed by the officers. His co-worker was translating that it didn't sound good! They dove into the nearest sand trap and started digging as bullets "chinged" all around them. Dad said, "It was like a John Wayne movie and we couldn't dig fast enough! Sand was flying as the bullets hit and we couldn't dig fast enough! We realized they were getting closer and our safety was jeopardized, so we got up and ran. We found some bushes and dodged under." They witnessed the Americans being stripped down to their underwear and corralled. They also witnessed men being lined up on the edge of a sand trap and an officer behind with a pistol, "BLAP!", Dad said, and each time he heard that a body fell down into the sand. The king had escaped. I don't know if the officer shooting was one of the King's men shooting cadets and coup officers or what. I assume it was. I was on a bus with the girl's softball team going to play at Sidi Yahia. As we were playing, some active duty guys who worked for my dad came over to relay the scant news and details of what had occurred. They said the US officers and men had been marched onto the base at Kenitra in their underwear with arms over heads. My father was missing they said. They didn't know if he was alive, captured or what. Big gulps. Game was called and on the bus ride back to Kenitra, I remember holding my hysterics in and looking by the roadside for any miracle, like my Dad on a scooter with his chin strap flying in the wind! I believe it took a day or two at our Mehdia beach house for us to finally hear that he was coming home (Ha! On the scooter I think...). My mother recalled the landlord who lived below us at the beach house coming up the stairs to the door and saying, "The King is dead! Now me as good as you!"

Jessie Smith Allen

I was in our house on 15 Ave de Marrakesh in Rabat, when I remember hearing planes overhead, my sister Chantal and I ran upstairs to the terrace roof to see what was going on. We saw airplanes chasing each other in the sky...someone said coup d'etat, we were very excited to watch. Later on we heard that it was four Northrop F-5 jets, acting on General Oufkir's orders, and assisted by the Commander of the Moroccan air force base at Kenitra, forming a rebel group that intercepted and tried to shoot down Hassan's Boeing 727 as it returned from France. Allegedly, the rebel pilots broke off their attack on the king's aircraft after the king himself grabbed the radio and told the rebel pilots, "Stop firing! The tyrant is dead!" Believing their mission to have been accomplished, the rebel pilots broke off their attack, and the King was landed safely at Rabat Airport. Afterwards, relations between Kenitra and the Palace were tense because of the role played by the Moroccan air base at Kenitra.

Margaret "Maggie" Gourlay

From the Honolulu Advertiser (Honolulu, Hawaii), 18 August 1972, Friday, Page 2:

rebel pilots held
Americans captive

KENITRA, Morocco (UPI) — Americans who trained Moroccan rebel pilots told yesterday how they were held captive for six hours during the pilots' attempt on King Hassan's life.

When the United States sold 14 F-5 Northrup fighters to Morocco, U.S. personnel trained the pilots. A few of those pilots Wednesday strafed the king's Boeing 727, the airport in Rabat where he landed and his royal palace, 40 miles south of this Moroccan air force base.

"At 3 in the afternoon Wednesday, Moroccan air force officers said all American personnel had to go to their homes or to the clubhouse and stay there," said one American base workers.

That order apparently came from mutinous officers. The attack of fighter aircraft from the Kenitra base on the king's plane began at 4 p.m. as the royal aircraft entered Morocco from Spain.

There are 700 American servicemen and dependants living on base, used partly as a Navy communications center. Some of them live in villas outside the base walls and they said they were rounded up and taken to the clubhouse as virtual prisoners during the attack.

"They told us if we walked toward the gate they would shoot us," one American said. "They would not let us walk past a curve in the road where we apparently could have seen the fighters taking off."

At 9 p.m., after loyal Moroccan army tanks rolled through the front and back gates of the base, their officers told the Americans they were free to go.

Eight rebels were arrested, according to official circles.

One American wife said some of the U.S. personnel were frightened. Mrs. Sharon Brady of St. Louis said, "My 7-year-old boy was downtown with my husband, so I was anxious."

Another American said, "We all got loaded in the clubhouse and tried to forget about it."

In 1971 the king was criticized by his opposition for allowing "an American base" in Morocco and U.S. personnel emphasized "this is a Moroccan base, not American, and it's not our business to say anything."

The 1971 Yearbook

Administration: CAPT Ernest M. Cadenas, USN (Base Commander); LT Floyd A. Huck, USN (School Officer); Mr. Ernest M. Morgan (Principal).

Faculty & Staff: Faculty: Mr. David Bass; Mr. John Conway; Mr. Robert Gawley; Mr. Burton I. Gloor; Mrs. Linda L. Gunberg; Miss Evelyn Guy; Mrs. Barbara Harmon; Miss Rachel Jacoby; Mr. Courtlandt C. Kauffman; Miss Constance Kowalski; Miss Barbara Lutz; Mr. Michael T. Meats; Mr. David Scott; Mr. Arthur Stoeberl; Miss Phyllis Thacker; Mrs. Mary L. Zamora Thompson; and Mr. Robert E. Thompson. **Staff:** Mrs. Mary Beth Morse (School Secretary); Mrs. Ernest M. Morgan; and SK2 Alan Catz.

The 23 graduating Seniors of 1971: Dan Hall (President); Debbie Beatty (Vice-President); Christina Michelle Allam (Secretary); James Russell Young (Treasurer); Najib Assed; Salah Eddine Achaachi; Greg Davis; Nola Dixon; Greg Catlin; Dave Dugan; Mark Ellinger; Robert Gerard; B. J. Gleason; Dennis Holley; Karen Christian Kelby; Peggy Player; Farley Snell; Michelle Santos; Dean Trovinger; Larry R. Walker; Joseph Yeo; Larry Smallwood; and Saddah El-Kalini.

Class of 1972

1972 was a black year in history due to the use of terrorism entering sport with the massacre of 11 Israel Athletes by Arab Gunman. 1972 also saw the beginning of the biggest political scandal in modern times - Watergate. On the other side of the Atlantic a worsening of the problems between the IRA and the British government see wrongs from both sides and innocent lives are lost. On August 16 Morocco King Hassan II's B727 was shot up during another failed coup attempt by General Mohamed Oufkir. Reportedly, King Hassan grabbed the radio and told the rebel pilots "Stop firing! The tyrant is dead!", fooling pilots to break off attack. Born on January 16 was Salah Hissou, Moroccan long-distance runner, and on April 2, Moroccan-British singer Chico Slimani.

I Remember:

I was there 1971-72, having arrived from Pensacola, FL, and finding myself at the Mamora Hotel for a couple of months. Was told to never go out by myself because they grabbed kids off the street and sold them into slavery. Then I heard it was only blonde females so I was safe. Lived in Kenitra in a house surrounded by a tall wall with shards of glass embedded in the top – and clothes still disappeared from the clothesline! The first year was "on the economy" where we got our canned goods from the commissary and fresh fruits and veggies from downtown – and couldn't eat anything until they were rinsed with bleach. I still remember the adage "one capful of bleach per gallon of water." The record player didn't run quite right on the Moroccan electricity so it was interesting to hear what some music really sounded like later on when we had the player converted to run normally! We lived in

Kenitra until the first attempted coup d'état of the King at the golf course in Rabat and found out the base gates were locked - no one in or out. That didn't sit very well with Mom, so we moved on base the second year, in time for the second attempt on the King's life (where he landed the plane on the base!). Had a great time with all new experiences - learned a lot from Dave Bass, Evelyn Guy (librarian), Mrs. Morgan (the principal's wife who got me into college!) and others. Hung around with Abderrahman Oumlil and Bob Beaver, and Paul Collins and Everette Dotson on our Flandrias. That little 49.9cc motorbike was a godsend that gave me freedom of movement and allowed me to move about on my own without being driven around. Loved to head over to Mehdia Beach and get a doughnut from the Doughnut Man. Man, they were good! Was usually on the golf course or bowling alley or working at the base library (next to the Teen Club) or up on the Strip after school engraving trophies and plaques. Of all the movies I went to at the indoor theater, I remember *Zachariah* – a comedy-western with Don Johnson in his acting debut (better known later for his role in *Miami Vice*). Took Diane Teece to my Junior Prom and Socorro Acosta to my Senior Prom. Also was a DJ at the base radio station on Sunday mornings. "Your voice of home, your sound of America, this is AFRTS CNL, 1484 on your radio dial...." Played a lot of Elton John, Eagles, America, Credence, Rod Stewart, Stones, Neil Young... Got Wolfman Jack or Casey Kasem records going for the Sunday late risers. Was one of three editors on the school newspaper – with Jessie Smith and Diane Teece. And for those that may still be wondering who "Dear Abby" was – it was Jessie! Secret's out.... When I graduated from Kenitra American High School, it was the 13th school I had attended since kindergarten. Such is the life of a military brat! I look back and find that there would be very little I would change if I had to do it all over again, especially my Junior and Senior years at KAHS.

Doug Campbell

NAS Kenitra gate.

I graduated in '72 and lived in Rabat (Avenue de Marrakech). Wore colorful clothes from the Medina, drank mint tea in the Oudaia and went to Mr. Bass' classes: he taught me English, Art and Art history. An excellent teacher! Found out that I couldn't whistle in tune from Frank Keen; had heated discussions with Chris McCarthy in history class and with his sister Peggy in Art class; marveled at Doug Smith's vocabulary. Went dancing at La Cage with the crowd, but with Cathy Wade danced ballet in Kenitra, and for the 'Amahl and the night visitors' production in a church. My family stayed on two more years. It was an unforgettable year!

Anne De Tarr-Lasius

Here are a few photos of the Rabat medina where Anne De Tarr bought "her colorful clothes."

I was in Morocco 1966-70 and would have been Class of 1972. Here is a quick overview of my 4 years in Morocco, a place I still hold dear to my heart. Traveling on the USS Constitution from New York to Italy and in a new VW bug from Germany, my mother and I arrived in Morocco in 1966. We were joining my sister and her husband, the Peace Corps Doc, in Les Oudayas, the old walled city of Rabat. On arrival in the city, we got lost trying to find the American Embassy. A gentleman, realizing the difficulty in communicating directions, rode his bicycle in front of our car and lead us right to the Embassy! I felt very safe in the Kasbah being the only blonde running thru the cobbled ways. There was a small shop at the end of our street where we bought fresh Moroccan bread and Danish butter cut from a huge block. Nearby, a communal well and an oven where women and children brought their bread to be baked. Bahdia, our Fatima, became like a second mother to me. We communicated in a mixture of French, Arabic and hand gestures. While in Rabat, I had one year at a girl's Catholic school, L'Ecole de Jeanne D'Arc, and one year of Calvert's Correspondence School at home. In the summer of 1967, our mother was traveling in Europe and left $200 with my sister in case of an emergency. We had an emergency! We had to buy a horse! Chico, a beautiful, high spirited, buckskin colored Arabian stallion was housed at the base stables and was my introduction to military life. After my sister and her husband returned state side in 1968, my mother and I moved to Mehdia Plage. My mother, Caroline Ezhaya, was dating a Seabee, George Podchelne, at the time. He bought a moped for me...from horses to motorcycles. I started school at Kenitra American High School and mother got a job on the base. The Oasis, Teen Club, movie theatre, outdoor theatre, pool, things were very different on the base. There was a group of wild and crazy motorcycle riding servicemen who frequented the beach. I have a photo somewhere of a group of us on the beach and another taken outside a nightclub in Kenitra. I remember dancing the night away and emerging from the club at dawn. Don't remember the name of the club, though. When we left Morocco in 1970, a piece of me stayed. For a time, a word in French or Arabic would come to mind and I would have to search my memory for the English translation. Thirty-six plus years later I still wear, almost daily, the gold hand of Fatima I treasure. I have not returned to Morocco but would love to do so. Bahdia did visit us in Massachusetts the year after we returned. She stayed with us for about six months and experienced a New England winter. She also visited my sister and family in Saudi Arabia when they were there in the '70's.

Ann Ezhaya White

I had the treasured opportunities of living off base at Mehdia beach with all the adventures it offered. I babysat for the school nurse and rode the bus in with her daughter on the Rabat bus in the mornings to school. Gendarmes came out early mornings when I was out on the beach and shot all the stray dogs. I'd see the fresh catch at the pier mid-mornings and then the tall brown man loping along the sand with his board of sunbaked donuts and outstretched hand wanting his payment for all the donuts you guys ate and then pointed to the girl up there on the 4th level! Thanks a lot guys! They were so good tho, weren't they? Doug Smith, Pat Hansard and Frank Keen would come out to the beach. I'd cook scrambled eggs in the cast iron skillet and drag that heavy thing out there. They'd play guitars and sing and we JUST enjoyed. Have you ever had a bite of French bread, a chunk of chocolate— chew them together and then follow up with a little sip of red wine? MMMMMMM or edam cheese, or Jarlsberg with French bread and wine? Nummmm—nummm GOOD STUFF! Dig a lounge chair out, sit it in the sand...the warmth on your back and bottom. Breeze in your hair, sand in your sunscreen and mouth. Who could've wanted more?! Faraj and Marabat and Salah would surf and show me parts of Kenitra and the medina that filled my heart! Mint tea, dates with almonds and I don't think they knew what to do with a girl who wasn't burka'd up! I couldn't get into the mosque, that's for sure!!

Jessie Smith Allen

My name is Abderrahman 'Ben' Oumlil and I entered KAHS in my Junior year and spent two years there as a student, graduating in 1972. Based upon my experiences, I consider KAHS to have been an excellent institution of learning. It offered me many opportunities to pursue my academic endeavors and my interest in sports. During my first year there, I did experience challenges due to the significant differences in cultural, educational and social mores.

From an academic perspective, I remember that my journey at KAHS began with only two years of basic English language training from a Moroccan / French school. The Moroccan education system is modeled after the French education system, which is without any elective courses or options. It is based on memorization while the American education system is oriented toward a more practical and pragmatic approach. Dealing with a limited knowledge of the English language should have led to a restriction of benefits enjoyed in all aspects of academic life and the general enjoyment of American school life. I do not think it did.

Although facing some academic and cultural challenges, KAHS administration (Mr. Morgan, Mrs. Morgan, etc.), staff members (Mr. Dement, Mr. Gloor, Mrs. Beth Morse, etc.), faculty members (Mr. Bass, Mr. Kauffman, Mrs. Sellak, Mr. Meats, Mrs. Brown, Mr. Thompson and Mrs. Thompson, etc.), and students worked diligently to create a welcoming environment conducive to learning and to finding solutions that worked and that helped me to get up-to-speed quickly (for an international student) so that each international student had the opportunity to study and benefit from the academic and non-academic experiences at KAHS. Having very dedicated administrators, staff, faculty members, and students helped international students, such as myself, overcome cultural and academic shocks. For example, teacher-student relationships and interactions were informal in the American education system in comparison to the French system.

Moreover, teachers and students interacted differently but also people interacted differently in an American academic and social milieu. Accessibility of teachers to students made questions easy to ask and learning fun.

I remember that it did take time to get used to this and to gain a good understanding of how teachers and students reacted to one another. Additional factors that helped to immerse one in the cultural, social and academic environment at KAHS were: 1) the ease in making new friends with American students; 2) looking to other International students as a support network and sharing and learning about common practices in KAHS and the American cultural/academic milieu; and 3) participating in the optional sports programs like wrestling and track and field, social events, field trips and outings, getting involved in student clubs at KAHS, and stepping out of one's comfort zone.

All these opportunities helped me greatly to get acquainted with my new school for the duration of my studies at KAHS.

Abderrahman 'Ben' Oumlil

The 1972 Prom:

Bottom left is Jessie Smith. Behind her and from left to right is Larry Yeo, Everette Dotson, David Morgan and Diane Teece.

From left to right – Bob Beaver, Socorro Acosta and Doug Campbell.

Left to right: Majid Slaoui, Frank Keen and Doug Smith "on the hill."

Frank Keen (Class of '72) and Majid Slaoui (Class of '73) smoking in the Roach Coach.

Who Remembers Their Favorite Teacher?

Mr. Seeke, my English teacher from 1973, was my favorite teacher. I did my best writing in his class!

Neil Thakur

Chorus was my favorite class and Mr. Gauley was my favorite teacher. Music was my only escape from many things in life and still is. I love it. He made it possible to have the joy of music in my life. He was always very kind and I feel a wonderful example of what I think a teacher should be like. He never showed favoritism or seemed judgmental. He was a very kind soul.

Beverly Lear Beardsley

Mr. Moroney, social studies.....His wry sense of humor.

John Quinn

A great memory at KAHS was my art class with teacher Mr. David Bass senior year (1971 - 72). But my favorite was Mr. Miletich hands down!!! He taught world history/social studies and was the adviser to the KAHS drama club during my senior year. Great guy!!! He drove a Javelin!! He also gave us our final exam with an open book test!!! Myself and Charlie Beggs got an 'A' on our final!! Woo hoo!!

Robert Oberkehr

Courtlandt Kauffman taught physics and always challenged you to think! Something we are missing in our schools and life today.

Tony Collins

Mr. Kauffman was one of my favorite math teachers. He had the best ability to explain new concepts and then followed them up with some practical examples. There were three of us about one year behind our normal grade level for various reasons, but we quickly understood concepts so he put us on an accelerated path which really help us catch up. He has probably passed on, but it is good to recognize his positive contribution to his students.

David Neumann

[Note: "Court" Kauffman passed away in December 2016]

I was so sad to hear that Mr. Kauffman died in 2016. He was a disciplined teacher, which now, I respect very much. I was one of the few young women taking the upper level science and math classes. Thank goodness for my Chemistry partners, Mike Morrison and Chakib Loudiyi, in Chemistry...and Majid, husband, for his tutoring in Trigonometry and Analytical Geometry!!!! I learned to feel comfortable in a "man's" world back then and that gave me the confidence to continue to strive and commit to my life's passion...teaching........... Lecture, over!

Nancy Lukas-Slaoui

My favorite teacher was Dave Bass. I used to look at art as only from an investment point of view or functional – "will it fit over the sofa?" Thank God Dave Bass opened my eyes to "art for art's sake" rather than "art for money's sake," although I still tend to be intrigued in how much art is worth. But now, having walked though some of the greatest art museums in the world (Prado, Hermitage, MOMA, Smithsonian...) I do silently thank him for teaching me about negative space, shadows, brush strokes, etc. He also taught English and we had to learn 10 new words a week! Many of which I still use today. Poignant, huh? HA! As to the path I took in life, Dave Bass guided me down the road and he doesn't even remember doing it. Mrs. Morgan, the principal's wife, took over as our Guidance Counselor and helped us with our college applications. I was accepted to two colleges (I needed to get into one that had NROTC), Vanderbilt and the University of Kansas. I had no idea which one so I asked Mr. Bass and he said "If you want to go to a school with a name, go to Vanderbilt. If you want to learn something, go to Kansas." I went to Kansas and got my degree in Journalism and a 23-year career in the United States Navy. Not a bad path to have gone down.

I must also say Thank You to our librarian, Miss Evelyn Guy, who passed away in 2014 (see note from Burt Gloor below). Having an excess of "points" needed to graduate (even by the end of my Junior year), I got to choose some other areas of interest for a class or two. One was working on the school newspaper. Another was helping out in the library. I learned a lot more than the Dewey Decimal System. I learned about book themselves and the words inside them. Whenever someone like the Officers' Wives Club wanted to censor a book or two–I think Abbie Hoffman's *Steal This Book* was one—Miss Guy would go on a rampage about censorship and eventually get her way—the books stayed. She fought to make sure students got to see the world as it was and not through rose-colored glasses. I believe we wound up reading Hoffman's book in our Social Sciences class.

Doug Campbell

KAHS teacher Burt Gloor wrote an email to Doug Campbell on the passing of Evelyn Guy. "I wanted you to know that Evelyn Guy passed away on Jan. 2, 2014. She had been to the gym that week with no signs of illness so her death must have been sudden. We had a celebration of her life with some of her DoDDS friends in January. In going thru her photo albums Mireille and I came across a kind letter that you had sent her, telling her what an impact she had on your life--your working for her in the library, training you on the Dewey Decimal system, etc. Your comment about Evelyn marching down the halls of TMWH brought back my own exact description of her. I would compare her "march" to that of a Nazi storm trooper. It was strange that we both remembered that loud "clack, clack" noise on the wooden floors of TMWH. She was a very independent woman who traveled the world. In going thru her album we discovered that she had worked in 18 different places and traveled the world during the summers. I recall one summer when she took a freighter (alone) along the coast of Africa-got off at Namibia and took a bus to the border of Angola (This was during the fighting for independence). Evelyn just walked across the border into Angola and "dropped in" on a Portuguese military outpost. She was the only person entering Angola. They didn't know what to do with her so they put her up in the officer's quarters and the next morning after breakfast asked her if she would like to "review the troops." She said, I felt like the Queen of England! Afterwards they flew her out on a military helicopter. Evelyn and I later worked together in Brindisi for 5 or 6 years. She worked hard, partied hard and loved eating at local restaurants."

Burt and Mireille Gloor

Always Mr. Meyer - History. Brought it alive. I also have to humbly thank Mrs. Sellak--she taught me skills that helped me land jobs and keep them through the years (even though I hated typing class). God does have a sense of humor! LOL

JeanMarie Sample

This little school was truly blessed with a rare gathering of not only talented but also very engaged teachers. I have been through exactly ten schools on three continents before I finally got my (German) high school diploma (Abitur) in 1977. I had the good fortune of having been a pupil at KAHS from 1970-1972. Let me give you a glimpse of how several teachers there have impressed me:

First: Miss Mary L. Zamora Thompson. This particular teacher was an example of dedication and great empathy to me. Because of her "regime" of constant testing I completely lost my "exam nerves" (Fear of testing or being tested). Man, we had tests every day: Little quizzes almost daily, smaller tests on a weekly basis. She really drove those fears out of me in a patient, caring and empathic manner. Also, she astounded me with her wardrobe! I never saw her with the same dress twice! ;)

Secondly: Mr. Gawley. He was my math teacher. Never before -and certainly never after- have I met a math teacher with this Zen-like patience. You could ask this man the abysmally most stupid questions and he would never lose his cool. He always reacted in a kind, patient and accepting manner. Because of him I lost my fear of math! Before I met this guy, I was always a bit uneasy with math. I was never really good in math and I kinda had already accepted that I wouldn't ever have any kind of liking for it. Mr. Gawley got rid of that. He made me gain confidence with math and from then on, I was never really bad in that particular subject. (Though I wouldn't say that math became the love of my life... ;))

Thirdly: Mr. Courtlandt Kauffman. He was the math teacher I had after Mr. Gawley. What I liked most about him were two things: His patient and empathic way of teaching and his really cool composure. For a young lad like me he was a perfect role model. I thought to myself: If I could become even halfway as cool and composed as this man I'd be doing pretty good...

Fourthly: Miss Constance Kowalski. She taught French in a way I hadn't experienced before. Mind you, I've had French teachers before but they were all a fairly drab lot compared to this lady! Miss Kowalski had all sorts of creative ideas on how to teach French. We learned not only the vocabulary and the grammar. We learned the culture, the savoir vivre, she asked us to write our own poetry or design crossword puzzles, sing French songs, learn

about French recipes. Apart from that she had the craziest
collection of very original glasses. She was gorgeous!

Fifthly: Mr. Stoeberl, the English teacher. I know that many of
my classmates probably didn't like him too much. Him coming with
Shakespeare's original "Julius Caesar" or Homer's "Iliad" at us.
But I loved it. I found it interesting and captivating and I was really
glad that he wasn't just teaching us English, but that he was trying
to build our vocabulary and give us an understanding of how words
are used and how they changed the world...

If I had more time I could probably come up with some more. I
also have fond memories of the school's librarian, Evelyn Guy.
She was also very patient and a high example of true dedication.

Manfred Kramer

French...M. Berard. He used to skip school to surf and catch
flies with his hand and eat them. Ha, ha! Loved him so much - I
got A's in French.

Cece Canton

French - M. Berard! He used to swim at Mehdia Beach with the
sharks! I loved him, you never knew what he was going to say!!

Kathy Cox West

Mr. Bogden, English - Strict but great if you did your job.
Mademoiselle Jacquemart, French - I learned fluently. Mr.
Mughrabi, Arabic - Wish I had a do-over. But have never forgot
Mr. Maroney, History - Just an all-around great teacher.

Gloria Kemery

David Bass...first crush! Loved his style, charm, self-
confidence, sense of humor! World view. Opened me up to
current events, art and humanities. Always made me feel a little
better than special. Held me to a higher standard. Called me Mata
Hari... ; -)

Jessie Smith Allen

David Bass allowed me and BJ Gleason to hang out in his
classroom, thus he became my favorite teacher and art became
my college major. I earned a Masters in Fine Art from Texas Tech

University (David gave me great advice during those years), and later I taught at two universities and several public schools.

Nola Fulkerson

I have two! Bonnie Crumpler, Biology (I still love science) and Mrs. Mary Thompson (So pretty, never wore the same thing twice and fixed her hair different every day).

Marguerite Golden Bright

Mr. Bass. He was the best ever, throughout every level of schooling. Creative, compassionate, brilliant, and hilarious. I will forever be grateful to him for how dedicated he was to teaching us and helping to develop the characters we were. David Bass will forever be a pivotal person in my life. He challenged us to journal, to step outside our comfortable creative boundaries and experience the fullness of cultures not our own. I just admire and love him and thank him more than I will ever be able to articulate. I think he had a gift for making everyone feel as special as he made me feel. I think back now on the teachers we had and many of them were so young and as naive as we were...what a great experience for them, too. I thought Miss Freeman was so very cool and I thought Miss Thacker was so earnest and tried so hard that it was impossible not to like her.

Barbara "BJ" Gleason Ford

As far as favorite teachers go I have to say I really enjoyed Mr. Kauffman's classes and Mr. Meyer's classes. I had Mr. Kauffman every year I was there for math and science and Mr. Meyer every year for social studies. I also really appreciated Mrs. Morgan for all her help in getting all my college applications sent in and for her life guidance. She was a special person.

Leigh (Crocker) McSwain

When it comes to remembering high school, I liked most of my teachers once I made it to 11th and 12th grades. My favorite teacher was Mr. Samson who taught the science classes. He once caught Richard Evans and I playing hooky. We had skipped the last period, picked up our golf clubs and were on hole number 3 when we encountered Mr. Samson cutting across the golf course to go home. He said that the basic rules of science did not allow us to be there if we left school as he did 20 minutes earlier.

However, he let it slide. I skipped my last class period several times. I was assigned to Public Works down the hill from the school. I was learning basic drawing and specification requirements from a 1st class who enjoyed my occasional absences. He was a good teacher and I a good student as long as we didn't have to be together 5 days a week.

Bob Bull

This photo was taken in 1971 depicting many of the students in what became the Class of 1972. Laura Beatty (bottom right) was the only one in this group photo who did not graduate with the others as her family rotated out. Carla Golden Callaghan says "OK, I remember the day we had this taken. We were out behind the school and it was the first time I went thru an art classroom to get there. I had no art classes and that room was so interesting."

The 1972 Yearbook

Administration: CAPT Joe F. Lasseter, Jr., USN (Base Commander); LT Floyd A. Huck, USN (School's Officer) and Mr. Ernest M. Morgan (Principal).

Faculty & Staff: Faculty: Mr. William Shepherd; Miss Barbara Lutz; Miss Bonnie Crumpler; Miss Karen New; Miss Susan Ervin; Mr. Courtlandt Kauffman; Miss Evelyn Guy; Mr. Pablo Mares; Miss Michele Barsodi; Miss Kimette Johnson; Miss Sandra Weary; Mrs. Janice Sellak; and Mr. David Bass. **Staff:** Mrs. Ernest M. Morgan; Mrs. Mary Beth Morse; SK2 Alan Catz; Bouchaib Ben Mohamed and Belaid Ben Abdeslem.

The 28 graduating Seniors of 1972: Brian J. Piantadosi (President); David Morgan (Vice-President); Jessamyn "Jessie" Smith (Secretary); Stephanie Staupe (Treasurer); Carla Marie Golden; Douglas Eugene Campbell; Abderrahman "Ben" Oumlil; Robert Oberkehr; Larry Yeo; Frank Keen; Josiane Andrews; Cathy Wade; Christopher McCarthy; Doug Smith; Paul Collins; Gloria Ford; Charles "Charlie" Beggs; Everette Dotson; Christian Andrews; Carlos Acosta; Alia Al-Dalli; Jody Smallwood; Diane Teece; Steven Branch; James "JJ" Jones; Katherine Myers; Anne De Tarr; and Robert Beaver.

CLASS OF 1973

1973 saw world inflation significantly impacting the lives of people around the world with the UK inflation rate running at 8.4% and the US running at 6.16%. This caused problems in every aspect of people's lives from the price of gas, food and bills, which in turn caused higher wages and the spiral continued, much of this caused by the Arab members of the (OPEC) restricting the flow of oil to countries supporting Israel as part of the Yom Kippur War. The start of a Recession in Europe caused increased unemployment and a 3-day work week in the UK. Meanwhile in the US, two important cases dominated the news with Roe v. Wade making abortion a US constitutional right and the start of the Watergate hearings in the US Senate. Due to the significant price increase of gas, the Japanese car manufacturers with smaller engines and more efficient continued to impact the US car industry. On March 10, Morocco adopted its Constitution. On December 23, a French Caravelle airliner crashes in Morocco, killing 106. Also in 1973 a Polisario movement was formed, aimed to establish an independent state in Spanish Sahara, a territory south of Morocco controlled by Spain. The group has Algerian support. Born on May 24 was the Moroccan tennis star Karim Alami.

I Remember:

I'm from the Class of '73 (as is my husband, Majid Slaoui). I lived on the Naval Training base (where the school was located) and Majid lived in Rabat and commuted with Embassy kids to school every day. Oh, my house was directly behind the fence of the outdoor movie theater, and the first house up the hill from the "Strip" with the PX and commissary. The street continued down to the school on the other side. One more thing, I attended KAHS from '71-73. Majid attended from '69-73. My sister-in-law, Norea Slaoui, was there from '69-75, and my brother-in-law, Omar Slaoui, was there from '74 until the base closed.

Nancy Lukas-Slaoui

I lived in Rabat from 68 to '73. Dad was a contract USAID.

Mike McSwain

Hi dear all. I am Faraj Benwahoud, Class of 73. Unfortunately, I missed the last few reunions but I see that they were superb "rencontres." I wanted to pay a special tribute to Debbie Gerth, a dear and generous Lady and friend and another dear friend, Khalid Benchekroun, who also left us. I was wondering if anyone has seen or heard from some of my classmates Robert Angelo, Peter L'Heureux and Eleine (in French it's Hélène) all the best to you all.

Faraj Benwahoud

Lived on the base in Kenitra from June 1969 to June 1971.

Karen Ruth Butler

Moved to Kenitra in October of 1972, lived in the Mamora Hotel for 2 months, then a Quonset Hut on base until summer. My Dad was a Warrant Officer so we couldn't live on Officer's Row and the base had to figure out where to put us. We ended up across the street from the hospital. My brother Gordon was class of '75, he passed away in 2004. All of our family has lived here in San Luis Obispo California since my Dad retired in 1975. Lots of fond memories of the people I met and the places we saw. Played tennis so got to go on trips to Spain and Germany.

Teressa (Knowles) Spring

I lived in Rabat from 1969-1973; graduated 1973. I REMEMBER:

- Drinking mint tea every night with my family after dinner.
- The smell of orange blossoms on the way to school.
- The muezzim's call to prayer several times a day.
- Hearing Three Dog Night on the bus going to and coming from school.
- Grapes that tasted like sugared sunshine.

- Paying 5 dirhams to go across the Bou Regreg River from Rabat to Sale in a blue rowboat.
- Playing in the coastal ruins of Sale and pretending to be a Barbary pirate.
- The smell of India ink and erasers when entering Mr. Bass's art room.
- Eating couscous every Sunday after church until I thought I would burst.
- Miss Guy's scowl if even so much as an ant farted in her library.
- Hearing the cannon blast from the Oudais Casbah every morning at 4:30 during Ramadan.
- Learning about gothic cathedrals in Humanities class and then going to see them years later.
- Hearing Pachelbel's Cannon in D in Mr. Bass's class and falling in love with classical music.
- Paying 25 cents to see movies at the Rabat American School on the weekends.
- The powder puff football games where the girls kicked footballs and the boys were cheerleaders.
- Majid Slaoui wearing my skirt when he was a cheerleader for the powder puff football games.
- The fetid smells of the tanneries in Fez.
- The snake charmers in Marrakech.
- Riding 30 miles to school every day in a grey bus driven by a Seabee.
- The salty mists of Mehdia Beach every morning on the way to school.
- My first hayride at a school dance.
- Watching the fighter jets take off from the runway on base.
- Walking through the Rabat Medina and wishing I could buy everything.
- Viewing the great plains where Volubilis stood and imagining wild lions and Roman legions.
- Seeing the sacred eels swimming in the pools of the Chellah.
- The students and faculty of TMW/KAHS who are my extended family and whom I will love until I leave this life.

Sandy White Bartell

My family lived in Kenitra from 1970 - 1973 - we first lived in the Mamora hotel for about 1 month, then moved into a villa across from the city bus, then moved on base - my father worked in Sidi Yahia during this time.

Margie Tyson

I was there from 71-73. My Dad was a corpsman ... he handled the Air Evacs at the hospital. There were many a night spent walking up the hill to the hospital to spend the night because the base was shut down and we couldn't get home from school (we lived in town). While I was in Morocco much later than all of you (at least, so it seems) there is a Moroccan (from Kenitra, believe it or not!) who owns a pizza place just off the boardwalk here at Virginia Beach. Most of the people who work there are family/friends of his from Kenitra. At first, he didn't believe me when I told him I'd lived in Morocco...but you should have seen his face when I started describing Kenitra! ("...go to the clock, go 5 blocks down Mohammed V, take a right...") It's amazing how I walked in to get pizza one day and I've grown quite a friendship with him and his family (they've even made couscous for myself and my girlfriend!) ... all because of my days in Morocco! If you're ever in Virginia Beach, it's Bella Pizza on Atlantic Ave (runs along the boardwalk) between 14th and 15th Street...Actually, it's the best pizza in town! Tell Ahmed ("Ed") you lived in/around Kenitra and Dean sent you...he'll talk to you for hours! I also remember the Christmas of '72 when the base radio station decided they would track Santa but wanted to put a "War of the Worlds" spin on it by continually breaking into the music with news updates of the Strategic Air Command tracking inbound missiles! Everyone thought there was a war starting.

Dean Longo

My name is Peggy Thomas Whitcomb and we arrived in Kenitra in 1970 and left in 1973. My father was RMCS William R. Thomas. I was just a young girl then but loved Morocco. We lived in a hotel in Kenitra for a few months, then my dad rented a villa near a section of Kenitra where diplomats lived. I remember a French diplomat family who lived near us and I would play with their kids. There was a little corner store across the street from our villa. I remember there was a coup of some sort and as we lived around the corner from the Kenitra courthouse we were told to stay inside. They executed some of the people involved in the coup at the courthouse. You could hear the firing squads. At some point my Dad was transferred to Sidi Yahia. We moved on base there. Besides his regular duties [as a Senior Chief Radioman] he was also in charge of one of the clubs. We would go eat pizza and play shuffle board there. There was another attempted coup on the King's life and I remember jets flying over the base. My Dad retired from the Navy there. I am wondering if anyone remembers him?

Peggy Thomas Whitcomb

My name is Bill Simpkins and I would have been KAHS Class of '73 but we left Morocco before that and I graduated from Woodham High School in Pensacola, FL. Reading some of the travel adventures folks had getting to Morocco reminds me of my family's trip to the kingdom. We actually drove down from Bremerhaven, Germany. My dad and mom, my brother, myself and Alf (a daschund) loaded up our 1957 Chevy and headed south for the African continent. No problems getting through France, except my dad wouldn't go into Paris so we could see the Eiffel Tower.

However, in Spain while making our way to Rota our car lights went out coming down a small mountain and by the time my dad could get the car stopped we were sideways in the middle of the road. My dad and brother with the help of one flashlight managed very carefully to get the car to the side of road. After a short time, a nice Spanish man stopped to help us. We limped down the side of the mountain following him in the glow of his tail lights. We ended up getting the car fixed on base at Rota and spent two days extra there while the vet figured out why Alf (the daschund) had become violently sick. My mom was swearing it was the water, but after a couple of days the vet came up with the solution, the dog was car sick. A couple of pills fixed that problem and we were on our way.

The next problem was a little harder to fix because it actually had to do with us getting into Morocco. After taking the ferry from Spain, the Moroccan government would not allow entry to my dad. The reason – he was in the military. So, my dad and mom had to come up with Plan B.

Plan B was for my dad to return to Spain via the ferry then make his way to the base in Rota (I believe he did that by bus). He was then to fly to Morocco via Port Lyautey, commandeer some form of transportation and meet us in Tangier. Meanwhile, my mom, my brother, myself and Alf (the daschund) were to cross the border in the car and meet him in Tangier at a pre-arranged place. Before departing my dad hired a Moroccan lad to guide us to the rendezvous (I threw that word in there because after all we were in "FRENCH Morocco") point, a hotel. My dad's ETA in Tangier was three days.

The Moroccan lad (that's right you guessed it) Mohammed, got us to our destination in Tangier safely and quite efficiently. Then we sat and waited. After about a day of sitting in the hotel my mother went temporarily insane (I think my brother and me were driving her crazy) and let us go with Mohammed into the city. He took us into every nook and cranny of the city, the marketplace (the smell still haunts me) the cafes (we sat at the bar and drank coke out of those little bottles) and down to the waterfront. What a great adventure. My dad showed up just about right on time and we moved on down the coast to Kenitra. We stayed three months at the hotel in town then moved to a villa off base. The interesting thing about this villa was the whole yard was concrete. Also, this is where we were living when JFK was assassinated, but that's a whole different story. We eventually moved on base near the Chief's club overlooking the airfield. My dad could actually walk to work at the airfield. I don't know why that impresses me so much, maybe because I have to drive 30 minutes one way to work these days.

Billy Simpkins

I remember Kenitra...in three vignettes!

First vignette – The Right Stuff

Navy flyboys used to begrudge the assignment to the Port-Lyautey navy base in the mid-1950's. It was a base for guys who were supposed to make "mail runs" into Europe, but surreptitiously would do high altitude espionage runs into Russia, up through the Black Sea...among other destinations.

When back at the base, the single guys (most of them) would compete for the attention of the French dames that would hang-out at the officer's bar, seeking a change from the town's terraces where most faces were familiar.

My mother Yvette was such a dame, one with a past. Widowed from a French officer who had been killed in Vietnam, single mother of a daughter who, like her, had been born in Rabat, she was a local beauty who had returned home from the Far East to take refuge with her family and raise her daughter, here in Port-Lyautey. Pushing to turn a page, exuberant and eager to laugh, she often made evening plans with friends when she'd drop her daughter off at her father's house. He, Louis Keriel, a wounded WWI veteran from Britanny, had come to this town in 1921 to run a boys' school, had married the daughter of the French North African Park Services director, and would eventually die there. Port-Lyautey, Kenitra-city as the Americans on the base called it, was home.

On a warm Maghreb evening, early in 1954, Yvette had driven around to pick-up a couple of her girlfriends in her father's '49 Studebaker coupe. Fashionable and elegant, they had headed off to the base where the MP's would raise the gate and the ladies would flash lipstick smiles.

In the bar, a 3-man combo would often play jazz tunes, else the juke box would string Ella, Crosby, Sinatra, the Platters, King Cole, Clooney, Bennet, Dean Martin's *That's Amore*. The room was smoky with cacophony, hued khaki with stripes, wet with gin and scotch, and filled with testosterone.

My mother seemed to be in the early stages of striking-up something with a Lt. Commander; he would much later be described to me as a "dweeb". For now, the cluster of Yvette, the dweeb, and the increasingly engaged swell of entourage was deep in fast exchanges of broken English, pig-French, zests of lemon and olive-spiked refills. As for the "dweeb" opinion, it was being spontaneously inflated by a dynamic and irresistibly charming macho flyer lieutenant who had just walked in.

Lt. Hartley had just come back from a round-trip mission to Germany, and he never wasted time to get to the action once he'd debriefed. That night, it was to be in the Officer's bar, down from the hospital on the hill where he had an optional date with a nurse. "I was immediately struck," says the Lt., "that the dweeb had the attention of the most mesmerizing girl I could remember setting eyes on. She was the life of the party, and I had to find a way to get her off his arm and on mine."

That he did. The affair was passionate, explosive, and impactful; she, still in love with another dashing young Lieutenant who had exploded on a mine to save his troops, one borne of a conservative prominent Bordeaux family and father of her child; and he, the flyer, engaged to a society-woman stateside, and strutting the arrogance of an Annapolis wrestler with wings, jet wings. It lasted months and became as painful as it was romantic. He was deeply suspicious of her, and she measured him against her dead husband, each clung to the other in the impossible circumstances of a torid affair, and each had the volatility and outsized energy to tear each other's heart apart.

While on a lover's fortnight escape at the Mamounia hotel in Marrakech, the Lieutenant once cause the ire of Yvette with various indiscretions. Walking back into the hotel from an excessive absence, we witnessed his open suitcase flying out of a second story balcony window, his shirts catching on to palm fronds on the way down like dangling flags of surrender, and after a beat his navy cap sailing out to land on the scattered wear.

The unfurling of the romance is beyond the context of this book, but the point of it is that my very being stems from the ground where lives of the people in this book converge. Only divine irony would bring me back there again.

Second vignette – The planet called "La base"

I wasn't born in Morocco, nor was I conceived there. It was in Rhode Island, at the Quonset Naval Air Station, the Lieutenant's next Navy assignment. My mother followed him there; the unmarried couple with a 6-year old in tow made fodder for heavy gossip. They lived together off-base for a few months and tried to make something of it. It was a miserable failure. On December 29, 1954, Yvette left the US on a freighter ship, daughter in hand, and pregnant… confused, embarrassed, afraid, regretful, wounded. The lieutenant wanted nothing of it. She considered my fate, her fate, our fate.

She would keep me. The ship would dock in Nice, France, and she decided to stay there a while to figure out how she was going to explain this to the world. Alone, living in a terraced apartment overlooking the Promenade des Anglais and the Mediterranean, she brought me into life as Philippe Keriel, her father's last name, and thus I was born a French boy of unknown father.

It was a year before her sister convinced her to get back to the ease and support of like in Port-Lautey. There I learned to walk, talk, go to school in French nursery, run, bicycle and become a small boy. But among my earliest memories are of the hospital on the base. Friends my mother had made on the base recognized from my early morphing physique that I was of Lt. Hartley's blood, and made arrangement allowing her to have medical care for me on the base and get shopping privileges at the PX. What seemed like a gigantic parking lot, in my 3-year old's perspective, separated the supply store on one side from the long drive that led up the hill to the hospital. Equally gigantic to me were the cars, monoliths with steel bumpers wider than my little body and level with my head, and grills that seemed to want to eat what came to it. And there, in that lot, was the site of my first accident, the featured story of the base paper the next day. I trotted out impulsively as little boys do, and boom, had a head-on collision with one of those ferocious steel beasts that was pulling out. Up the hill I was rushed. I remember the strange ramblings of officious-looking white-coated individuals there. Speaking no English, exchanges on the base were mysterious. But today still I keep three scars from that hospital: the first from said incident, and the other two being out-sized vaccination scars on the left side of my left thigh, like dollar tattoos of silver.

So as a little boy, a pre-schooler, my memories of Kenitra include the Mamora forest where my mother and sister rode at the stables under the tutelage of an ex-pat Russian cavalry officer, of the basin at the foot of my four-story building where swans seemed to reign, of the drive up to my grandfather's villa where shutters would always keep our the brutal heat of the early afternoon, and of the American base. My forming brain looked upon it as an efficient place, a place only certain people could come into, a place where men and ladies looked different, spoke differently, and to which my mother seemed to attribute superlatives. In the base there were no people in Djellabah's, no people in sirhouals, no feet in baboushs, no people speaking Moroccan or French, no gendarmes. Men in blue called 'sailors' wore funny white bob hats on their heads. Fast planes took off as if to return to another world. And at the PX, candies were like none I saw on the other side of the fence.

Prelude to the third vignette-

Three continents separate us from the next vignette in this tale, as well as a geo-political pivot. By the time I was 5, the world had changed. Algeria was independent and the French protectorate of Morocco had ended. My grandfather died and our properties were disposed of in fire sales. Moroccans, like all North Africans, began expressing strong anti-French feelings, and the French colonial economy the world over came to an end. Yvette "repatriated" us to Paris.

I began feeling the hole in my belly, a dull pain I did not know how to explain. I became a little Parisian boy, playing with my bourgeois friends in the 16th quarter while my mother earned a living finding housing for all the French returnees from North Africa. My longing for a father found a soothing balm in my selfless maman's descriptions of a man of great attributes, a flyer, an athlete, an American man in a uniform of whom I reminded her intensely.

I was 11 years old when my world exploded in dimensionality. DeGaulle was still President, but France was moving to a post-colonial future and my mother grew wary of the Paris hubbub. She longed for le Maroc, its lazy days and easy life. She had corresponded about that with a friend of hers from Kenitra who had ended-up marrying a whimsical Navy captain and had been whisked half-way around the globe to a promised land called California, and a city of the future called Los Angeles. "There are places here called Palm Springs, called Santa Barbara, where you will feel like you are in Morocco; same vegetation, climate, pace." Suitcases were packed, belongings sold, and I was taken out of school. We were going to the other side of the globe, to California!

During the Air France jet plane ride to the first stop, New York (might as well have been Mars so far did is seem), a screen was pulled down at the front end of the aisle by an elegant stewardess in a tight chignon and crisp white shirt, and I sat up in my crisp white shirt and tie to watch a movie (a movie, on a plane!). It was Walk Don't Run, a Cary Grant love story which takes place at the Tokyo Olympics and involving competitors in a walking race. Half-way through it, my mother seemed really disturbed. She pulls the stethoscope looking hearing apparatus from my ear and points to the screen. "I think that's your father…" My what? Who? Where? I follow her finger and some character comes back on. "Him!" she whispers loudly. "I'm sure that's Ted…That's your father!" But, that guy is Russian, thought I, confused and bewildered. "He's not Russian, he's playing a Russian" explains my mother, sensing my confusion. My eyes were transfixed on the elusive appearances of the Russian guy. My mother scans the end credits, and it was confirmed. I had, for the first time in my life, seen and heard my father...proof he was alive, and existed. The rest was completely unclear.

Skipping volumes in the tale, my father had in fact left the Navy, moved to Hollywood and become an actor, was living a life of glamorous bachelorhood, convertibles, tennis, soirees and tabloids. A listing in the telephone company White Pages confirmed that he was, in fact residing exactly where fate had taken us.

A long-ruminated phone call by my mother to the listed number caused a powerful turn in all of our lives. Now retired Lt-Commander Hartley, upon facing me, could hardly deny the obvious: he had a twelve-year-old son, and I looked exactly like him. What ensued can be contained in a headline: Parisian boy meets Hollywood father, mother is odd person out... Six months later, hurt and disillusioned by a relationship that never seemed to bring nothing but pain for her, Yvette points herself back to Morocco in search of a lifestyle and comfort mode rooted in her system. She takes me back with her and we settle in Rabat where I live in Agdal. I attend Lycee Descartes, at the very top of the hill of that villa community. It was the last year of my total Frenchness and my view of Maroc through those lenses, hanging out with pied-noirs buddies, roaming the streets with my bicycle gang, rock-throwing fights with Moroccan street youths, lush summers at the Skrirat hotel, on the beach next to the king's Summer palace. It's where I was when I watched Neil Armstrong take the most famous step in human history. Glued to the spectacle with my French and Moroccan buddies on this North African resort hotel lobby, I felt different from them, now personally linked to the flag that had been planted on the moon. It seemed impossible to understand, but it was now part me.

As I entered puberty, I wanted to explore life with the person who was my father, in a land far far away. My father wanted the same thing. My mother, wise to what she had sown with the fateful telephone call, relented. Today I cannot fathom the pain it must have caused her to agree to hand my future over to the man who had failed to support her, who had turned his back on my childhood, and sent her 13-year old boy out of her life. At the end of the summer, now my 8th grade year, I moved to California, was immediately enrolled in a private ROTC boarding school, and retro-actively became an US-born citizen. My name was now Phil Hartley, but I did not speak English.

The development of the father-son relationship did not go well, despite amazing exposure and discovery for me. Those were by far the loneliest years of my life. I could not relate to classmates, could not find the relationship I had wanted with my new and only father. I lived for the weekly "three minutes for $10 phone call" at a phone booth with my mother. But, like the willow that bends from the swinging of boys on its branches, an American I did become quickly, in culture and thinking, in attitude and style. After 3-years of California private school education, my father's and my relationship came to a head. Without consulting Yvette nor me, my father decided I needed to go back to live with my mother. He found that the base at Kenitra was still operating, now in conjunction with the Moroccan, and that it still hosted a high school for military and diplomatic dependents. A bus even transported the embassy kids from the capital to the base, there and back daily 35 miles each way, he'd been told. As the dependent of a retired US military, I was enlisted while still in California, and that was that.

Third vignette- Déjà vu all over again, at KAHS

I was to enter my junior year when I arrived back in Rabat; maman now lived in a small apartment at the top of Avenue Mohamed V, a block from the railroad station and the King's Palace. Morocco and I had both moved away from France, and changed.

At 6:35 AM in August 1971 morning, a grey US Navy unmarked small bus, strangely out of place in the streets of Rabat, picked me up at the corner of avenue Alla Ben Abdellah and rue Benzart, the foot of my apartment building. Half-a-dozen strangely American teenage physiques sat strait-backed and silent in scattered formation. The young sailor at the wheel found his way through the oblique streets on this first day of school. With additional stops familiarity of returnees brought banter in the cabine. I remember Doug Smith and Brian Piantadosi, relative neighbors and seniors, being the firsts to carry on about something and the ice was broken. By the time we got on the road, past the bridge to Salé over the Oued Bou Regreg, with the romantic Kasbah des Oudayas overlooking Rabat beach at the North, I had begun my integration into US ex-pat society, an American boy and military brat in the land that had cradled the French colonial I had been before on these very roads.

We drove along Mehdia beach, under the large power lines that fed the comparatively large needs of the base, and I remembered seeing them as a little boy because of the large spheres that were strung along them so air traffic taking off and arriving into the base would have eyes on them. For odd reasons, that triggered my sense of familiarity with the place. When we pulled up to the military gates, those I had last seen raised by PM's as a small French boy whose mother had PX privileges, it all rushed back. The hospital on the hill, the parking lot, the Quonset huts that had disappeared from my visual vocabulary, the trotting Marines in formation, the strangely Americana scenes transposed as if misplaced in the land of fantasias, the sounds of jets from the runway, which I would rediscover behind the school. But I understood the words spoken, and shared roots with the people, and felt entitled. Soon my pliable adolescent heart left behind my relationship to Morocco as my grandparent's settlements, and I embraced it as an American teenager's excellent adventure.

The school, the bus, the life! This amazing little school brought us privileges and opportunities which seemed unbelievable to most children anywhere. As a member of the cross-country and tennis teams, I got to fly to Spain and Germany for meets on US bases in those countries. As a member of Mr. Seeke's flag football team (which I quit, for which I was shown shame), we got to play against adult Navy guys, had meet-ups like vs. Admin, or vs. Marines, or vs. Supply. I loved that so much effort was made to run the school as closely as possible to what a normal life in a small-town US high school would be: cheerleaders, homecoming, band, shop class and debate, the Sultan yearbook, dances and senior privileges, city council and pranks.

As students we gave little thoughts to the choices teachers had made to find themselves in this small Department of Defense Overseas Dependents School (DODDS). Yet in retrospect I'm amused to think of how so many of these folks had jumped at the opportunity to spend a couple of years in Morocco by taking a teaching gig. It was de rigueur for those who hungered for knowledge, like David Bass, who brought so much fresh air and nuance to our classrooms. I want to say that I have a lot of memories of our time together with Mr. Bass. One of many I might share with you: the way he would, during Art History lectures, refer us to a particular page in that voluminous text book which, in his own book, would be marked by a sheet or two of toilet paper. "I like to be comfortable when I prepare my lesson plan," he'd say as he snapped the flimsy paper out of its Bayeux tapestry page!

Then there were other excellent but more traditional teachers like Mr. Meyer, who taught government and history, and could have taught at any US school. What had he and his wife come to do, here, in Morocco, beside discover the Atlas? His contribution to my education was the singlemost useful little exercise anyone has every given me: pick an article from a leading periodical on current affairs, any article, and create a list of all of the impacts that this event would have on all levels and aspects of society, politics, economics and culture. The world is a set of dominoes, it forced me to observe, and I've used the skill throughout my life to predict trends and developments.

Base residents had a more confined world that I didn't know, because I never once spent a weekend there, and the base kids never came to Rabat. With all my base resident friends, I had primarily a school-ground relationship, save for the occasional trip to get a root beer at the PX. So friendships were built on the grass in front, or the park across the street. My mother did not have a phone in her apartment, so once I left the base, there was no interaction with those who lived there.

But there was one dramatic incident that directly linked the two poles of my life, the base and Rabat: the August 1972 coup d'etat against Hassan II. I had been on the base to pick up my senior year books and have some sort of orientation prior to the start of school. In the early afternoon, I had heard planes taking off from the base, though had not paid attention. As I was getting ready to get back to Rabat on the bus, the base was put on shut down. The bus got clearance to get through to drive the students back to Rabat. By the time we arrived, we understood the gravity of the situation. The Moroccan commander of the Kenitra base had been the right hand to the coup's leader, the Defense Minister General Oufkir. As Hassan II was returning from a trip to France, F-5 jets had taken off - from the same runway my father had once used - to intercept the royal Boeing. After taking fire, the king got on the radio and called out to the attacking pilots as if he'd been a friendly rebel on board the large jet and called out "Stop firing! The tyrant is dead!" Rebel jets escorted the royal plan...which landed safely in Rabat airport. In Rabat, tanks had taken to the streets and exchanges between rebel air forces and ground equipment pockmarked the façade of my apartment building, across from the military academy and one of the grand entrances to the Palace.

The rebels had taken the national radio station, and a street battle ensued. The bus amazingly avoided all of that and dropped several students off at the US Information Agency office, and others one block up at the door of my building, after which it could go no further. After nightfall, I needed to drive home one of my fellow students on the back of my 2-stroke 49cc motorbike. With no phone at my place, there was no way to let her parents know her whereabouts, so I needed to get her back to her house in the Hassan neighborhood toward the US Embassy. To do so, we had to ride right past the radio station, power center of the simmering fight. We ended up looking down the barrel of machine guns as we were ordered off the bike. A very tense long moment ensued. I had no idea which side of the fight these men were on, but all I could think of was that I could not let them know I was French.

Through the long daily rides, those on that bus became my community...Wade, Smith, Piantadosi, White, De Tarr, Slaoui, McSwain, Gourlay, Acosta, Mesfiwi, McCarthy, the names are like an old quilt blanket...a small clan of boys and girls with roots outside of the 50 states, most of whom were products of deep American culture but had lived in the US barely more years than I, and none as recently as I. These Rabat kids came from US families that had been on assignments across the globe, in years of post WWII expansion of American political influence. Many of their parents held jobs with titles that seemed legitimate, but which I understood later might in fact have been distractions for other government activities. These kids had moved around the globe, like me. As a boy without roots, I felt at home on this grey bus riding with them through this particular country.

Eighty miles each day through Morocco ties that bus gang together, through romances, fights, cramming sessions, songs and dances, pranks and impromptu happenings, like a hot spring late afternoon, travelling on the N1 back from the base, somewhere between Sidi Taibi and Bouknadel: our bus passed a crate truck filled with oranges on the two-lane highway. Majid Slaoui, who looked like a man in his 20's when the rest of us still had pimples, leaned out the window and screamed in authoritative Moroccan at the truck driver to pull over, which he promptly did. Then he told the young sailor, himself a teenager, to stop in front of the truck. On any given day, we were probably 18 or so in that bus, and all of us ran out and climbed on the truck to pick up oranges. As we got back on the road, of course an orange peel fight broke out.

Out of the bus, there were train trips to Marrakesh, lazy days in the souk, sipping mint tea at terraces overlooking the Mediterranean, and ski trips to Oukaimeden in the Atlas (where I once discovered a bunch of bumbling snowplowers all dressed in camouflage white on a lonely mountain face, only to find out it was the British mountaineering troups in training).

The music of the time was a mixture of Moroccan percussion, Elton John, the Moody Blues and Carly Simon, teenage guitar and drum sessions, and the newsreel fanfare before the featured movie started at the theatre (it was always about the King's activities, of course, as he was shadowed by this little boy, always dressed exactly like his father, who today is King Mohammed VI).

The seeming ease of the US diplomatic life in Rabat, to which I was exposed with rose-tinted glasses, inspired me such that I ended up going to the Georgetown School of Foreign service, intending to enroll into the State Department. That never happened, New York and Wall Street having eventually lured me with promise of greed satisfaction and easy access to Studio 54. My mother moved back to France to live in Antibes. The US Navy left Kenitra for good, and all roots seemed lost, save for our Moroccan school mates and one cute cheerleader from Florida that stayed behind. But the common appreciation of my follow Sultans for those fairy tale times have, thanks to the timely rise of electronic media, kept the smell of mint swirling in my head and the taste of tagines in my heart, inchallah!

Shoukran K'nitra, shoukran bezef

Philippe Hartley

What was your Favorite Hangout on the NTC Base in Kenitra, Morocco?

The Hilltop Club and that swimming pool!! Also; the outdoor theater!!! The swimming pool at the Hotel Mamora was also a great memory from the summer of 1971.

Robert Oberkehr

Loved the outdoor theater and the pool! Did competitive diving one summer! It was so fun!

JeanMarie Sample

Pool, Hilltop Club, Tennis Court/Racquet Ball Court, Oasis, Teen Club and, of course, Mehdia Beach.

Michele Fetterly

Everything Michelle said and indoor theatre.

Marguerite Golden Bright

Outdoor theater. Mehdia beach of course. Life-guarding at the pool was fun too.

Rhonda Thompson Driver

Pool and movie theaters!

Betty Slaughter Gurganus

Every day that they were open!

Gina Mantlo

Enlisted Men swimming pool! I perfected my belly flop off the high dive there...(not on purpose I might add)

Bill Simpkins

The pool, gym playing basketball and jumping on the trampoline. But my most unforgettable times were cycling around the base.

Mardy Navalta

At the pool I was on the synchronized swim team but any free time was at the Teen Club. Indoor or outdoor movies. Mom was always an officer of the NCO Wives Club so yep, there's a lot!

Gloria Kemery

The Oasis, Teen Club and library were my favs. Our library at Sidi was much smaller!

Kathy Myers Strange

All of the above plus the tennis courts!

Terri Spring

The Outdoor theater and the Halsey indoor theater!! I remember when they announced the moon landing at the Outdoor theater!! Also, my sister Maxine had their graduation there at the Outdoor theater in 1969.

Michele Fetterly

The bowling alley with the pin ball machines. The bowling pins were set up by hand, not machine. If you threw some dirham down the gutter the guys would help you bowl a great score! HA! It was fun bowling in the 230's and not even trying!!

Doug Campbell

I liked the bowling alley too. Sidi's only had 2 lanes. And I liked the Teen Club, pool, and movie theaters.

Kathy Sheppard

The Teen Club, the pool, and the Outdoor Theater.

Dean Longo

The pool when I was younger, the Oasis when I was a teen.

Kathleen Therese Campbell-Marble

The hill, Oasis, the roach canteen.

Ali El Mesfiwi

Teen Club, Pool, the Halsey and the outdoor theater.

Brenda Cozad Nutt

The only place I remember was "The Oasis"... I wasn't there too often but the times I was there I loved it.

Manfred Kramer

Teen Club for sure. Remember when the Carney's ran it? I still have a letter, on cork paper, that Lynn Carney wrote to me.

Viki Lasher

I guess I have to say the Oasis since I was only on base during school hours or after school events. Also, the bus ride to and from the base.

Mike McSwain

Me too - I think the bus rides were the best to and from Rabat.

Sheila Bright Roberts

Mehdia Beach, Teen Club, Pool, the Halsey and the outdoor theaters (in our backyard!) and my Flandria motorbike.

Bob Bennett

Plage de Mehdia! And the donut man!

Barbara Ford

YES!!! The donut guy was great, and the charcoal grill guy who had skewers of lamb chunks and a piece of flat bread for 1 dirham per skewer!

Bob Bennett

I loved those sugar donuts. After a while, I stopped telling my mother I was eating donuts and chicken sandwiches at the beach. She thought for sure I was going to die of food poisoning! I've eaten a lot worse since then.

Marguerite Golden Bright

You can still get the donuts. The Mehdia Beach really hasn't changed much over the years except the good restaurant in the Portuguese fortress is closed. For the dirt bikers, that area in the forest behind the beach is still there by the lake.

Nancy Lukas-Slaoui

Well off the base it was that little French pastry shop and that upstairs French salon where they took this gangly child and made her feel like a young lady.

Gloria Kemery

The outdoor theater!

Charlene Coke

Remember the apple tarts? Flaky pastry filled with some kind of vanilla creamy pudding and covered with thinly sliced apples and brushed with a sweet, light glaze? I can still taste them!

Viki Lasher

The base golf course. Hazel Parker and I could be found there any weekday morning. John David says I should tell the story of the Sunday golf tournament when I played on Captain Counihan's team...so here goes: The golf tournament that Sunday was a "team of four" format - man/woman/man/woman. Captain Counihan was head of the entire Port Lyautey base and he was rough and tough, to put it mildly. He saw me in the Commissary one day and approached me, saying "Do you want to play on the 'old man's' team Sunday?" I replied "Absolutely not, I'd drive you crazy. I'm the worst player on the base!" He said "Don't worry, I'll see that you get the best man player for your partner." And this was when we drew names out of a hat, but somehow Captain Counihan drew the best woman player (a 16-year-old daughter of a Marine officer) and I had the best man player....his first name was Bill as I recall. the Captain insisted that I play, so I gave in. I managed to hang in on the first two holes and the #3 hole was a par 3. My partner, Bill, made a magnificent drive, actually hitting the green, but unfortunately it was on a steep, straight up and down "cliff" and the ball rolled down and dropped straight down into a sand trap. I knew it was hopeless, so I just hit the ball as hard as I could and lo and behold, the ball tipped the green and rolled down to 5 inches from the cup. Captain Counihan cursed a blue streak and yelled "That's the best #$% &+#$% damn golf shot I've ever seen in my entire life!" But that's Golf.

Joan Ellen Bernard

Teen Club, then pool!

Cece Canton

The Oasis, and it was still there at [2000] reunion!

Chloe Camry

The 1973 Yearbook

Administration: CAPT Joe F. Lasseter, Jr., USN (Base Commander); CAPT C. L. Staigle, USMC (School's Officer) and Mr. Ernest M. Morgan (Principal).

Faculty & Staff: Faculty: Miss Bonnie Crumpler; Miss Karen New; Miss Susan Ervin; Mr. John Forster; Mr. Gerald Curran; Mr. Courtlandt C. Kauffman; Liz McSween; Mr. Pablo Mares; Miss Michele Barsodi; Fred Myer; Philip Miletich; James Seeke; Nancy Terry; Miss Sandra Weary; Mrs. Janice Sellak; and Mr. David Bass. **Staff:** Marjorie Cosson; Phyllis Coomber; Kathy Lowry; Mrs. Ernest M. Morgan; and Louis Richwald.

The 29 graduating Seniors of 1973: Philippe Hartley (President); Chakib Loudiyi (Vice-President); Nancy Lukas (Secretary); Dan Iwata (Treasurer); Maria Socorro Acosta; Robert Angelo; Nadia Assed; Salah Assed; Saad Bennani; Faraj Benwahoud; Deana Marie Bowden; Gayle Bowden; Michael Dugan; Aun Faizuliabhoy; Joanna Fuller; Deborah Gerth; Chantal Gourlay; Teressa Knowles; Peter L'Heureux; Peggy McCarthy; Mike McSwain; Steve Meadows; Gary Migliacci; Susan Reason; Mona Riley; Michael Senf; Abdelmajed Slaoui; Kevin Smallwood; and Sandy White.

Class of 1974

1974 saw the IRA begin a bombing campaign on mainland Britain - bombing the Tower of London on July 17th and the Houses of Parliament and pubs in Birmingham. Following Watergate Scandal impeachment hearings started on May 9th, Richard Nixon becomes the first US president forced to resign. He did so on August 9th. On October 30th, the much-hyped boxing match between George Foreman and Muhammad Ali (for Ali to regain his heavyweight title) takes place in Kinshasa, Zaire (Democratic Republic of the Congo). The Kootenai Native American Tribe in Idaho declares war on the United States. Stephen King, a 26-year-old author, published his debut novel "Carrie," during April of 1974. The 55 MPH Speed Limit was imposed to preserve gas usage US-wide. The Sears Tower in Chicago became the world's tallest building. The World's Population reaches 4 billion. In Morocco, Moroccan athlete Hicham El Guerrouj was born on September 14. In August 1974, Spain formally acknowledged the 1966 United Nations (UN) resolution calling for a referendum on the future status of the Western Sahara and requested that a plebiscite be conducted under UN supervision. A UN visiting mission reported in October 1975 that an overwhelming majority of the Saharan people desired independence. Morocco protested the proposed referendum and took its case to the International Court of Justice at The Hague, which ruled that despite historical "ties of allegiance" between Morocco and the tribes of Western Sahara, there was no legal justification for departing from the UN position on self-determination. Spain, meanwhile, had declared that even in the absence of a referendum, it intended to surrender political control of Western Sahara; meanwhile Spain, Morocco, and Mauritania convened a tripartite conference to resolve the territory's future.

I Remember:

As the years fade away, and my memory fails me, I frequently reflect back to the days I remember most vividly. It was a short period of time of no more than 24 months. I pack a lifetime of memories worth reliving every 2 years or so at every Kenitra American High School reunion. The stories get livelier and embellished a little more as I retell the memories of my youth.

We lived on the base from 1970-1972 and I would have been Class of '74. We first lived in the Quonset huts across from the parade grounds that were directly in front of the school and later moved in the house across from the Exchange.

What I remember most are the number of "first's" in my life.

My parents gave me my first real independence. I was given permission to do and go just about anywhere I wanted to go. Looking back on this freedom, I did not realize the gift I was handed. I was in a foreign country but my parents were smarter than I thought they were. I was given the freedom but had no money or job. I was only 16. So I stayed close to home like most of my friends. I spent many hours on the back of a Flandria tooling to and from Mehdia Beach. Today, I find that I seek out beaches wherever I go. Sitting in my beach chair, I just close my eyes, feel the wind and sun on my face and think about Crosby, Stills, Nash and Young's music in my head. I'm transported back in time where I'm greased in baby oil, decked out in a red and white polka dotted bikini (I'm sure it was itsy bitsy too!). The sounds of the surf crashing on the shore are so vivid. I think it's because the surf sounds the same at most beaches. The taste of those sugar donuts sold by barefooted vendors approaching every red-faced teenager along the beach shore have never been duplicated in my life's travels. I remember they never dropped a single donut in the sand.

I remember going to my first "R" rated film at the outdoor theater on the base (M*A*S*H*). If was our gathering place every summer night. The Moroccan soldiers occupied about a third of the outdoor venue and smoked strong-scented cigarettes. The cigarettes had such an unusual smell. It was like a cross between geraniums and gas station hand soap. Smells bring back memories. I would like to smell those cigarettes just one more time. We would walk to the open-air theater with our blankets. We would sit next to our boy (friends) on the ground at the back of the theater. This is where I had my first really noteworthy "make out session." Since this is not a "tell all" memoir, no names will be mentioned but I innocently want to thank a couple members of the wrestling team for their continued efforts to mold me into the "kisser" I am today.

I remember the first time I dove in the base pool and attempted to swim underwater the whole length of that Olympic sized pool. I was not successful. Eventually, I tried enough times that I would swim that pool many times. Even today, I still enjoy swimming a couple of times a week. I can solve all the world's problems with my head under the water. I hear nothing but the pounding of my heartbeat in my ears. It's like waking from a dream. When I get out of the pool, I don't remember what problems I solved. So every day is new to me. The problems of yesterday are new today for me to think about.

I learned to play tennis. I'd like to think I can still play but I'm also of the mindset where I think I can stand on my head or do cartwheels too! Really, it's all in my head. It was at Kenitra that I saw a buxom sister of a friend of mine on the tennis courts, running a very good game. She was going one way and her boobs another. She probably thought she had a killer game going on with the crowds that were gathering but no one wanted to tell her that even though braless was the fashion statement in the 70's...braless on the tennis court was a whole other game. We all silently thank the inventors of sports bras today.

We used to fill up our metal tennis ball cans with 'water fountain' water and bring it to the tennis courts to drink. No pesky water bottles for us. Today, I would find it appalling to drink water from a fountain. This is what we did before bottled water and no one cared or gave it a second thought. How are we still standing?

I remember never making my bed. We had a lovely "Fatima" named Zanib. She came to us in our first weeks at the Mamora Hotel. We all cried when we said goodbye to her 2 years later. Looking back, she was a wonderful, caring person. She never said or did an unkind thing to our family. Instead, she faithfully came to work 6 days a week and made my bed. Our house was never dirty because my mom kept a nice house so I'm thinking Zanib thought it was a pretty good arrangement too. I remember she would take time for herself every day and take a bath. She did not have a bathtub where she lived and enjoyed this part of the day. She cooked the best food. My mother was a terrible cook. Those two years of Zanib's cooking was like eating at a restaurant every night. It was like being at Club Med every day. We all learned from Zanib's dedication and love. She showed me that cultural differences bring families together. Thank you Zanib. You left an impact on me in a way you will never know.

I developed my love of the sciences at school. I "pithed" frogs, grew bacteria in petri dishes, looked under microscopes, gathered insects and studied anatomy. I'm still curious like that. I like looking at innards and seeing how things work. Thank you, Bonnie Crumpler, for awakening that question mark in my head. You answered all my questions with confidence and ease. You never know as a person how you are going to impact another person's life. She left her lasting imprint of science on me.

I developed lifelong friendships. I had started collecting "friends" years before coming to Africa, but I collected my favorite friends while gathering shells on the beach, marching in my first homecoming parade and eating French fries dipped in mayonnaise at the Oasis café. These friends I do not see often enough. The bond of these friends is stronger than I can describe. At every reunion I attend, we pick up right where we left off. We are 16 again, youthful and full of promise. We have a common bond of growing up together. Every Kenitra alumni knows what I'm talking about. Every person at the reunion is my new "best" friend. Even if I only knew them as acquaintances in high school, they are more than that at the end of each reunion.

Lastly, I experienced falling in love and the first of many broken hearts. I recovered to only have it happen many more times. Having 2 sisters and raising 3 girls meant this would happen more times than I cared to count. In our family, the only way to mend a broken heart is to go shoe shopping. Sometimes, I would just get a nudge and a tear from one of my daughters and everything seemed better with a new pair of shoes to look at. This, along with the promise that things would get better and it's his "loss." My daughters have tons of shoes. Shoes are good for the soul. Shoes build character. In our family, shoes help mend broken hearts.

I know now that boys are fragile. I learned that lesson from Mr. Wonderful. He has since made sure our 3 girls are aware of this fact. I cluelessly ignored Mr. Wonderful in high school and if he hadn't "schooled" me in the emotional vulnerability of young teenage boys, I might have missed out on the best part of my life. He told me that the handsome guy that wouldn't talk to me probably had a crush on me. He wasn't being rude, but awkwardly shy. The lesson he taught me and continues to pass along to the young women we have raised is to smile, be kind and positive to those quiet boys because, those shy boys become confident men.

So later in life, that quiet shy boy who sat behind me in Miss Ervin's English class, who played Romeo to my Juliet in our class play, grew up to be my soulmate. Even today, he tells me that when he sat in the desk behind me all those years ago, he knew we were destined to be together. He told himself that all he had to do was be patient. Patience is a virtue. His patience paid off. This girl did talk to that shy boy and my heart was never broken again. His imprint on me is everlasting even today.

Marguerite Golden Bright

My father was stationed in Morocco on NCTC Kenitra for 3-and-a-half years from 1971 to 1974. I and my sister were students at the elementary school there. I enjoyed living overseas and the time in Morocco has totally changed the way I look at the world.

Michael Overboe

It is funny how small the world can be. Since I left Morocco in 1974, I have run into one person that knew somebody I knew in Morocco (a student of mine that had been to Morocco with her father who was on business and met the person that I sold my horse to…) and later through the website, I emailed someone I was friends with in Morocco, whose brother actually lives less than 5 minutes from my house…. I guess we learn about the 6 degrees of separation…

Nellie (Hoffman) Mills

In October 1974, we arrived at Mohammed V Airport in Casablanca bound for NCS Sidi Yahia, a small, isolated Cold War-era outpost located about twelve miles inland from Naval Air Station Kenitra (Port Lyautey) in western Morocco. The base, which opened in the mid-1950's, was located just east of the village of Sidi Yahia el Gharb on Highway N4. To ease the tension with Russian and other Muslim countries Sidi Yahia (and the other American bases) was actually dubbed a Moroccan training center and its American military occupants were "instructors." To add to the legitimacy American flags were not flown outdoors except on special occasions. In the past the country had also played host to several U.S. Air Force SAC installations including Sidi Slimane, El Nouasseur, and Ben Guerir.

NCS Sidi Yahia had a small main area with housing surrounded by a massive antenna field. The U.S. Navy utilized the small base, as a receiving station in conjunction with a transmitting station at nearby NCS Bouknadel, to maintain secure communications with the assets of the U.S. Sixth Fleet. I'm sure these bases were also utilized to keep tabs on Russian naval traffic entering and exiting the Mediterranean Sea through the Straits of Gibraltar. The sprawling bases totaled 4,800 acres of land. The country had also played host to several former U.S. Air Force SAC installations including Sidi Slimane, El Nouasseur, and Ben Guerir.

Outside of NCS Sidi Yahia sat a local pulp (paper) factory, which my dad said was used as a front for a Russian surveillance operation that kept tabs on the nearby American presence. This facility, which went into operation in 1957, is still visible (with its stacks of lumber) on satellite maps if you look directly north of the base.

I attended the second grade on base in a small schoolhouse divided into four rooms and known as Sanford G. Hooper Primary School. I believe the older kids were bused to nearby NAS Kenitra for classes at other schools including Thomas Mack Wilhoite High School.

Like pretty much every family we had a Fatima or maid who helped out around the house. The Fatimas, who were screened to work on the base, were dropped off by a bus at the front gate of the base every morning. Most of them served as in-house maids but others worked at the exchange, bowling alley, or movie theater. Our first Fatima was a rather large woman who did not speak much English. My mom believed she may have stolen money from the house so before long we had a second Fatima. Her name was "Asha," she was twenty-nine years old, spoke fluid English, and was quite pretty. My mom really liked her. Asha was married at age twelve and had nine kids - the first one at age thirteen! She was paid $2 a day as was the norm and did general cleaning and cooking around the house. My mom would give her food and clothes at times but would have to write a note for her so she could take the items off base.

Other things I remember from Sidi Yahia include the German Shepherds and their U.S. Marine handlers that guarded our base, watching my parents play tennis, listening to Suzi Quatro songs at the Fourth of July base picnic, learning the French phrase tout de suite, going to the on-base movie theater, going without TV for six months, collecting American comic books, the terrifying haunted house on the parade grounds during Halloween, an unusual weekend fishing outing to a secluded lake in the Atlas Mountains, eating French Brochettes (which my family still loves today!), and roaming around our small base with my friends.

When we first arrived the American military presence in Morocco was already being phased out due to advances in satellite communications. I think the alliance with the Moroccan king and his ministers was weakening as well. We departed even earlier than expected and were only in Morocco for six months. NCS Sidi Yahia was vacated by the end of 1977 and is currently under strict control of the Moroccan Royal Air Force.

Jeff Bales, Jr.

I remember Mehdia Beach! In 1973 or 74, on a very hot day on the bus going home from Kenitra to Rabat after school, Tex the bus driver accedes to a chorus of demands to stop at the beach. So Tex detours from his usual route and exits toward Mehdia Beach. We arrive at the beach streaming out of the bus and running into the ocean fully clothed. After dousing ourselves in the warm waters, back on the bus soaking wet and onward to Rabat.

I remember the Drama Team! In 1973, Peter L'Heureux and I take our one-act play to Rota, Spain, as part of the KAHS drama team. I am Ann Bolynn and Peter is Henry the VIII. We have done this play so many times. I think I am very eloquent, but I still get put in the Tower of London and lose my head.

And I remember Mr. Meyer! In 1973-74, Mr. Meyer, the US history teacher and tennis coach, kept us fit on the tennis team by having us run around the base three times a week and then tennis practice on the Kenitra courts the other two days. In his own games, Mr. Meyer has an inspiring assortment of colorful headbands that he switched out between games to psych out his opponents. A quote of his that sticks in my head, "Tennis is 10% physical and 90% psychological."

Margaret "Maggie" Gourlay

I am Manfred Kramer and I would have been from the Class of 1974 like Marguerite (Golden) Bright, Bob Bright and Warren Boomer. I was there my freshman/sophomore years between 1970 and 1972. I had the name Manfred K. Vogel back then because my stepfather (whose name was Vogel of course!) didn't want too many people asking too many questions (Never really understood that part, but that's what they told me back then).

I remember one another German boy in the same class – one Wolfgang Schober. He was the son of the German cultural attaché at the time (I think). We became friends then before he left the next year. I was a bit jealous of him because he was a very suave guy who was very popular with the girls while I was rather brash and somewhat coarse/blunt in comparison.

We lived in Rabat at the time. Every morning I was picked up by that yellow schoolbus and then – after about a half hour of picking up the other students in the city, the bus set off for Kenitra where we arrived about half an hour later.

One of my earliest memories was the fact that I had quite a difficult time at the beginning understanding the American variant of English. I remember how surprised I was that I – who had spent two years in an English-speaking school in Ghana(!) could barely understand this "chewing-gum" English being spoken by the students and teachers at KAHS.

Anyway, I adjusted quickly and found out soon that this little school was a very good one, with well-behaved classmates and dedicated teachers. I have – with just one small exception – only fond memories of my time there.

I remember, for example, my teacher Miss Thompson. She taught me Geography. I remember her especially for two things. One: She had this regime of constant feedback with quizzes, tests and exams. That was her method of making sure that we remembered the stuff she taught us. This was – I think – on a daily basis. At the time I suffered quite a bit from exam nerves. This constant testing made me lose my exam nerves bit by bit. She literally desensitized me with this constant barrage of little quizzes and tests. I am still grateful to her for that! In later years this would help me greatly in keeping my cool in other (more weighty) testing situations. The other thing I remember her for was an observation I made about the clothes she wore: She was, what one would call today, a real "fashionista". She NEVER wore the same dress twice! I remember that I was quite intrigued by that. There was no other woman (or girl) in the whole school who did this. Most other teachers, male or female, had their favourite attire which they would only vary slightly. The men, especially, had the least variety in their style of clothing. Mr. Kaufmann for example (my math teacher and one of the best I ever had!) always wore white shirts with a tie with either grey/beige or black-colored trousers. Miss Kowalski, my French teacher, was in love with costumes and cardigans and also seemed to have a large assortment of elaborately formed spectacles in all kinds of colors. What I liked about Miss Kowalski was her unconventional approach to teaching a language. We didn't just learn the words and the grammar. She would make it a point of bringing us closer to the culture of the French "savoir vivre". We would learn French songs, learn a bit or two about the history, the food and the society. That was quite unusual for me at the time.

This is one of the details I still have very vivid in my memory: The quality of the teachers. Their dedication and their creativity in teaching us was quite extraordinary. Not before and not after that particular time had I met such amazingly engaged teachers. You see: When I finally made my (German) "high school diploma" (the so-called "Abitur" which you attain after a minimum of 13 years on german secondary schools) in 1977, I had been through exactly 10 schools on three continents with three different school systems (the German, the British – West-African – and the American system). So, I had some background to compare...

Let me say it again, without any exaggeration or glossing over: KAHS was the best school of them all! If I had to name a handful of teachers which have impressed me of being the best I ever had during my whole school days the majority of those would be teachers from that school. I have given you some names already above. Those three were not the only ones by the way. There was also our English teacher, Mr. Stoeberl, who made a very good class in telling us about Shakespeare's "Romeo and Juliet," where he encouraged us to replay certain scenes. I remember one scene where Marguerite Golden played "Juliet" and Bob Bright played "Romeo." Little did they know that years later they would become a pair too! I played "Mercutio" rather lamely – but that was to be expected. I have been, I am and will always be: A lousy actor! Also we read "Julius Caesar" and (with much groaning from most of the class) the "Illiad." Mr. Stoeberl would push us to try our best to comprehend what was really going on in those masterpieces of times gone past and it is to his credit that he invoked an interest in literature in me which I hadn't felt before.

Also there was my math teacher, Mr. Courtlandt Kauffman, who I remembered had a seemingly inhuman amount of patience with us. I was never too good at math really. After about half a year in his class I was rapidly getting much better. You could ask this guy really anything, anytime, and he would always give you a patient and detailed answer. This man got rid of my fear of math once and for all just by being patient and empathetic.

Another thing that impressed me a lot were the social acitivities in that school. Every class seemed to be involved in all kinds of parties, "sock hops", cake-sales etc. I never experienced that before in any of my previous schools. Those were a bit more conservative times (and schools) where I was before. The scope of participation in daily school life was really something special to me. I was delighted! Although I was way too uptight to fully enjoy all these activities, I was nevertheless charmed by the laid-back style of it all!

I mentioned one "small exception" which in hindsight was not really that negative – just weird. It's a small story but at the time really jolted my not very well-developed self-esteem. Anyway, here goes: Our class once decided that they wanted to hold a "Slave-Sale." Everybody thought it was a great idea that would flush some money into our notoriously near-empty class cash register. We debated for some time which rules should govern this whole endeavor. It was, for example, set down that one would only be a "slave" for a day and within certain behavioral boundaries. It was decided that there must not be any abuse of any kind. Any "slave" could refuse to do something which would go against his/her morality or cultural identity (whatever that means).

And so the day came: In the assembly hall the whole school was there to appraise the "slaves" who were all members of our class. One older student played the auctioneer and began selling us off. To be brief: It was a smash. With a lot of ballyhoo and hooting from all sides, all "slaves" were successfully sold. Majid Slaoui, a student one or two classes higher than me, "bought" me for $2.50. The next day I would be his "slave" for the whole school day and would have to follow his biddings. Little did I know what awaited me...

The next day Slaoui intercepted me before I made it to Miss Thompson's class. He shuffled me to the boy's toilet and opened a bag. In it were some girl's clothes. He told me that I should undress and wear those instead. From what I remembered there was one pink Tutu and some glitzy blouse. He actually wanted me to get rid of my trousers and wear this flimsy Tutu, but that's where he hit my personal bounderies. I was already quite shocked but not that shocked. I told him in no uncertain terms that I would certainly not get rid of my jeans and he'd either accept that I wear this Tutu over my jeans or not at all. I was quite defiant over this detail. He finally accepted, teeth grinding. You can imagine the giggling and hooting when I entered class with this outfit. I was quite embarassed and everybody could read that off my face. When break-time came Mr. Slaoui took me to the "Oasis" where running the gauntlet continued. I had to get him all kinds of stuff and serve it to him at the table. He really seemed to enjoy my embarrassment. During other break-times he would make me run a couple of laps on the athletic grounds. Also, he enjoyed watching me doing the sit-ups and push-ups he asked for.

Man, that guy sure seemed to have the time of his life... I was really quite glad when it was all over. I was actually even a bit proud of myself that I didn't give up and thus reduce my class' cash by $2.50. I am sure a lot of people were quite amused seeing me like this... When I saw pictures of Majid from the Santa Fe reunion I remembered this little story about the two of us. I realized that I had a smile on my face when his pictures reminded me of this only bit of common experience between us. You see, apart from this little adventure we hardly really interacted with each other. He was just another student in the school. Of course, I don't hold any old grudges against him, although I would still like to ask him today: "Why did you pick on me!!?"

Manfred Kramer

The 1974 Yearbook

Administration: CAPT Joe F. Lasseter, Jr., USN (Base Commander); CDR R. E. Bentley, USN (Schools' Officer); and Ernest M. Morgan (School Principal).

Faculty & Staff: Faculty: Mr. Frederic Meyer; Liz McSween; Carol McQuistion; Karen Moujjen; Linda Myers; Dale Nichols; Janice Sellak; Michele Barsodi; Pat Blake; Mary Byars; James Corey; Howard Dearing; John Forster; and Courtlandt C. Kauffman. **Staff:** Marjorie Cosson (Secretary)

The 18 graduating Seniors of 1974: Tony Collins (President); Latifa Louise Sefiane (Vice-President); Mark Roberts (Secretary); Warren Boomer (Treasurer); Mona Al-Mudhaf; Houssine Benjelloun; Haluk Binkaya; Abbie Cogan; Charles Croker; Walter Cosson; Charles De Tarr; Margaret "Maggie" Gourlay; Malika Hammoumi; Ramin Khoshatefeh; Randy Kiddy; Dennis Migliacci; Rene Morgan; and Rhonda Thompson.

CLASS OF 1975

1975 saw inflation in the UK continue to spiral out of control reaching 24.2% - the price of gas increased by nearly 70% in one year, but the US sees its inflation decrease to 9.2%, both governments use interest rates as a way of trying to control inflation with the US Federal Reserve at 7.25% and The Bank of England at 11.25%. Meanwhile, one of the true success stories of modern times begins when Bill Gates and Paul Allen create the company Microsoft. The first of the new hobby computers are starting to appear including Altair 8800 and the battle for video recorder standards (VHS vs. Betamax) starts. This is also the year the Vietnam war finally ends. 1975 saw the first disposable razor, Jimmy Hoffa (the ex-Teamsters boss) disappears, the Suez Canal reopens, and Dutch elm disease decimates elm trees in the UK. In Morocco, on September 9, a chartered Boeing 707 crashes in the Atlas Mountains and 188 die. On November 6 King Hassan orders 350,000 civilian volunteers to cross into Spanish Sahara in what was called The Green March. On November 14 Spain, Morocco and Mauritania sign an accord about the Spanish Sahara. In December Spain agreed to leave Spanish Sahara, soon to become Western Sahara, and to transfer it to joint Moroccan-Mauritanian control. Algeria objected and threatened military intervention; Moroccan forces entered and occupied the territory. The Moroccan-Indian actress Laila Rouass was born on June 22.

I Remember:

I lived on base in Kenitra from 1967-1969. Dad (Dick Mantlo) was in Supply. We lived up from the grade school and across the street from the Pirrachi's. Mom (Judy Mantlo) worked in the library near the Oasis and across from the mini-golf. Many of my favorite childhood memories were of Morocco: adventures in the Captain's gardens, experiencing an earthquake, buying a kilo of potassium nitrate for a quarter (to make gunpowder), finding a skeleton, and camping by the Sabu eating old K-rations. We watched the moon landing on a 6-inch TV with a several yard-long tin foil antenna and listened to the audio on the American Armed Forces radio.

Nathan Mantlo Class of '75

Lived in Kenitra in a Villa from 71-74. Then moved into new housing on the base. Dad ran the Pharmacy, Mom worked at the Exchange. Brother Steven graduated in 72, I graduated in 75. Brother Greg and sister Linda also went to school there. We loved Morocco. It was a wonderful experience for our family and I wouldn't take anything for it! I am delighted that we are getting in touch with each other again!

JeanMarie Branch Sample

Lived in Rabat from 1969 to 1973. Attended 9th and 10th grade at KAHS. I am Sandy Bartell's (Class of 1972) younger brother.

Tom White '75

I was Class of '75. We lived in town in Kenitra '70 – '72. Dad was a CTR stationed at Sidi Yahia.

Ted Miller

I arrived in Morocco in 1972 and left after graduating from Kenitra American High School in 1975. I lived in Rabat in a neighborhood called Souissi out the Route De Zaire on the way to the King's golf course, Dar Es Salam. I spent many hours riding the bus to and from Kenitra for school and made so many great friends on that bus! It was almost a magical time for me. I don't know if it was because of the difference in the culture, or that I lived there during those formative years on the cusp of becoming an adult, or that it was where I met my first true love whom I later married, but Morocco has always had a special place in my heart. I have only been back twice but hope to go again before I'm too old to travel that far!

Some of my fondest memories include going to see movies at the Cinema Za'wa, shopping in the Medina, drinking green tea at the Kasbah Des Oudayas, eating beignets on Mehdia beach, dancing at La Cage and downing espressos at La Jour et Nuit, gorging on pizzas at La Mamma's and having Noisette gelato afterwards at La Dolce Vita, riding on the back of Guy's Honda 50 and hanging out with some of the coolest people and listening to the best music ever! I also remember cheering on our flag football teams and going to school dances with the disco ball twirling and eating lunches at The Oasis listening to the Bee Gees on the jukebox. Those three short years I spent in Morocco had a huge impact on the person I am today and I wouldn't trade them for anything!

Leigh (Crocker) McSwain

The 1975 Yearbook

Administration: CAPT William I. Parrish, USN (Base Commander); CDR R. E. Bentley, USN (School's Officer); and Ernest M. Morgan (School Principal).

Faculty & Staff: Faculty: Kitty Miller; Karen Moujjen; Dale Nichols; Steve Osborne; Betty Rebarick ; Janice Sellak; and John Vecchio. **Staff:** Marjorie Cosson (School Secretary); and Alice Carter (School Supply).

The 33 graduating Seniors of 1975: Leigh Crocker (President); Ali Mesfioui (Vice-President); Terri Sanders (Secretary); Guy McSwain (Treasurer); May Al-Mudhaf; Edward Arnold; Wafa Al-Karbouli; Khalid Assed; Bennaissa Benaghmouch; Saud Assed; Driss Benslimane; Jean Branch; Sunyong Choi; Abedl Ilah Hajji; Abdeslem Houmina; Gordon Knowles; Bob Howard; Khalid Loudiyi; Miriam Mestoura; Zahara Mestoura; Khalid M'Rabet; Glenna Murdock; Hassan Rachidi; Driss Najidi; Magdalena Rybinska; Witold Rybinska; Nejma Sefiane; Habiba Barbara Sefiane; Nora Sefiane; Rachida Sefiane; Noria Slaoui; Tony Taylor; and Vicky Clauch.

CLASS OF 1976

1976 saw inflation continue to be a problem around the world. The supersonic Concorde entered commercial service and cut transatlantic flying time to 3 1/2 hours. One year after Microsoft is formed Apple is formed by Steve Jobs and Steve Wozniak. Nadia Comaneci scores the first ever perfect score in Gymnastics. In South Africa riots in Soweto on June 16th mark the beginning of the end of apartheid. In music the first of the Punk Bands appear The Damned. Major News Stories include NASA unveils the first space shuttle, Fidel Castro becomes President of Cuba, the US $2.00 bill was issued, Notting Hill Carnival Riots, Cod Wars between Iceland and UK, United States Bicentennial celebrations, and the first encounter with Legionnaires Disease. In early 1976, Spain ceded the administration of the Western Sahara to Morocco and Mauritania. Morocco assumed control over the northern two-thirds of the territory and conceded the remaining portion in the south to Mauritania. An assembly of Saharan tribal leaders duly acknowledged Moroccan sovereignty. However, buoyed by the increasing defection of tribal chiefs to its cause, the Polisario drew up a constitution, and announced the formation of the Saharawi Arab Democratic Republic (SADR), and itself formed government-in-exile. The Moroccan government eventually sent a large portion of its combat forces into Western Sahara to confront the Polisario's forces, which were relatively small but well-equipped, highly mobile, and resourceful. The Polisario used Algerian bases for quick strikes against targets deep inside Morocco and Mauritania, as well as for operations in Western Sahara. In August 1979, after suffering military losses, Mauritania renounced its claim to Western Sahara and signed a peace treaty with the Polisario. Morocco then annexed the entire territory and, in 1985 built a 2,500-kilometer sand berm around three-quarters of Western Sahara.

I Remember:

I was Susan Walker and I was in Morocco from '68 to '71. Attended the Elementary School for 5th and 6th grade then on to TMW for 7th grade. I would have been in the class of 76. We lived in a hotel in town for a few months then moved on to base down the street from the Elementary School. Returned to States and finished school in Pensacola, Florida where my dad was stationed until retirement.

Susan Walker Powell

My father is Moroccan and retired with his family in Lawrence, KS. I was there when the school closed in 1976. Actually, they had planned to close the school in 1975 but at the last moment decided to keep it open one more year. This meant scurrying about trying to get all the needed books, etc., for another year of high school. I would have been KAHS Class of '78.

Karima Zhiri

I was Class of '76, in country between 1969 and 1973. Went from the Astor, to a very nice villa in Kenitra, to base housing right near the base hospital. Fantastic four years for a kid turning into a teenager!

Steven Finster

I am Carmen Hedges (Carmen Acosta) sister to Aristeo Acosta ('77), George Acosta ('75), Socorro Truchan ('73), and Carlos Acosta ('72). I would have graduated from KAHS in ('76) but we left after I went through freshman year. Arriving in Morocco made me a better person. I learned about other cultures as well as life, at an age when most teenagers are getting jobs or going to friends' houses. In a nutshell I am grateful and have good memories of living in a new continent. I look back and am grateful for it, yet I was quite happy when we came back to the USA. I remember the Medina and the stores downtown. It seemed like an oasis when I walked in the stores and would see the inside patios and decorations unique to this land. I also remember the local cuisine, harira soup, cheeses, fruits, breads, meats. So different from the food I was used to eating, going to the local bread ovens was such a learning experience! I was living a life I hadn't planned on, yet it made sense to understand it, for it was a different place and time that today any teenager gets to live – starting with studying in a different system altogether, making friends from different countries, and different homes, transportation, food and language. I was in for a big change! We lived in Rabat and attended RAS [Rabat American School] before KAHS. My first year was tough for I had no friends and communicated in a school with other cultures. I used to have a bilingual education, with classes in both Spanish and English; these were the only languages I knew. Here the local culture was Moroccan and I had no knowledge of the French or Arabic language! I was going to have to learn French to communicate with local people. I remember when we first arrived. We stayed at the Tour Hassan hotel and we rode the yellow school bus to school. It seemed like such a change from my usual walk to school! The KAHS Years were very different for not only did we have a pass to enter the base but we only knew it as students. So all of the classes were in English but speaking only English made it different for me. I looked forward to dinner time at home just to hear about everyone else's day in my family. I look forward to catching up with some of my classmates when I am able to meet up. I hope this may help those that had a similar experience share their own.

Carmen Hedges (Carmen Acosta)

Attended KAHS from '74-'76. Lived on "Captain's Row", just up the hill from the school. Transferred to Rota after KAHS (boo), but returned to the base for the closure ceremonies :(

Scott Coppess

It really was a great place to be a kid...I was so angry (and still am!) when they closed the high school and I had to come back early...wished I'd opted for boarding school in Zaragoza instead. Woulda, shoulda, coulda...dumb kid! Anyone remember the store outside the Base run by the man everyone called "Barney the Jew"? I just loved that man; he was always so nice to me, so friendly and liked to tease me a lot about haggling with me. He always told my parents "she's the Jew, not me". I always knew it was just his salesman schtick and there was no way I was getting anything past him, but he was so much fun. I was a really tiny thing and had blond hair and green eyes...my mother always made me go to Town with her when she went shopping because the shop owners and the merchants in the medina always gave me things. (But never Barney the Jew--haha, he never gave me anything free.) There was a merchant just inside the door of the medina, an old man (seemed old at the time, he was probably only 60 or so) -- he was on the right as you went in. He gave me so many things, mostly toys like camels and Berber dolls--I still have some, one camel and a Berber water merchant are my faves. He also gave me a ton of bracelets and necklaces. We all 3 loved going to town so much. So were constantly there so we got to know so many of the merchants and shopkeepers. The more we came, the more gifts they gave me. For some reason they were nuts about my hair and eyes. Our Fatima Habiba was always telling me they were trying to buy me from my parents...never doubted her and I still don't, haha. They were always talking to my parents but giving me the goodies, loved it--but I sure wasn't going to town by myself--I was taking "at least" a friend, even if there wasn't an adult, dumb kid me just felt safer. I Realize now that there were so many times I seriously could have been grabbed and gone. But I was smart enough to know to never go to certain places in town without Habiba. We lived across the street from the elementary school. Habiba always got onto me for going into town without her or my parents. She kept telling me someone was going to "steal" me & sell me. Definitely always believed her, she was not teasing me. But was stupid enough (and fortunate enough) that that never happened. Probably more like enough people knew me and liked me so that was why I was safe. For some odd reason Mother never believed her up to the day she died, she always thought it was so funny and a big joke. Habiba would get so upset with her and kept telling her not to let me go to town without one of them, but, she always did. She, I guess, just was really naive about it. She had been a very protected way-out-in-the-country girl growing up, was always convinced everyone was her friend and no one would hurt her. She was also convinced that because we were American, everyone loved us and would never do anything to us. Shook my head at that then and still do now. I just knew instinctively that the way Habiba acted about it, she was dead serious, dumb kid or not.

Betty Linda Johnston DeGrauwe

Do You Remember Adjusting to Life After Morocco?

I missed the rise of the hippie/"long hair on men" generation. So imagine my confusion when Daddy had a porter taking our luggage through JFK whose hair was longer than mine. Daddy got stopped to clear our cat through agriculture, but the porter kept going so I had to chase him down. Only thing is I was doing it in French and called him Mademoiselle.

Deborah Robin Kafir

To this day (I graduated TMW class of '60), when asked where I am from, I just answer "I am a Proud Military Brat!" It's a lot easier and has started lots of interesting conversations and friends.

Patricia Thomas Elliott

For me there was no adjustment at all. I graduated and came back to the States. My graduation present was a Greyhound Bus ticket "All You Can Ride" and I spent the summer riding all over the USA on my own. I think it was a 90-day ticket and I guess they don't do that anymore. Can you imagine letting a teenager do that today? It was the greatest gift ever! Then off to college... I was heading to the University of Kansas and I was on my own - another grand adventure! What I had to adjust to was being surrounded by students who had never been to the ocean, never tasted salt water or had it sting their eyes, heck, many never even left their STATE or COUNTY (not country, county!) and the biggest thing that ever happened to them was traveling across COUNTY LINES (remaining in Kansas) to attend college. OMG! I told them all the places I'd been, things I saw, etc., and they looked at me like goldfish out of water... I guess there was one adjustment – when I graduated from KAHS it was my 13th school – the life of a military dependent! And now I was spending four years in one place. Really felt odd – like after two years I really should be packing up everything and moving on!

Doug Campbell

I went to college within 2 months of returning to the US. As a freshman, there was a lot of activities where you had to meet with others from your State. . . I was told to sit with the foreign students. After many years, I just introduced myself as a Military Brat from all over! I just was so young and didn't know how to answer or what to say--it took a lot of years for me to come to the full realization of what a blessing my Dad's career was for all of us! We had some rare and amazing experiences for kids in the early 70's and we are so grateful for it!! One thing – on base we were not able to display our American flag--that was sad, and when I got stateside after four years and people were disrespecting and burning our flag it really frosted me! People have NOO idea what they have and what they are disrespecting when they scorn our flag and our country!

JeanMarie Sample

I enjoyed our time in Morocco. Our family of six moved from 3 years in London England to Sidi Yahia in 1972. It was quite a culture change for me as a 15-year-old but having moved 9 times previously we just looked at it as a new adventure. We spent the first two weeks living in the Mamora Hotel in downtown while waiting for on base housing. It was an adventure just to walk around downtown Kenitra. Nothing had a fixed price. You bartered for almost every item you bought. Seeing the base at Sidi Yahia for the first time was quite a shock. You could literally see the back fence from the front gate! It was about one square kilometer but the Navy did a great job keeping us entertained and busy. There was an Exchange, cafeteria, movie theater, two-lane bowling alley (with human pin setters that could be bribed to help your score), two baseball fields, outdoor movie theater, horse stables, picnic and playground area, swimming pool, wood working shop, automotive shop, small gym, tennis and basketball courts. They even had a Boy Scout troop which I belonged to shortly. Thinking back, it must have been quite the undertaking to build it. Even though we were not allowed to display the American flag it was our home away from home. We had our own sewage and water treatment plant, electric plant, radio station, fire department, church and such. It was a small city ringed by dual barbed wire fences and a perimeter road that was patrolled. When we arrived, our new home (duplex) was in the very back corner of the base. I lost two bicycles and many clothes off the clothes line to fence jumpers based on our home's location. We were informed that the house came with a Gardner and a Maid. My father told his sponsor that he was not certain he wanted or needed a Gardner or Maid. We had a Maid on one of our 3-year tours in Japan but that was when my dad was out to sea and my mom could use the help with four children. This was shore duty. We were informed that they sort of "came with the house" (for a fee of course). We could decline but that would shake up the entire hierarchy of Maids (Fatimas). The CO had his maid, the XO had his and ours was the third in the hierarchy. If we declined the maids would have to change households based on their positions in that hierarchy. He reluctantly accepted. The Gardner turned out to be a little shady (our Fatima ratted him out) so he did not last long. I forget what he did but he was let go. Probably petty theft. The locals had so little. It was sad. Having our Fatima turned out to be a wonderful experience. Her name was Hadesha. She was a large, happy woman that really enriched our experience. She accompanied us on many trips. She served as tour guide and interpreter as we spoke little French and no Arabic. From the local souk and meat market to trips to the Atlas Mountains, she was there to share the experience with us. Here is a funny story about her: Hadesha arrived each morning at 8am on a US Navy shuttle bus from her home in Kenitra as did all the other Fatimas. They all wore the full-length Burkas and veils with just their eyes showing while in public, but once she was inside our home she was comfortable lowering the hood and removing the veil. She always had a smile and was good natured. Anyway, one day my father came home for lunch and decided to make himself a salad. Hadesha had been working with Americans for over 10 years so she was familiar with American cooking. Breakfast, Lunch and Dinner. She offered to make his salad but he politely said no thanks. As he finished making the salad he added some bacon bits to stop it off. She had never seen bacon bits before and asked him what they were. He told her they tasted like bacon and offered her some. She was alarmed! She threw up her hands and said "No Mr. Counts, I cannot eat bacon, I will go to hell!" He explained that there was no real bacon in them. They are made of soy and just taste like bacon. She looked perplexed and puzzled. After some persuasion she reluctantly tried some. Upon which she proclaimed: "They do taste like bacon!" Realizing what she just said her face turned bright red with blushing and she asked to go home for the day. That story makes me chuckle and I often ask my dad to share it when I visit. I think of Hadesha fondly and often. I wonder what became of her when we closed the base in 1976. I read somewhere that one of our requirements of us leaving was to make certain the locals that had worked there were taken care of. I sure hope that is true. God bless you Hadesha wherever you are.

Jerry Counts

At TMW, girls' basketball was played full court so Stateside I kept fouling out until they let me play roving forward. Also, in 9th grade TMW, I took Business math but that was a Senior class in North Carolina. I was terrified being the only Freshman. Hated it

Gloria Kemery

I think the biggest shock was when we flew into D.C. at night. There were all these white headlights. I was blinded! I had a terrible re-entry after 5 wonderful, formative, "No TV" years at Port Lyautey - ages 11-16. Came back as a senior ('66) to a very cliquey, richer area school in Arlington, VA. The place I could shine, because I was very athletic, was sports. I went to the VA State tennis championships in '66 and our basketball team was great! But, I made no close friends and hated the D.C. weather. A few great friends from Maroc, like Sandy Hansen, moved there the next year and we had a lot of fun. Penny Wickham lived in Quantico, so we were still friends. Patty Dilucido lived in Pennsylvania too. But, then college was a totally freeing, great time. So, one year of hell and off I went!

Cece Canton

I had a very hard time adjusting when we got back to the States. Coming from a tiny school and going to a college where there were sometimes 100 students in a single class was almost overwhelming. Also, we had been raised in another world—one where the Vietnam War, race riots, and the counterculture revolution were some distant thing we read about in magazines. It was difficult to relate to peers with whom I had no shared experiences. I felt very lost and alone my freshman year in college. Eventually, I adjusted as we all did in our own ways, but never seemed to quite fit in. In my older years, I have found many niches that I fit into quite nicely, but I am forever grateful for those few years I had in a special place with some exceptionally fine people.

Sandy (White) Bartell

I graduated and stayed in Morocco as a dependent for another year! Loved it! But I, too, had some adjusting to do returning from Morocco both times. I was in a small town in North Georgia for 9th grade and one of two people in the school not from that county. I was put in mostly sophomore classes and I enjoyed the challenge. Their ways were radically different though. Girls would want to fight me because their boyfriend spoke to me! I was too lady-like for that and told them so. LOL. Anyway, during the next two years (two states) there were racial issues in those big schools. I didn't understand what the problem was. I had gone to school with many different nationalities. There were knifings, drug overdoses and all kinds of issues that kept me nervous and on my guard. Not a fun couple of years!

Kathy Myers Strange

I left Maroc in February '63 headed for South Louisiana. I would have been Class of 1965. As luck would have it, Bob Zaborski and Mike Vanness were there. Enrolled at an all-boys' school. Was way behind socially and academically but managed to adapt. Seems we Military kids make friends easily. Transferred to another all-boys' school for Jr. and Sr. years. That was great. My dad retired from the Navy and up to Seattle we went. University of Washington followed...then Navy Flight School. Morocco was fantastic. I have great memories spending 3 years there.

Patrick Foley

After graduation in 1971, what I noticed about returning to the U.S. was the noise. Cars, traffic, radios. I had to learn how to drive. Also, it was lonely, even surrounded by 30,000 other students. I was the first in the entire Dixon family to go to college, so it was a huge leap for me. If it hadn't been for some amazing teachers (Mr. Bass) and BJ Gleason as a best friend, I would've been content with a secretarial job. They encouraged me to stretch and grow and be confident. Art was my go-to, so I wound up graduating from Texas Tech U with a degree in art education and a Masters in Fine Art. The experience of being in Morocco taught me that I could do anything I set my mind to. If I had stayed in the States during the Vietnam War, I would've been like Jennie in the Forrest Gump movie. Life really did hand me a box of chocolates and God protected me with a host of angels. I'm so grateful for those amazing years in Morocco.

Nola Fulkerson

I stayed another year and helped establish the library at Bouk. I was librarian until the next fall when I came back stateside to attend University of South Carolina. Best year of my life at that time. Funny story, 40 years after Morocco, here in Aiken, SC, I went to see a doctor for a colonoscopy of all things and he saw I was wearing my Fatima hand necklace. He asked about it and what do you know? His name is Mark Meyer and he was there and went to grammar school a few years before I was there. So we exchanged yearbooks and became good friends. Small world.

Bonnie Arey Fowler

Upon getting back to the States my school records were evaluated. I was so far ahead in school that I only had 2 classes a day as a senior. I was done each day by 10am. Thank you USDESEA. Fine job! When we left Morocco, we flew to Lisbon and on to NY, NY. I had not been in the USA for over 5 years. We had heard of the gas shortage but when we approached NY from the air it was amazing! Millions of lights dancing in slow motion. My thoughts were..."So much for the gas shortage." When I got to my new high school in CT there were 1500 students! Quite a change from KAHS which I think had 50 students from grades 7 thru 12. The school was so big that I was late to my Chemistry class on the first Day. I had gotten lost. The teacher wanted to make an example out of me and ordered me to stay after school for being late to her class. I never liked Chemistry after that. Shame.

Jerry Counts

I went from KAHS and 150 students to a Senior Class of 450. I didn't even make the yearbook, but after 2 weeks of evaluating my DOD school records I got to drop most of my Senior courses and just had 12th English and an Elective for an Academic degree.

Deborah Robin Kafir

A+ for our school in Kenitra, but when we came into the harbor in New York and I saw the Statue of Liberty, tears ran down my cheeks and my heart just seemed to burst. I wasn't expecting that.....it was like 'my country, tis of thee.'

Joan Ellen Bernard

I graduated in '69 and almost immediately went to summer school at the University of Maryland, Munich. Then I attended 3 semesters before dropping out and joining the Navy, Stateside, in '71. When my father retired, we all came home by ship MV *Michelangelo*, with our car in the hold. Arriving in NYC but destined for Tampa Bay, Florida, we discovered that the car's starter had been damaged in transit, perhaps by using the starter to move the car aboard the ship. So, with yellow headlamps and yellow Moroccan tags we awkwardly drove the car south, pushing it to start every time!

Andy Milot

I graduated in '61, stayed with dad until he received his orders (to Washington DC) and left in '62. After graduation I managed the 2-lane bowling alley as Sidi, Morocco. Came back to the States, joined the Navy and went to Radioman A school.

Wayne Lawson

I left after graduation and worked that summer as a waitress in a resort in the Poconos. Then to college and nursing school that fall.

Susan Bernet

I went off to college - which was totally strange. I had been gone for so long I didn't fit in anymore. One of my early deals...

"We're going to see America!"

"That sounds like fun how will you be going?"

"We're driving"

"How long are you going to take?"

<weird look> "Just the evening".

[the band America, not the continent I figured out much later]

Jack Parker

I really didn't want to leave Maroc and I remember crying on the plane as we flew into New York, then LA, because of the smog!

I just thought everything in the States was going to be as grim as the sky. As all military brats do, I adjusted and made friends, but I was way ahead academically and moved schools again the next year. The huge class sizes were pretty intimidating at first. I remember going into my French class junior year and telling about my summer in French and the other kids just looked at me like I was from Mars! So many things were very different - had to deal with race riots and police on campus and fear of getting beat up daily; not ever using the restroom for fear of getting beat up - and that was the better school in town! I could have graduated early but didn't want to go to college at 16. Anyway, I was still in touch with Jennifer Miller, my best friend from Rabat, so that helped.

Sheila Bright Roberts

It's been a long time since I last walked the streets of Kenitra; however, I can say that the memory of those days is as fresh as the day I was there. The experience provided a great deal perspective over the last 30 years!

Robert Seddon

After Kenitra, moved to California for a year and then to Kentucky until 1985. Joined the U.S. State Department's Foreign Service and have been travelling around the world since then. Have lived in: Tokyo, Niamey, Lima, Conakry, Rabat, DC, Kinshasa, Addis Ababa and now in Ft. Lauderdale. Have a son, 21 years old, and 2 dogs (Blondie and Ace) and a cat (Ollie). Looking forward to retirement in the next 5 years or so. Plan to follow passions and take care of dogs and cats that are handicapped and/or the ones nobody wants anymore.

Theresa Everett

We didn't move very far. We actually drove to our next place, which was the U.S. Naval Station (USNAVSTA) at Rota, Spain. The school was much bigger and I did have a hard time adjusting to that and finding my place.

Carmen Byrd Bohn

I remember we came back to the States after I was in 9th grade at Kenitra. I had enjoyed the classes and sports in school yet wasn't ready for High School. I made a great impression on the others in French class though - so that helped! I also made foreign friends so much easier than American ones.....maybe I was just shy? I appreciate the experience and all I learned during my years in Maroc. Life had great opportunities in languages when I graduated and when I went to University, I tested out of all French and Spanish language credits!!! Thank heaven for the life my parents offered us! I just wanted to share that with everyone!

Carmen T. (Acosta) Hedges

I didn't have any problems adjusting to "Life after Maroc." The year at the University of Maryland campus in Munich probably served as a good transition - being with other "brats." After some exploring in Switzerland, I headed back to the States using Space A military flight out of Frankfurt. Arriving at Andrews AFB, I took a bus into Washington, DC. I felt right at home. I feel very fortunate to have had the time at Maroc and the Navy Brat Experience.

Bob Bull

I think there were about 30 or so seniors in my graduating class, and probably only a third of them were American citizens so we were a small, close-knit but diverse school where everybody knew everybody whether you were a freshman or a senior. Going off to The University of Texas at Austin was scary and overwhelming at first. It took me awhile to learn how to cope with the huge class sizes and sheer number of students after our small school at Kenitra. In a way, though, I felt better prepared than many of my college peers, some of whom had never been out of the state of Texas, much less exposed to a foreign culture and people before. It seemed like everyone was trying to dress and look like everyone else instead of celebrating diversity. Living in Morocco taught me many things, but most importantly it taught me that people from different cultures and backgrounds can learn so much from each other and also that we have more in common than we think!

Leigh (Crocker) McSwain

The 1976 Yearbook

Administration: CAPT William I. Parrish, USN (Base Commander); CDR R. Y. Coppess, USN (School's Officer); David

Bensen (School Principal); and Robert Kubarek (Assistant Principal).

Faculty & Staff: **Faculty:** James Corey; Annette Goode; Joanne Johnson; Rita Klemp; Janice Sellak; Courtlandt C. Kauffman; Loren Lorenzetti; and Karen Moujjen. **Staff:** Lois Haskins (High School Secretary); Karen Strunk (High School Librarian); Betty Newman (Elementary School Secretary); Carolyn Maxwell (Elementary School Librarian); Alice Carter (High School Supply); and Sharon Koritar (Elementary School Supply).

The 22 graduating Seniors of 1976: Zineb Benjelloun (President); Jeanne Neptune (Vice-President); Linda Foster (Secretary); Moattassim Lamdouar (Treasurer); Nadia Anwer; Riad Al-Assad; Frances Demain; Jean-Marc Doyle; Tahar El-Korchi; Ouafa Eloifer; Shamoel Faizullabhoy; Shireen Faizullabhoy; Sherif Henein; Robert Keen; Rod Lubasky; Souheil Merhege; Christopher Prest; Laura Salisberry; Charles Smith; Mike Taylor; Bob V. Whitaker; and Cynthia Woods.

Class of 1977 and Beyond

1977 saw the movie Star Wars open in cinemas, the first Apple II computers go on sale, and the Television mini-series "Roots" go on the air. Elvis Presley dies of a heart attack at the age of 42, NASA's space shuttle undergoes its first test flight, UK Jubilee celebrations, Roman Polanski is arrested and charged, and the Alaskan Oil Pipeline is completed. 1977 also witnessed the New York City Blackout that lasted for 25 hours; and Quebec adopted French as their official language. Jimmy Carter is elected as the President of the United States. The precursor to the GPS system in use today is started by US Department of Defense.

I Remember:

I first came to Morocco in summer of 1965. Dad was a newly commissioned officer after working his way up through the ranks. We lived in a hotel upon our arrival and for a 6-year-old that was a blast. Then we lived in some apartments off of Rue Mohammed V, then moved out to Sidi Yahia directly across the street from the elementary school. I did 1st grade at TMWS elementary with Mrs. Horowitz as teacher-second grade at elementary on base at Sidi with Mrs. Nelson. Finished our 1st tour there in '68. I have 3 other siblings: Kathy Myers, Bo Myers and Connie Myers. Kathy was a new teenager of 13 at Sidi, Bo was in 3rd grade and Connie started 1st grade. We went stateside and returned to Morocco for our 2nd tour in 71. I finished 6th grade (we came in April and I had my 12th Birthday in the Hotel), lived in a villa in town for just a few months and then out to Sidi - once again a house near the elementary school. LOL. We had the first house in the row as you turned onto Officer's Row. Our neighbors were the Fuquays.

Rode the bus to KAHS were I did 7th, 8th and the beginning of 9th grade. A holler out to Counts, Donovich, Koehler, Gamble, Little and anyone else from Sidi that rode the Bus. I hated having to leave Morocco both times in my life. If I could have I would have just stayed and lived out the rest of my life there. Our Fatima was named Boughbia. Loved my Boughbia. Had her the 1st time and 2nd. When we left in 67 I cried and cried, I wanted to stay with her and her family. Actually, went and stayed at her house in the Medina several times. I miss her every day. Wish I could find out about her and the family.

Pamela Jean Myers Richert, would have been Class of '77

Hi, my family and I moved to the Kenitra Base in 1977 when I was 2 (Father was an officer in the Maroc AF). That place is such a big part of my life. I had my 2nd, 3rd, 4th and 5th grade graduations in the chapel in 1985 and I ran and roamed all over the base (except for I wasn't supposed to go). I lived there until I finished High School in 1992. I always wondered what had happened there in the years before my family moved there. I don't even know where to start, but A BIG THANK YOU is due to all of you who helped in building and maintaining that place. It was such a pristine area for me to call home. I learned how to swim at the same base pool that is in the pictures. I learned how to ride the bike on those streets and when I fell and scraped my knees, I went to the hospital to get all fixed up. I played in the trees and found some very old Budweiser bottles that made me wonder "who drank this here?" Living on the Kenitra base always made me want to visit the US because it looked so different from the rest of Kenitra and Morocco (granted that it's a very beautiful country in its own ways). Nevertheless, I ended up getting a degree from Auburn University in Alabama and I now live in Birmingham with my wife and new child. THANK YOU ALL SO VERY MUCH from a grateful civilian.

Hicham Sori

We were in Kenitra from '69 to '73. We started out at the Mamora Hotel, then a villa in Kenitra and then on base in Kenitra. I attended Thomas Mack Wilhoite for 7th grade and I am class of '78. I was there with Steve Kiser, Joe Wayne, Greg Branch, Nancy Wright, Pam Haines, Nancy Wirth and Melissa Mabe off the top of my head. The Ducks were our next-door neighbors for a time on base. I had Ms. Judar for 4th grade, Ms. Jones for 5th grade and Ms. Hansen for 6th grade. My Dad, Arlen Schall was a CTC O Brancher stationed out at Sidi. We returned to the States and I finished school in Pensacola, Florida, where my dad was stationed until retirement and still resides.

Kim Schall

I came to Morocco in the summer of '66 (if I am counting fingers and toes correctly), and we came to Virginia in '75. I would not trade my youth in Morocco for anything. The friendships I made there are the enduring life friendships I treasure today. We initially lived in Kenitra, on Rue Zim Zim and later moved to Sidi Yahia. I was fortunate enough to have a Dad with a gypsy touch, so we travelled/camped every square inch of it. From the Sahara / Marrakech, to the ski slopes in Ifrane to the beaches of Tangiers. Met so many amazing people, some of which are here. Shout out to Vicky, Tonya, Betty, Debbie, Pam, Scott, Laura... you know who you are. I would like for folks to know that my sibs include Marian Campbell (deceased), Shawn Campbell (deceased) and Gwen Campbell, still around, thank God. We lived in Officer's Country, down on the cul-de-sac. Since then, I became a registered nurse and have raised my family here in Virginia. For those who know me, it's great to catch up. For those who are new to me, I look forward to getting to know you better. GO SULTANS!

Kathleen "Kay" Campbell, would have been KAHS Class of '79

I would have been Class of '79. In 1961 I was born on base Kenitra, lived on base in Sidi and attended Stanford C. Hooper K-3. In '69 moved to Kenitra-Rue Imam Ali and attended TMW Elementary 4th through 6th grades; then KAHS 7th to 9th grades before it closed in '76. I came stateside and attended 10th at Jacksonville, NC, 11th at Florence, AL, 12th was split between DeSoto, MO and finally graduated in Bedford, IN. I left Morocco for the last time in August '78. My siblings are Michael, Patricia, & Greg Davis and they all attended and/or graduated from there. Since I'm not positive on their actual graduating years I'll just base theirs off mine and get close. Respectively theirs would be Class of '66 for Michael, Class of '68 for Patricia and Class of '71 for Greg.

Tonya Davis Himmelspach

My father, RMCS James S. Steele, my mom Beryl, my sister Kim, and I were stationed at Bouknadel from 1970 - 1973. I would have been Class of 1977. Sadly, I must say that my dad passed away June 2011. We were introduced to John and Paulette Mendez (daughters Maria and Christian) who ran the Astor Hotel and owned some villas by another Navy family, Robert and Patricia Reed (daughters Terry and Sheila). We spent the first year or so living in a huge villa off of Rue Mohammed V in Kenitra before moving on base in Bouknadel. The Reeds also lived downtown for a while and then moved to the base at Sidi Yahia. Man, what great memories I have of those 3 years!!!! We made lifelong friends of the Mendez family as well as several Moroccans who adopted us as their own and treated as like royalty.

I remember many, many weekends packing jerry cans of gas in the trunk of our Toyota Corona Mark II (bought in Norfolk before deploying to Morocco) and travelling the highways and backroads of the four corners of Morocco. Fez, Meknes, Casablanca, Rabat, Marrakesh, Tangier, Azrou, Ifrane, Volubilis, the gardens outside of Bouk..... and so many more! What crazy trips, the four of us stuck in that little Toyota with our family German Shepard Fritz, listening to 8-track tapes of Johnny Cash, Elvis, Lee Greenwood, Diana Ross, Roberta Flack, the Ventures, Creedence, and who knows what else while caravanning with the Reeds in their huge Pontiac Bonneville convertible and other friends!!! As a side note, our dog also travelled to Cuba and Italy with us too. One of my favorite vacations was when my grandparents flew to Morocco from Pennsylvania and spent two weeks touring with us. We even took the ferry across Gibraltar to Spain and drove the Costa del Sol and stayed in Malaga. When we were transferred to Naples, Italy from Bouknadel in 1976, we drove to Tangier and took a drive-on cruise ship tour of the Mediterranean Riviera before offloading in Genoa and then driving down Italy to Naples. Oh, also can't forget the long bus rides from the jr./sr. high school on Kenitra back and forth to Bouk. Talk about fun trips - the school bus doubled as the station shuttle and used to go from the high school to downtown Kenitra by the souk and market shops before going back to Bouk. We used to get off the bus at the market, buy a baguette of French bread, some kettle chips, oranges, and gouda cheese to snack on the way home. Mom used to get so mad at us for not eating our dinners!!!

I remember being on lock down on the base at Bouk during the three attempted Coups in early 70s. One by the Army, one by the Air Force, and the other caught before it got started. Marines in their battle gear and us being told to be ready to leave on a moment's notice, leaving everything we owned behind. We could hear the helicopters and machine gun fire in the distance as the rebels were hunted down. I remember being at the high school and watching the fighter jets take off when the rebels tried to shoot down the king's airliner too.

I remember my parents playing softball and bowling in leagues a lot there too. My dad was an avid golfer and spent lots of time on the golf courses in Kenitra and Rabat. It sure was fun being a junior high teenager there! I think I still have the Moe stick that I traded who knows what to get!!! We used to barter all the time with the local Moroccan kids for chameleons, walking sticks, and trinkets. Usually involved swapping candy, sodas or cigarettes that we had swiped from our parents! Many summer hours were spent bicycling around the base, playing sandlot ball games, and at the base swimming pool learning red cross safety stuff, racing, and diving.

Some of the Bouk family names I remember are the Brinkmans, Cashers (kids David and Paula), Crosbys (kids David, Selena, and Marlene), Mastantoneos (son Tony Jr. - I used to babysit him), Wrights (daughter Nancy, can't remember the son's name), Porters, Pipers (kids Tracy, Brian, and Jeffrey), and Smallwoods (kids Kevin, Audrey, and Jody). Another thing about Bouk: it was pretty wild that the base was in the middle of a cork oak tree forest! Us kids loved climbing on the soft cork bark and swinging on rope swings on those huge oak trees! Not too bad for memories from 40+ years ago!!! I still have many of the vinyl albums that I bought in the little base PX on Bouk. Spent lots of quarters and dimes in the little geedunk and 2-lane bowling alley too. Who can forget the evening matinees to watch High Chaparral, Mannix, and other shows either.

My first paycheck job was at Bouk in 1972 or 1973.... Worked part-time as a base librarian for minimum wage, I think $1.72 an hour! The Christmas holidays there were very special times - spent them with the Mendez family and the Reeds. Bob, Pat, Terry, and Sheila Reed were our "adopted" Uncle, Aunt, and cousins. One of my best friends there was Lon McGuffin, who's family lived downtown for a while and then I think moved to Kenitra. Ok, I think I have rambled on enough for now. Thanks again for this trip down memory lane!

Jim Steele

The Triumphal Arch of Caracalla is one of Volubilis' most distinctive sights. Nearly all TMW-KAHS students had a road-trip to see this – and to giggle at the remains within the House of Ill Repute.

Francis Ford Coppola's Patton, *starring actor George C. Scott as General George S. Patton, was released in 1970. A portion of the movie was filmed at Volubilis – as you can see from the Triumphal Arch behind him. Photo courtesy www.movieboozer.com.*

Doug Campbell taking a photograph of Robert Beaver (with camera) taking a photograph of Carla Golden – all Class of 1972 on our Class road-trip to Volubilis.

We lived in Sidi Yahia from 1972-1975. I would have graduated from KAHS in 1979.

Debbie Donivan Lich

I lived on base from late '73 to '77...My dad Chester Taylor ran the Commissary Store. My siblings are as follows: Tony; Michael; David; Angus and the Taylor Sisters (as we were known as) Anna and Laura...My mom cooked for the base in 1976.

Laura Murphy Taylor

I remember living off base in a villa and every morning and evening my job was to break up fruit crates and light the fire under the hot water heater so we could take baths. Then in the morning after I did that I would go just around the corner to a bakery and buy fresh bread for our lunches. I remember Saturday and Sunday afternoons during the summer after spending most of the day at the pool or gym, hanging out at the enlisted men's club listening to the bands they brought in, usually from England. Happy days. I remember hanging out in the Oasis, listening to music and eating fries with gravy on them; playing ping pong at the Teen Club. My mom and Ferne Ballard were running it at the time. I remember the basketball and baseball trips to Spain and riding the ferry across the Straits of Gibraltar. I spent one weekend in Gibraltar with a bunch of guys from the base. It was my first trip to a casino. I was 16 and still naive to the intentions of this old man that took me around showing me how to play the games. I realized what he was about when I saw him looking over the urinal at me. That cut that night off short!

Bill Bradley

My name is Thomas Campbell and my dad was stationed at NTC Kenitra from 1970-72. While there I attended 6th and 7th grade; my older brother graduated from KAHS in 1972. Later I graduated from high school (Pine Forest High School, Pensacola, FL) and I eventually enlisted in the Navy and became an Electrician's Mate. I later retired after a 20-year career in the Navy. One of the highlights of my career was being stationed on board *USS Bristol County* (LST-1198), a Tank Landing Ship, in E Division as a First Class (E-6), from December 30, 1993 to August 17, 1994. During that brief 8-month stretch I was one of five US Navy sailors that took the ship to Casablanca, Morocco (under a Moroccan crew), from San Diego, CA. I had an Officer's "State Room" for my living quarters while underway! You see, *USS Bristol County* was decommissioned and struck from the Navy's inventory on July 29, 1994 and disposed of through the Security Assistance Program (SAP) - transferred via cash sale as an ex-US fleet hull foreign military sale to Morocco. The Moroccans renamed her *BDC Sidi Mohammed Ben Abdellah* on August 16, 1994. Mohammed Ben Abdellah al-Khatib was the Governor of Marrakech in 1750 and Sultan of Morocco from 1757 to 1790. There exists a letter written by George Washington to Mohammed ben Abdellah in appreciation for his signature on the Treaty of Peace and Friendship signed in Marrakech in 1787. The new name for *USS Bristol County* seems to be most appropriate! And officially, for at least one day, I became an American sailor serving aboard a Moroccan-flagged ship! No wonder the US Navy screwed up my pay, but that's another story! I made fast friends with the Moroccan crew and was treated like a long-lost brother. We sailed out of San Diego taking with us possibly every available bicycle, washing machine and any other appliances that could fit on the ship! Someone was going to make a killing reselling all that I bet! We sailed through the Panama Canal and tried to use a U.S. Navy supply chit to pay our way through, but it didn't work! We went through the Caribbean Sea to Norfolk, VA, and then across the Atlantic Ocean, what we called "crossing the pond." While the ship was tied up to her pier in Casablanca I ate lunch out in town - $5 for a whole chicken and fries! But the hotel was $200 a night. I was able to travel over to Kenitra and see the base I used to live on as a military dependent. Back in the early 1970s I remember living out in town with glass-embedded walls all around the house and a small yard and the maid always coming back for her shoes she left behind. I never understood that! Then we moved on base. I remember my brother John being born at the Naval Hospital there and I remember going to the movies every Saturday and being in the play *Oliver*.

Tom Campbell, would have been KAHS Class of '77

Do You Remember the Base Closure on September 31, 1978?

From the *Santa Cruz Sentinel*, Santa Cruz, CA, 1 October 1978:

U.S. Abandons Its Last Military Foothold in Africa

KENITRA, Morocco (AP) – The United States quietly abandoned its last military foothold in Africa on Saturday with a low-key ceremony that ended a 36-year military presence in Morocco dating back to "Operation Torch," one of the turning points in World War II.

The signature of Navy Capt. William Parrish – commander of the American-run communication bases centered on Kenitra, 25 miles north of the Moroccan capital of Rabat – formally handed over to the Moroccan government all that remained of the multi-million-dollar installations.

Parrish and four other officers were the last in a succession of tens of thousands of American troops who have served here since Gen. George Patton's GIs stormed ashore Nov. 8, 1942, and captured Kenitra – then called Port Lyautey – from the forces of Vichy France after a bloody three-day battle.

There is no monument here to the 567 Americans who died in crushing the bitter resistance of French troops under the Vichy's regime Gen. Charles Nogues.

Greatly expanded and modernized by the United States, the bases at Kenitra and neighboring Sidi Yahia and Bouknadel were placed under nominal Moroccan command in 1965 to counter Communist and Third World criticism. But they remained firmly under American control.

At the height of their importance in the 1950s, the bases served as a major arms depot, intelligence listening post, staging point and communications center, with a garrison of more than 2,000 troops and dependents. The bases were downgraded in 1965 to a "communications facility," but the number of American troops was only slightly reduced.

Anxious to keep a low profile, the troops and their families lived almost entirely on the bases with their own hospitals, club houses, tennis courts and Olympic-size swimming pool.

In a much-publicized exchange with Soviet leader Leonid I. Brezhnev, Morocco's King Hassan II blandly asserted there was no such thing as an American military base in Morocco. But the leftist campaign against the U.S. presence continued until two years ago when the United States decided to "disestablish" the bases costing more than $7 million a year to operate and replace them with satellite facilities.

Sidi Yahia, the radio receiver station, was turned over to the Moroccans with a flag-lowering ceremony in December.

In the nine months since American troops left Sidi Yahia, the unguarded base has been looted of all usable equipment left there by the Americans. Refrigerators, light fixtures, door handles, virtually everything that could be moved, have disappeared. A gap in the fence is wide enough for trucks to drive in and out undisturbed.

Moroccan officers have assured American colleagues that this will not be allowed to happen to Kenitra and Bouknadel.

Although the U.S. Navy and Air Force removed the most sophisticated electronic equipment, the bases were handed over in fully operational condition. They include fully-equipped housing for thousands of troops, a functioning harbor and airport, long-range antenna fields, generating plants, movie theaters, school buildings, firefighting equipment and even a complete milk processing plant.

American and Moroccan officials declined to make an estimate of the value of the facilities. "We took great care to turn everything over in working condition," an American officer said.

The Moroccan government paid nothing for the bases. Its only obligation, in the handover document signed by Parrish and the Moroccan base commander, Lt. Col. Abdelkader Ramdani, was to maintain the aircraft warning lights on two towers at Kenitra and to pass on generous American dismissal indemnities to more than 1,000 Moroccans once employed on the bases.

Once a brat always a brat -- My dad, Ernie Marcurio, was stationed in Kenitra from June 1976 until the base closed in 1978. He was an electrician there. We always joked that he had to stay until the base closed to turn out the lights. The high school closed just as we got there so I was part of the Maroc group that went to Zaragoza and Torrejon. Great times.

Ginine Marcurio

A TEACHER REMEMBERS

I Remember... Teaching and Living in Kenitra

My name is Mary Armao McCarthy. In 1968-69 I was a teacher at the Thomas Mack Wilhoite Elementary school. I was twenty-one, just out of college, and a newly minted Navy wife. My husband Kevin was a yeoman in the base Security Unit. When school administrators learned I had my teaching certification and was on a Federal civil service list, they offered me a choice of three jobs — full-time teacher, high school secretary or substitute teacher. I opted to substitute, as it provided extra income but still gave us time to enjoy being newlyweds and to see Morocco. Substitutes were needed at the Thomas M. Wilhoite (TMW) school, which had recently transitioned to a dedicated elementary school, separate from the high school.

Teaching TMW Students

The students at TMW were bright and eager. I enjoyed teaching there. Reading was my favorite subject to teach. I loved sharing and developing the enthusiasm of young schoolkids for books. They would focus with my help on reading the words in the children's books, and I would enjoy watching their faces light up when they saw a special picture or a surprise as they turned the page. Most students were dependents of US military with a sprinkling of children of Embassy staff and Moroccan VIPs. The only downside to substituting was that by wild coincidence the absent teacher always had playground duty at lunch time, so I was required to fill in. Sometimes I wondered how the other teachers kept a straight face as they broke the news. I knew I was being gamed, but I didn't mind as I was young and enjoyed being outdoors with the kids while they had fun on the swing set and played games.

Boy Scouts provided a special touch of home on base. The Scouts had uniforms and regular activities. Kevin and I lived in one of the base Quonset hut apartments, and it was a happy pop-up of home one day to have a Boy Scout in full uniform knock on the door selling candy as a fundraiser for his troop. The base diner, the Oasis, provided a similar, simple touch of home.

My husband Kevin's duties as a base policeman included manning the main gate, preparing reports for investigators, issuing passes and guarding the Navy warehouses and ammo dump. He remembers that the two Chiefs in the Security Unit had bubbly teen-age girls who would visit the office after school. Occasionally an enlisted man would date a teen from the base, but this was Frowned Upon. Kevin is happy to report that there were no problems with American students during any of his police watches.

R&R and Holidays

The military made an effort to provide a variety of activities and entertainment for troops and dependents. The Olympic-sized swimming pool complex was a favorite hang-out for students and servicemen. Touring USO bands sometimes played poolside. We never rated major celebrities, but bands just starting out visited us. On the patio, we could buy tasty Moroccan brochettes, small skewers of beef or lamb cooked on barbeque grills, the scent floating on the breeze and calling to you.

Also on base were indoor handball and paddleball courts, a bowling alley, a stable with horses for riding and two movie theaters. Because the weather was dry for nine months after the rainy season, a large outdoor movie screen with rows of white wooden park benches for movie watching had been built in years past by Navy Seabees. One night, under a starry African sky, we watched Boris Pasternak's epic story of the Russian Revolution in the Hollywood version of *Dr. Zhivago*. It was a cross-cultural explosion.

Oh, say can you see by the dawn's early light… The Star-Spangled Banner played before each film at the indoor movie theater on base while an image of an American flag was projected. The theater and the mess hall were the only places on base to see a Stars and Stripes flag. American flags were not allowed to be flown at that time, because technically the facility had transitioned to a Moroccan training base. The flag grew to be a stronger symbol for us in its absence. We might not have missed the sight of our country's flag if we were simply travelers amid a bustle of new experiences in a foreign land. But being forbidden to see it created an entirely new perspective. The Stars and Stripes fluttering on the theater screen brought a strong rise of emotion and forever strengthened the meaning of flag and country to us.

For me, everything in Morocco had the charm of being slightly different. Houses were villas, the first-class train cars we rode had rich wood interiors, and even soda bottles were unique. On their red caps and the upper curve of glass, Coca-Cola was written in Arabic script.

The military tried to make holidays away from home as authentic as possible. For Christmas, the monthly supply ship delivered real evergreen trees. We couldn't fit one in our Quonset hut, but there were plenty of decorations to choose from in the Exchange. A small, artificial tree with red ornaments and pretend snow became our first Christmas tree. We brought it back to the States and put it out every year after until it finally died of old age.

The Commissary ordered lots of turkeys to help us feel we were having an American Thanksgiving. We celebrated with friends and neighbors. Our friends Ron Updyke, Dennis Foley, and others carted the dining room table of Dawn and Larry Blankenship from four doors down the street to put next to ours so we could all squeeze in. Even though we were far from home, we had a happy Thanksgiving Day in Kenitra, Morocco, enjoying a feast of Tom Turkey, gravy, mashed potatoes, assorted other dishes and most of all, friends.

Picnics on base with belly dancers and horsemen were a unique combination of cultures. These were held on the fields by the back gate. All but the most essential base functions would close at noon. American hamburgers and hot dogs were served alongside Moroccan lamb brochettes and couscous. Swaying gently to traditional music, with arms graceful and fingers chiming castanets, belly dancers removed outer layers of gauzy veils but remained fully clothed in blouse and colorful pantaloons. A Fantasia by Arab horsemen completed the entertainment.

Kevin's commanding officer, Lt. Commander Melendy and his wife were warm and hospitable to the enlisted men, sometimes including them for holiday dinners and once holding a reception at their home for the Security Unit. The commander flew the twice-weekly mail plane to Rota, Spain. At the Melendy's reception, I was awed by their ornate Spanish punch service from Rota. I sipped delicately from one of the engraved silver cups set out around the matching footed serving bowl. It was the best punch I ever had.

Beaches ~ Mehdia and Bouknadel

Mehdia Beach wore all the colors of the rainbow on its stucco villas. I loved to study the saturated colors that trimmed the homes. Low fences were made of decorative concrete blocks that were painted white on the outside with the interior faces painted tangerine or azure or other intense shades never used on buildings at home. Most villas were simple square buildings, shining very white in the strong sun and trimmed in kaleidoscope. We would park on the street by the houses closest to the beach. Getting out of the car, we would be greeted with the tousle of breeze off the Atlantic, along with a sunbath of brilliant light under a blue Moroccan sky.

The beach at Mehdia still testified to its military role in World War II. Abandoned gun battlements hunkered on huge stone jetties that curved from the sand into the Atlantic, bracketing sunbathers and swimmers in an eerie contrast of times. The battlements seemed to whisper to us with reminders and foreboding.

Bouknadel. I don't know the translation of the word, but Bouknadel Beach was a place from a fairy tale. Unlike the level shoreline at Mehdia, the beach was down a long slope. You didn't arrive--you made an entrance--passing through a long, reed passageway that created an exotic contrast from its darkly shadowed tunnel to the brilliance beyond. A tall rock formation curved gracefully into the sea, with a natural arch large enough to walk through. Rollers extended back and beyond, layer on layer into the sea. There were no homes, just unmarred open beach as was so often the case in Morocco. The only structure was a restaurant hugging a curve of boulders. There we enjoyed cold drinks served on a stone patio that spilled onto the sand.

The Morocco-US Naval Training Command

I was impressed to learn that Morocco was the first country to officially recognize the newly independent United States of America in the year 1777. Morocco and the United States had a long history of cooperation and support, and the port of Kenitra on the Sebou River had served America and the Allies since World War II. Despite past and current alliances, the U.S. presence now was not embraced by all Moroccans. Because of this, civilian clothing was always worn off base. Military uniforms were forbidden in town, even for the shore patrol. When Kevin was assigned to the Security Unit, he was issued a khaki base police uniform with no markings of U.S. military service. Kevin was one of two yeomans in the Security Office which handled police functions, main gate security, warehouse watches and detective work for more serious crimes.

Kenitra was rated by the Navy as hardship duty because of its isolation, a status rarely given to land assignments, and one that brought a slighter higher pay scale. We first lived in a garden apartment in town but then moved to housing on base, where superior amenities included potable, running hot and cold water and direct fuel hook ups for our heat and stove. In town I used bottled or boiled water as there had been cases of hepatitis treated at the base infirmary. Our housing on base was in a Quonset hut, a small but cozy home that met all our needs. It was a duplex, split mid-way into two apartments, with another Navy family living on the other side. Our income was modest. In fact, we earned too little to even pay federal income tax, but our dollars went far due to the difference in American and Moroccan cost of living. Compared to the average Moroccan, we were wealthy. Many families in the countryside were poor, and the doctors on base sometimes treated local children with malnutrition.

In photos from Morocco now grown old, friends are all young and playful. Beneath those sunny surfaces was a constant recognition that the Vietnam War was going on, that guys sometimes disappeared in the middle of the night for reassignments, and that the medics on base were there for training before shipping out to hospital or helicopter or field assignments in the war zone.

Technically, we were on a Moroccan training base. The U.S. had officially withdrawn its forces from Morocco five years earlier in 1963 but needed to maintain its communications facilities based at Sidi Yahia and Bouknadel. The main base, officially named The Morocco-US Naval Training Command, was the supply installation and thus a Navy function. Kevin and all military were issued red diplomatic passports, allowing the government to say they were not armed forces but diplomats. In keeping with the title of a training base, a contingent of Air Force personnel provided flight training for the Moroccan military. I remember diving to the floor behind our couch one day when a training flight needed a little more altitude. A few years after we returned home, there was a clamor in the American news questioning the U.S. presence in Morocco followed by elusive bureaucratic explanations.

Robert Kennedy's Assassination

We were in Morocco on June 5, 1968, when Robert Kennedy was shot in Los Angeles the night he won the California Democratic primary for the presidency. The assassin was Sirhan Sirhan, from the Middle East. The entire base was locked down for a week and radio broadcasts were censored for fear of American retaliation. We were not allowed to leave the base, and radio broadcasts would go blank if the USA news were broadcast. We had no television or Stateside newspapers, and we never saw images of Robert Kennedy bloody and still. Perhaps the news black-out did its job. I heard no angry sentiments toward Moroccans.

Saying 'Good-bye' to Kenitra

My last trip into Kenitra before we left was on the bus, affectionately known as the Green Monster. As I waited for it at the bus stop to return to base, I stood and memorized the scene in the center of town. Morocco always pleased me with its flowers, both wild and planted. There were individual and municipal plantings along roads and throughout town. The main square in Kenitra was beautiful, with red and white flowers circling its green lawn. On that day, I closed my eyes and breathed in my presence, registering the sounds, the scents, the sights, mentally recording it all. I chanted silently to myself, "Remember this, remember this. Remember what it feels like to be in Morocco, this time and place."

And I do.   *Mary Armao McCarthy*

A Salute to Our Reunions

To date we have had these major reunions. Some of the mini-reunions may still need to be identified.

1982 – First KAHS Reunion, Greensboro, NC (10th Anniversary Class of 1972)
1992 – Greensboro, NC, July 4th weekend, 1992 (Largest reunion to date, some 200 alumni including friends/spouses)
1993 – Virginia Beach, VA
1997 – Vienna, VA, September 13
2000 – Old Town, Alexandria, VA, May 6
2000 – First one in Rabat, Morocco
2001 – Imperial Beach, CA, June 22-24
2003 – First Orlando, FL, February 7-9
2005 – New Orleans, LA
2007 – Sarasota, FL
2009 – Cruiseship Reunion, Seattle, WA
2011 – Las Vegas, NV, Labor Day Weekend, September
2011 – Wrightsville Beach (Wilmington), NC, October 27-30
2012 – Pensacola, FL, March 30 - 31
2012 – Second Rabat Morocco Reunion, June
2013 – Second New Orleans Reunion, June
2014 – Second Orlando, FL, EPCOT Center
2015 – DC/Alexandria, VA
2018 – Santa Fe, NM, July 19-22 (With Dave Bass 75th Birthday Bash)

While the 1992 was the largest gathering to date, it was the smaller 2000 Reunion in Morocco from June 30 to July 2 that captured the true essence of all our Reunions. I believe the author is Alice Scully, who sadly left us in 2011.

The journey to find our "inner teenagers" began for most of us at JFK International Airport on June 29th where we met up with those who were going to the reunion on the charter flight. Tahar Meddoun from the class of '68, who made all the travel, hotel, and banquet arrangements for us in Morocco, was there to greet us and hand us our tickets for the JFK/Casablanca leg of the trip.

Our flight over to Casablanca on Air Maroc was smooth and many of us spent the whole time catching up with old friends and talking excitedly about the reunion. We landed in Casablanca around 7:00 a.m. the following morning.

When we reached the Safir Hotel in Rabat, there was quite a crowd of former alumni and faculty gathered about in the lobby. People registered at our reunion registration table, picked up their reunion t-shirts, and then socialized or went up to their rooms to rest after the long trip.

Many of our reunion gatherings and meals took place on the Safir's roof which had a beautiful outdoor pool and a penthouse-type room. The room had all-glass walls with magnificent views of Sale, the Bou Regreg River, the old Rabat Medina, and the Oudaias Casbah.

We had this whole floor of the hotel almost completely to ourselves for the whole reunion. Just looking over the balcony into the streets and over the city you could see how much the city has changed over the years. Rabat now has a rush hour; with the growth in population have come huge swells of traffic. The Bou Regreg River still has the same old wooden fishing boats but swirling in among them are jet skis. Apparently the new (and young) king, Mohammed VI (they call him "M6" for short, or the "Cool King") is a real jet ski fan and he introduced them to Morocco. Sometimes he goes jet skiing himself on the Bou Regreg.

Our 5:30 Happy Hour on Friday was a very nice affair. The hors d'oeuvres were a mix of Moroccan and American goodies: popcorn, peanuts, and Moroccan and French pastries--another one of the many examples of how Tahar had gone out of his way to make sure everyone felt at home. The Happy Hour was a relaxed way for people to get reacquainted with each other after all these years.

The highlight of the reunion for most of the students occurred the next day when we took two chartered buses to our old school in Kenitra. Arranging this trip was a major undertaking on Tahar's part because the base is considered a sensitive military area. He had to get permission up through the highest ranks of the Moroccan military brass and finally even had to get the King's signature. We didn't get the final permission until two days before the reunion!

We drove through the town of Kenitra and went to one of the base's gates down near the Sebou River. There was some discussion with the Moroccan guards and we were told to enter by the old familiar gate on the other side of the base. The gate looked much the same except the American military insignias had been replaced by Moroccan ones. We spent about 10 minutes in the buses while Tahar and the Moroccan soldiers had more discussions. Even though all the official permissions had been granted, there was still some reluctance to let us freely sail on through. Anyway, it all got settled and we began the journey into our past.

The groves of eucalyptus trees were still there on either side of the road, as was the old football field on the right. However, straight ahead of us, between the fork in the road, was a new-looking mosque. It was nicely painted and surrounded by flowering bushes. The buses drove down past the old dispensary on the hill and the PX on the left. The dispensary was covered with Mickey Mouse graffiti and the PX parking lot was completely empty. The building looked like it was locked up and unused.

Proceeding down the main road (still lined with date palms), we passed the old base chapel. The stained-glass windows in the front had been boarded up. It was being used for something because soldiers were milling about it; however, the identity of the building was painted in Arabic, so it was difficult to tell what it was being used for.

Then, the final and glorious appearance of our old school. We pulled up in front and there was more discussion between Tahar and the Moroccan soldiers. After a while we filed off the buses and went to look at the front of the school. At first the soldiers were reluctant to let us take pictures or walk around much, but after a while they relaxed and let us take any photos or videos we wanted.

The front of the school looked pretty much the same, with taller trees of course. The Marine Parade Ground across the street (around which we had to run tortuous laps for P.E.) had some kind of stone monument in its center with a Moroccan flag; all the big, old, beautiful eucalyptus trees around it had been cut down.

There was more discussion again between Tahar and the soldiers and they decided to let us in to see the inside of the school. This was a very generous act on their part because there was a group of pilots in our old auditorium taking exams. We tried to be as quiet as possible when we filed in. We walked in through the front entrance where our athletic trophies used to be displayed, then to the right down the hallway towards the old library. Everything looked much the same though the walls were now painted grey instead of Navy pea-green.

The floors still had the original black tiles but were not polished as they used to be. We actually walked back into some of our old classrooms and they also looked familiar. The doors to the downstairs portion of the school were locked and we were not allowed to go down there. But we didn't care; we were thrilled that they let us in at all. After we went back outside we split up into different groups to wander around. One group walked up the hill toward the base chapel to find the very first high school (apparently there was another one before this one came into being). The back of the school was terribly run down and paint was peeling all over the walls. There were lots of scrubby bushes, and the field out back where we used to have P.E. and build bonfires was covered by a grove of Eucalyptus saplings. The view out over the Sebou River was still relatively unchanged however.

Eventually, we climbed back aboard the buses and drove over to the officer's housing section, then to the old elementary school which many of our students also attended. It is still in use as a school, probably for the Moroccan children who live on the base. We drove all over the base, passing by the Quonset huts on the way to the movie theater.

Our next stop was the swimming pool which is in excellent shape and still in use. The soldiers got the keys to our old gym and let us in. It too, was in very good shape. In fact, it smelled EXACTLY the way it used to! The ghosts of our athlete's perspiration must still be wafting around there. A few of the students shot a few baskets while others broke into some of the old school cheers we had during our games. Finally, we all gathered by the bleachers for a group photo.

Our last official stop on the buses was the golf club where the Moroccan military brass had a very touching and warm reception for us. Long tables were set up on the verandah with all sorts of soft drinks and munchies. The wing commander gave a short speech in English, welcoming us back to our old school and homes. It was VERY moving. Many of the folks in our group had tears in their eyes.

On the way out, we stopped off at the old Oasis cafeteria, our hangout for good American greasy fries and burgers. It looked rundown and was obviously not in use anymore. The old sign was still up above the door with some Arabic writing painted over it. Through the door you could see the dusty interior which looked as if it had closed its doors the day the base was turned over to the Moroccan government. The old aluminum grills were still there in the back.

When one of our former Moroccan students was queried about why the initial reluctance and suspicion changed so dramatically into a "no-holds-barred" attitude later in our visit, he said there were two parts to our visit from the Moroccan point of view. First were the "official" permissions we had to get from the military / government bureaucracy. Then there was a judgment call from the wing commander who supervised our visit. After talking with us for a while in front of the school and observing our behavior, he concluded we were no threat and did not want to steal military secrets. When he could see that we only wanted to visit our old school and see our old homes, there was almost nothing he wouldn't do for us.

After leaving the base, we drove back by way of Mehdia Beach, which like the rest of Morocco, has grown considerably. It has many commercial beach establishments down by the water, but you can still see the old French cottages up on the hill. The field trip took much longer than any of us had anticipated, so we didn't have a whole lot of time before the gala banquet at Tahar's house that evening. Most of us relaxed by the pool or wandered about in the medina which was only a block away from the Safir.

About 7:00 we boarded the buses to the gala banquet at Tahar Meddoun's house. We drove past the Challah and on into Souisse. The road into Souisee which was only a two-lane road when we were there is now a 6-lane highway!

Tahar's house was on a quiet residential street. The buses dropped us off in front of his gate and when we entered you could see why he had chosen his place for the banquet. His yard is ENORMOUS with large, open, grassy spaces shaded by lovely fruit trees. There were round garden tables shaded by large umbrellas with gorgeous place settings. Tahar had hired a special band to play all the American hits from the 50s through the 80s-- representing all the decades of students at the reunion. The band was situated under a large, traditional Arab tent. We got there about 7:30 p.m. and spent the next two hours shooting the breeze, enjoying munchies and drinks, and taking group photos.

Around 9:30 the waiters began serving what was to be a spectacular 5-course dinner. Here's what we had:

Harira Soup (tomato, beef, rice, and chick peas)
Lamb Tagine (with prunes and sesame seeds)
Chicken Tagine (with lemon and olives)
Couscous (with seven vegetables and beef)
Takhtoukha (pastry leaves with crushed, roasted almonds in a custard sauce)

People gorged until they were spent and couldn't shove another thing in. After the banquet, acknowledgments and gifts for the people who had helped make the reunion come together were given. Each person was presented with a handmade pen with 24-carat gold-plated fittings. Tahar was presented with a pen and also a wood platter with an engraved plaque for the EXTRAORDINARY lengths he went to make this reunion such a flaming success.

After the acknowledgments, we danced to tunes from our old school days. Around midnight a bunch of us decided it was time to call it a day, so one of the buses took us back to the Safir (the other one left at 3 a.m.).

The official reunion brunch took place on Sunday around 9:30 a.m. so people could sleep in bit after the previous night's banquet.

And what a spread it was! It was like something you would find on a fancy cruise ship with everything so artfully arranged it seemed like a shame to eat it.

In the afternoon, most of us went over to the American Embassy's 4th of July picnic to which we had all been invited. The American club, just a few blocks from the American Embassy, was huge with several nice buildings and nicely landscaped grounds. It was held outside where they had all sorts of typical American fare like grilled hamburgers and hotdogs. They even had a small McDonald's stand with Happy Meals for the kids. Ambassador Edward Gabriel kicked off the festivities with a short speech and even gave us a special welcome. Then the Marines had a short flag ceremony and everyone made a beeline for the games and the food. The weather was beautiful and not too hot.

The next exciting event was a chance to go into a traditional Moroccan home to enjoy mint tea, pastries, and entertainment. This event was sponsored by Tahar El-Korchi '76, whose parents graciously invited us to their beautiful home. A group of us gathered in the Safir's lobby around 6:45 to walk over as a group. Although we had a map, most of us felt better about walking together; the medina can be very confusing with its small alleyways--even with a map. Several folks in our group had bought Moroccan outfits which they wore to the party. The women wore belly-dancer outfits (they got quite a few interesting looks as we walked along the medina wall) and the men wore djellabas and fezzes.

We entered the old Bab Challah gate and were immediately caught up in the bustle and exotic smells of the medina. After a couple of turns we were on a narrow street in front of a large, heavy, very old, wooden door that was slightly ajar. We assumed this was the place and had our guess confirmed when the first person in our group stepped over the threshold and wild drumming began from within. We walked through a narrow hallway and into a huge, sumptuous room that looked as if it had appeared straight out of an "Arabian Nights" fairytale. This home was actually three stories high with the top two floors containing run-around balconies overlooking the enclosed, courtyard. At one time, we heard, this courtyard had been open to the sky. This home has been in Tahar El-Korchi's family for 129 years. All the floor and wall surfaces were richly tiled, there were lavish Moroccan couches all around the main room and in all the surrounding rooms. A mint tea pourer sat on a hassock next to a table groaning with all sorts of wicked pastries. A group of lively musicians robed in blue djellabas were singing their lungs out and having a rip-roaring good old time. It didn't take long for a group to get up and begin dancing.

Soon the waiters came out bearing drinks: water, freshly squeezed orange and apricot juices, and of course, mint tea. Then they came out with trays and trays of both sweet and savory pastries. In one of the side rooms a soccer game (Morocco's national obsession) on TV engrossed the attention of several people. Whenever the whooping from that room reached a certain pitch, the musicians would stop briefly so people could peek in and see the score. After several hours of nonstop eating and merriment, we bade our hosts goodbye and thanked them for a spectacular evening. Tahar El-Korchi's parents could not have been kinder or more hospitable hosts to invite such a horde of us (over 60 people!) into their beautiful home; it was an evening none of us will ever forget.

On Monday, quite a few folks left to travel in other areas of Morocco. The only official reunion activity left was the trip to the Hassan II Mosque in Casablanca. One bus was all we needed for this group event. The mosque itself was exactly as Tahar had promised it would be: one of the premier architectural marvels of the 20th century. It is one of the few mosques in Morocco that non-Muslims are allowed to enter.

We had an excellent English-speaking guide who made this an incredibly fascinating 2-hour tour. It was interesting to see the juxtaposition of traditional craftsmanship and new technology. All of the carvings were done by hand; however, the enormous ceiling is retractable and on clear, still nights it opens to the sky and stars in only 5 minutes. Sensors in the ceiling automatically retract the ceiling when winds reach a certain speed. We were awed by its immensity and the fact that part of it is actually resting out over the ocean. No expense was spared for this building and all the materials came from Morocco at the taxpayers' expense. It is the third largest mosque in the world and certainly one of the most opulent.

This concluded a most fantastic reunion, one which none of us will ever forget. Most of us never even dreamed we'd be able to see our old school again and visit some of our old homes and haunts on the base. What a special privilege and treat it was to do be able to do that! Not only did we reestablish old bonds, we made new and dear friends from other classes we had never met before. Although it will be hard to top this reunion, we plan on having reunions until we all croak! Stay tuned for announcements of upcoming reunions and until then....*ma' as-salaama*....

INDEX OF NAMES

About the Editor

Douglas E. Campbell, Ph.D., was born on May 9, 1954, in Portsmouth, VA, and grew up as a Navy Brat, traveling all over the world and living next to U.S. submarine bases at such places as Holy Loch, Scotland; Rota, Spain; Pearl Harbor, Hawaii; and Charleston, South Carolina. The oldest of six children, he graduated from Kenitra American High School, Kenitra, Morocco, in 1972 – his 13th school. He received his Bachelor of Science degree in Journalism from the University of Kansas on May 24, 1976; the following day was commissioned at his Naval Reserve Officer Training Corps (NROTC) Unit as an Ensign in the United States Navy. He joined the U.S. Naval Reserve Program as an Intelligence Officer in 1980 and was transferred to the Retired Reserves as a Lieutenant Commander on June 1, 1999.

Dr. Campbell received his Master of Science degree from the University of Southern California in Computer Systems Management in 1986 and his Doctor of Philosophy degree in Security Administration from Southwest University in New Orleans, Louisiana, in 1993. Dr. Campbell is president and CEO of Syneca Research Group, Inc., a veteran-owned small business incorporated in 1995 supporting several Government and commercial clients. He currently resides with his wife Trish in Southern Pines, North Carolina.

Dr. Campbell recently completed a 3-volume set of books on U.S. Navy, U.S. Marine Corps and U.S. Coast Guard aircraft lost during World War II outside the Contiguous United States (CONUS). His 600-page book investigating the loss of the U.S. submarine USS DORADO (SS-248) during World War II as a result of "friendly fire" has received critical acclaim (www.ussdorado.com). For a complete list and abstracts of all his books go to www.syneca.com.

Other Books by the Editor

MILITARY & U.S. HISTORY

Volume I: U.S. Navy, U.S. Marine Corps and U.S. Coast Guard Aircraft Lost During World War II - Listed by Ship Attached
ISBN 978-1-257-82232-4; eBook ISBN 978-1-105-16346-3

Volume II: U.S. Navy, U.S. Marine Corps and U.S. Coast Guard Aircraft Lost During World War II - Listed by Squadron
ISBN 978-1-257-88139-0; eBook ISBN 978-1-105-19671-3

Volume III: U.S. Navy, U.S. Marine Corps and U.S. Coast Guard Aircraft Lost During World War II - Listed by Aircraft Type
ISBN 978-1-257-90689-5; eBook ISBN 978-1-105-20089-2

USS DORADO (SS-248): On Eternal Patrol
ISBN 978-1-257-95155-0

BuNos! Disposition of World War II USN, USMC and USCG Aircraft Listed by Bureau Number
ISBN 978-1-105-42071-9; eBook ISBN 978-1-105-53059-3

Patent Log: Innovative Patents That Advanced the United States Navy (co-author Stephen J. Chant)
ISBN 978-1-105-62562-6

U.S. Navy, U.S. Marine Corps and MATS Aircraft Lost During the Korean War
ISBN 978-1-304-61073-7; eBook ISBN 978-1-304-69633-5

U.S. Navy, U.S. Marine Corps and MATS Aircraft Lost During the Korean War: 2017 Edition
ISBN 978-1-365-47063-9

FLIGHT, CAMERA, ACTION! The History of U.S. Naval Aviation Photography and Photo-Reconnaissance
ISBN 978-1-304-47173-4

U.S. Navy and U.S. Marine Corps Aircraft Damaged or Destroyed During the Vietnam War. Volume 1: Listed by Ship Attached and by Squadron
ISBN 978-1-329-02165-5

U.S. Navy and U.S. Marine Corps Aircraft Damaged or Destroyed During the Vietnam War. Volume 2: Listed by Bureau Number
ISBN 978-1-329-05653-4

Save Our Souls: Rescues Made by U.S. Submarines During World War II
ISBN 978-1-329-69702-7; eBook 978-1-365-02679-9

Letters from a Soviet Prison: The Personal Journal and Correspondence of CIA U-2 Pilot Francis Gary Powers (co-author Francis Gary Powers, Jr.)
[Published Privately]

VPNavy! USN, USMC, USCG and NATS Patrol Aircraft Lost or Damaged During World War II - 2018 Edition
ISBN 978-1-387-49193-3

United States Navy Patrol Aircraft Lost or Damaged During World War Two
eBook ISBN 978-1-387-66188-6

CYBER & NATIONAL SECURITY

Compu-terror: Computer Terrorism and Recovery from Disaster
ASIN B00071D2XO

Building a Global Information Assurance Program
(co-author Raymond J. Curts, Ph.D.)
ISBN 0-8493-1368-6; eBook ASIN B000PSJ9CW

Computer Terrorism
ISBN 978-1-105-22289-4

Cybersecurity Policies and Strategies for Cyberwarfare Prevention
(edited by Jean-Loup Richet, contributing author Douglas E. Campbell)
ISBN 978-1-4666-8456-0

*Continuity of Government: How the U.S. Government Functions After All Hell
Breaks Loose*
ISBN 978-1-365-61442-2

NATURE & TRAVEL

On the Potomac River
(co-author Thomas B. Sherman)
ISBN 978-1-304-69872-8; eBook 978-1-4834-1491-1

*A Remote Sensing Survey to Locate the Remains of USS DORADO (SS-248) Off
of Bahia de la Ascension, Quintana Roo, Mexico*
ISBN 978-1-329-09883-1

*The Identification of Potentially Hazardous Material Discovered In and Around the
Mesoamerican Reef Region of Mexico's Yucatan Peninsula*
ISBN 978-1-329-85639-4

Shipwrecks and Submerged Cultural Resources In and Around Pensacola, Florida
ISBN 978-1-365-41505-0